Co

Editor's Preface

The re-issue of a series of books after fifteen years' exploitation of its field invites justification and prompts reflection. The justification – other than what lies in the qualities of the books themselves – is simply that no comparable series has appeared to replace it. Our purpose was to sum up what had so far been achieved in the rather new study of 'war and society' and to make it available as an attractive accompaniment to the Fontana and other general series on the history of Europe and its empires. That we were right to sense a need for such enlargement of view on the military side, has been amply confirmed by the army of historians and history-minded social scientists who have continued active in the field, and whose relevant contributions will be duly noted in our revised reading lists. Some of them, especially in the United States, march under the banner of 'the new military history'; which however boils down to much the same thing as was meant by the 'war and society' pioneers, a generation ago. The more recent writers evidently having shared with the earlier ones the aim of distinguishing their historical operations from those of the 'old' military history, it seems worth while to reconsider what I wrote about the series' purposes and principles, fifteen years or so ago.

The 'war and society' movement took shape in the 1960s, to make good what had come to be felt as something missing in the traditional style of histories of wars and warfare. Although the latter had paid much attention to what armed forces did to one another in war, they normally showed little interest in how those armed forces related to the societies from which they were drawn and in what war itself – the experience of it while it was going on, the perhaps huge net effect of it once it was over – did to the societies which engaged in it. The years 1935–1945 were crucial to the new perception. Each of the Second World War's major participants experienced social mobilization on a scale of totality historically unprecedented. Even before it was over, official histories of it were being planned to do justice to everything that happened away from the firing lines as well as on them; and those who survived it tended to feel sure that it must have caused great social changes. Particular inquiries into this latter possibility were what brought to the forefront of the movement the historian who more than anyone else launched 'war and society' as a viable and (to the limited extent that any area of historical studies can be so) self-sufficient branch of historical studies. Arthur Marwick effected this notable step forward when his history department at the Open University produced in 1973 its famous third-year course 'War and Society', in which pretty well every apposite part of the field came into view. About five thousand students took this course during its six years' lifetime, the teaching units expressly produced for it acquired a wide circulation, and some of them remain among the best things so far written. (Nor is that the end of the story; over six thousand students have, by the time of writing, taken its successor 'War, Peace and Social Change'.)

This new approach to war history's popularity was no doubt partly because it offered to those who disliked war (numerous indeed after the Second World War, and subsequently under the shadow of nuclear weapons) a way of studying war without what seemed to them its rebarbative and retrogressive aspects. From certain morally committed standpoints the new approach might appear to be positively progressive. After all, it was happening during the same years as the movement within the social sciences to learn more about the causes of war – and thus a hoped-for preventability of war – than had been made apparent in the well-established genres of political and diplomatic history. From the traditional point of view, these were the very novelties and connections which invited criticism. Practitioners of military history proper, continuing to work within the parameters of the tradition, pointed out that the new fashion, too enthusiastically followed, failed to do justice to certain inescapable historical facts: for instance, that war was about the use of force, that force normally made itself felt as armed violence, and that books about war without the battles which usually brought it to a close were not to be taken seriously. That such books, ignoring what they did not like to recognize, did surface on the further edges of the field, cannot be denied. Our series, however, seeks to avoid such imbalance. Far from rejecting, we gladly acknowledge the parallel labours of those (one of the most distinguished of them, a contributor to this series) who prefer still to be known by the honourable title of military historian. Their campaigns and commanders, their armies and battles and the ways in which they were fought are all to be found here, in proportionate relation to the societies which supported them and which would in the natural course of events be affected by them. All that is missing is, inevitably, space to dwell as much on any of the many relevant aspects as keen inquirers may wish; and for them, our up-dated reading lists will show the way forward.

There are some passions for military history and war studies which the 'war and society' approach will never satisfy. Believing that the place of war in the world is best studied with as much detachment and objectivity as can be managed, it avoids the nationalistic and hyper-patriotic attitudes which were the norm in military history writing (one might just as well say, in national history writing) before the early twentieth century, and which continue to colour many of its popular productions. Nor can 'war and society' history appeal to men who find excitement and stimulus in tales of violence and in the contemplation of instruments of violence: all those guns and knives, etc. which fill a certain class of magazines and picture books, and which (along perhaps with innocent interests in military uniforms and model soldiers) are evidently what many 'militaria' fans alone are interested in. In the face of those interests, and in obvious contrast with them, our war and society approach is no doubt better suited to the interests of the peace-minded than the military enthusiast. There is no reason why it should not prove interesting to military persons – indeed, one volume in the series has seemed interesting enough to the Spanish Ministry of Defence to have been translated into their language – but it will not long hold the attention of the militaristic.

The attractiveness of the kind of war studies which this series has helped to popularize is no doubt partly because it matches the very common civilian feeling that war and soldiering – ancient, admirable and 'normal' though they may seem to be – are worth more critical inquiry than military men and their numerous admirers used to seem to like, and the not uncommon realization by thoughtful people that war and peace, after all, are two sides of the same medal. Ideal as a title would be 'peace, war and society'. That alone comprehends the two poles of moral and historical interest between which 'war and society' studies oscillate. Why do wars happen at all?, is a question much more likely to be in the mind of a historian now than it was before the Second World War. Like the post-war boom in 'conflict analysis and peace research', it is related to the preoccupations of the generation born under that shadow of the mushroom-shaped cloud.

But it is nothing new, that the more reflective of our humankind should ponder upon the idea of war itself. War and the imagination of it are the ultimate link between armed forces and society. Human society, politically organized, becomes a State; and States have traditionally distinguished themselves from other States, to put it bluntly, by their abilities to defend their borders and, should they be of the expanding sort, to extend them. Whether there is something congenital in the natures of men (I say 'men' deliberately, because women may be different) and States which impels them towards competitiveness and conflict, is an enormous field of inquiry which has for long engaged the attention of some of the most thoughtful and caring of our kind. The idea of war may, to many living now, have become repulsive, unnatural and essentially destructive. The historian has to note that this marks a big change from the past. War appeared in quite a different light through the greater part of history. It was the normal accompaniment of State-making and almost inevitably the means by which States gathered empires around them. Societies which benefited from these processes thought nothing wrong in them; societies which lost out, bemoaned only the failure of their fights to defend themselves. Win or lose, the literatures and traditional ethics and (if they had them) written histories of societies throughout all history before the twentieth century accepted war as a fact of international life and admired the heroes who were good at it. War may not wholly begin in the minds of men (a lot of it begins simply in material need or greed, and in the gross appetites attached thereto) but a good case can be made for saying that it begins there more than anywhere else. The idea of war therefore, the place of war in what the French and many of the rest of us call *mentalité*, is of itself a matter of giant historical importance: how at particular epochs and in particular societies the idea of war is diffused, articulated, coloured and connected. Only by way of that matrix of ideas about God and man, nature and society, can come full understanding of the causes of wars that have happened, and of the armed forces which have for the most part conducted them.

Ideas, then, we consider to matter at least as much as the social and economic history of war and of readiness for war; they form the, so to speak, cultural and material envelope within which exist the armed forces whose existence and activities lie at the centre of our common interest, and about which something more must be said. Armed forces are a very special sort of social organization. They can be more nearly 'complete societies' than any other of the 'secular' associations and interest groups which structure society within States so far as governments permit. Their internal life is by nature peculiarly structured, tough and ritualistic; their business – discipline, force, violence, war – makes them exceptionally formidable; by definition they subscribe to codes of behaviour – honour, loyalty, obedience, etc. – which emphasize their solidarity and reinforce their apparent differences from the societies beside and around them. It is not difficult to understand why so much that has been written about them (not least, by 'old' military historians) has treated them as if they were absolutely different and apart.

But of course they are by no means wholly so. Except in cases where an armed force or a coalition of armed forces succeeds in totally militarizing society, or where a 'war-minded' ideology possesses a whole society to the extent that every citizen is as much a soldier as any other, there are bound to remain differences and distinctions between armed forces on the one hand, and the societies from which they spring on the other. And yet, while there are differences and distinctions, there must also be relationships and interactions. So they can and to some extent must be studied 'on their own', because in their own right they tend to be so remarkable and influential; but in other respects their history, nature, and influence demands that they be studied in their relationship with the world they belong to. We try, within the limits of our enterprise, to acknowledge both demands.

War, to sum up, is a unique human interest and activity, with its own character, its own self-images, its own mystiques, its own forms or organization and, to crown all, a prime place in determining the standards of national societies and their political viability as States. Such is our case for picking out of the whole seamless web of history the scarlet warps of war, for putting the more social and cultural of them under a magnifying microscope, and for writing about them in a way which the general historical reader, who is not normally a 'military buff', will appreciate. This was brilliantly done in miniature by Michael Howard in his *War in European History* (1976), a few years before this series began to appear. At that time, there was not much of similarly relevant character that had to be pointed out besides his book, the pioneer classics by Alfred Vagts (*A History of Militarism, Civilian and Military*, 1937) and Preston and Wise (*Men in Arms: A History of Warfare and its Interrelationships with Western Society*, 1956), and such specialized periodicals as the American periodical *Armed Forces and Society* and the *War and Society Newsletter*, since 1975 an English-language annual supplement to the celebrated German periodical *Militärgeschichtliche Mitteilungen*, and an ideal way to scan everything that is published year by year. A good deal has come out since then (besides the Open University material already mentioned) and this general preface may appropriately close by highlighting some of the most useful items.

Conspicuous among the war-and-warfare publications of the past twenty years are some of encyclopaedic type, worth mentioning because they should be available in most libraries and because within their broad spans of coverage, particular war-and-society interests may find satisfaction. The most impressive is the improved English-language version of what was begun by the most eminent French historian in the field; it now appears as the *Dictionary of Military History and the Art of War*, edited by André Corvisier, revised and expanded by John Childs, translated by Christopher Turner (1994). Still international, but slighter and more conventional is Charles Townshend (ed.), *The Oxford Illustrated History of Warfare: the triumph of the west* (1995); of national interest merely are David Chandler (ed.), *The Oxford Illustrated History of the British Army* (1994) and John Pimlott (ed.), *The Guinness History of the British Army* (1993). Another feature of the past twenty years or so is the appearance of several periodicals dedicated to the history of war in its broader sense: probably most appropriate are the Australian *War and Society* and the British *War in History* and the *Imperial War Museum Review*.

Of the writing of long-span histories of war and/or warfare, especially by retired generals, there is no end; the only ones known to me as doing justice to the war-and-society aspects of the subject are, in their different ways, William H. McNeill, *The Pursuit of Power. Technology, Armed Forces and Society since AD 1000* (1983) and John Keegan, *A History of Warfare* (1993). Readers with an understandable curiosity as to how the outbreaks and conclusions of wars have been conditioned by the practices, customs and laws of the society or States, a.k.a. international society, within which they were all contained, will find instruction in F.H. Hinsley, *Power and the Pursuit of Peace* (1963), Kalevi J. Holsti, *Peace and War: Armed Conflicts and International Order, 1648–1989* (1991), and (though the title hardly suggests it) Martin Wight, *International Theory: The Three Traditions* (1991, ed. G. Wight and B. Porter). Two ambitious works of sociological inspiration with pockets of the suggestively relevant in them are: Michael Mann, *The Sources of Social Power* (2 v., 1986 and 1993), and David Evan Luard, *War in International Society* (1987). And it is good, at the last moment before going to press, to be able to mention Peter Paret's very instructive and finely illustrated book *Imagined Battles. Reflections of War in European Art* (1997), which begins in the Renaissance and comes right up to the present.

Geoffrey Best
Oxford, 1997

Author's Preface

Geoffrey Best, in his Editor's Introduction to each of the volumes of this series, has called attention to the very welcome widening of the historian's view of warfare and its significance which has marked the writing of recent decades. Until then much of the published discussion of the history of war and armed forces had been the work of army or navy officers, serving or retired; and at its best this writing could in its own way be excellent, particularly as it often benefited from the personal experience of the authors and the feel for the demands and problems of service life which this gave them. But it could also, as Professor Best points out, become a somewhat limited though detailed narrative of military or naval operations or even a discussion of service minutiae of only specialized interest. The cataclysms of 1914–45 and the way in which they devastated and transformed the life of Europe have made it impossible to think of war in the modern world simply or even mainly in these limited terms; and in recent decades this widening of view and deepening of understanding has been extended backwards in time.

No period of European history has benefited from this transformation more than that which is the subject of this book. Throughout the seventeenth and eighteenth centuries conflict between States, and the demands of all kinds it made on the peoples of Europe, had consequences which ramified throughout the life of the continent and profoundly affected it. The Europe upon which the French Revolution suddenly burst was a different world from that of Philip II or Elizabeth I; and nothing had done more than war to bring about this difference. Since this book was first published in 1988 the output of excellent academic work bearing on its subject, particularly perhaps in article form, has been steady and growing; but I do not think it has made necessary any significant alteration of anything I then wrote. The text therefore remains as it was. I have, however, tried to include in the Bibliography the more important relevant publications of the last decade. At the same time, in an effort to prevent a disproportionately long list of books and articles from overwhelming a relatively concise text, I have taken the opportunity to delete from the Bibliography a few items which now seem to me either a little outdated or arguably of somewhat secondary importance.

I must thank Professor Best for inviting me to write this book. It was a task which I found, in the immediate aftermath of retirement, both stimulating and enjoyable. He also read it in draft and made valuable suggestions for its improvement, while I am particularly grateful for the detailed criticisms and comments of my former colleague at the London School of Economics, Dr Derek McKay. It is scarcely to be hoped that I have succeeded in avoiding completely all errors of fact or interpretation: for any blemishes which remain I am of course alone responsible. I have tried not to be self-indulgent in the matter of footnotes, that temptation of so many academic authors, and to use them sparingly: a high proportion identify the sources from which I have drawn quotations. I have benefited much from the resources of the British Library, the London Library and, as over so many years, the British Library of Political and Economic Science, the fine collection of the London School of Economics. To all of them I express my gratitude.

M.S. Anderson
London, October 1997

War and Armed Forces in the Early Seventeenth Century

War, pervasive but undefined

In early modern Europe almost everyone regarded war as a normal, perhaps even a necessary, part of human life. Events seemed to bear out this view; in the period 1618–60 every year saw serious armed conflict between states somewhere in Europe, and during a large proportion of it destructive struggles were being waged simultaneously in several parts of the continent. The ubiquity and apparent inevitability of war meant that serious discussion of its causes was rare. As an integral and unavoidable aspect of existence it was received like bad weather or epidemics, as something clearly beyond the power of the ordinary man to avert, something demanding acceptance rather than analysis. Luther's dictum that 'war is as necessary as eating, drinking or any other business' reflects in typically blunt terms this matter-of-fact and fatalistic attitude. Nor was there much grasp of the deeper and more lasting effects it might sometimes have. It was only too obvious that in the short term it meant for many death, destruction and loss. But against this was put the venerable and well-established argument that prolonged peace weakened the moral fibre of a society, making it lax, slothful, even corrupt, whereas war focused and mobilized energies, called forth many of the better qualities of man, and had a generally tonic and purifying effect. It was clear also that a successful war could heighten the personal prestige of a ruler; the vindication of claims put forward by monarchs to disputed territories, to alleged hereditary rights, even merely to precedence over rivals or to specific symbols of such precedence, were by far the most common ostensible causes of conflict. Occasionally it was realized that war might have important long-term economic results, that it might foster the trade of a victorious state against that of its defeated enemies and that economic rivalry might be one of its causes.

Struggles inspired simply or even mainly by this kind of material rivalry were not frequent in this period but they did take place: the Anglo-Dutch naval conflict of 1652–4 is the clearest case, while the Spanish government recommenced the long struggle with its rebellious Dutch provinces in 1621 largely in an effort to slow the threateningly rapid growth of their trade. However the idea that war might, through the demands it made on societies and the impetus it gave to the growth of powerful central governments, help fundamentally to change these societies, was still a strange one.

Moreover in an age when international law as an organized intellectual structure was still very much in its infancy ideas about war lacked in many ways the clarity which we can now take for granted. It was still possible for European powers, or at least bodies which represented them, to be actively fighting one another in the Americas, Asia or Africa while they were at peace in Europe. The English and Dutch East India Companies, for example, were bitter and active rivals in Indonesia and south-east Asia, conducting hostilities on a significant scale, decades before the war of 1652 began. In the long run these extra-European conflicts, if they were active and durable enough, merged into European struggles. This had happened to Anglo-Dutch imperial rivalries by the 1650s and to Anglo-French ones by the 1690s. But this was a process which took time, especially where Asia, more remote from Europe than the Americas, was concerned. Nor was the distinction between international and civil war always clear. The Thirty Years War, the complex series of struggles which covered the years 1618–48, was primarily an international conflict. In this sense it was a series of efforts by some of the German princes, Denmark, Sweden and finally France, sometimes with Dutch and even English backing, to weaken Habsburg power in Europe and to profit from its weakening. Yet it was also at the same time a kind of civil war in Germany, the seat of most of the fighting. In the same way the revolts which broke out in 1640 against Castilian rule in both Catalonia and Portugal were important aspects of the great Franco-Spanish struggle which had broken out in 1635. But they too were also civil wars (though neither the Catalans nor the Portuguese had any feeling of themselves as part of the same nation as the Castilians). Just as the French government after 1640 supported the Catalans and the Portuguese against Castile, so eight years earlier, to much less effect, the Spanish one had encouraged a member of the French royal family, the Duc d'Orléans, to rebel against the regime of Cardinal Richelieu, while sixty years later, after the English revolution of 1688–9, Louis XIV and his ministers used the bitter civil war in Ireland which that revolution produced as a weapon against the new regime in London. In all these cases there is a merging of rebellion and civil conflict with inter-state rivalries.

Finally, a clear-cut distinction between war and peace, a dividing line whose crossing was instantly recognizable, was something which was only beginning to emerge. The position of neutrals was still ambiguous, their status poorly guaranteed by embryonic international law and liable to frequent infringements. There was a general belief that a belligerent had some right to march its forces across neutral territory if it made good any damage they caused in the process (the right of *transitus innoxius*). Frontiers were still poorly defined, zones of contact between neighbouring powers rather than lines clearly demarcated. The hold of central governments over officials and commanders in border areas was often still incomplete, so that in these areas locally inspired acts of oppression and outright violence could frequently occur, though usually without involving the states concerned in formal conflict. In this violent age incidents of this kind formed a sort of grumbling undertone to international relations, seldom actively menacing peace between states but always a potential threat. In one area in particular where the powers in contact still felt themselves to belong to different worlds and irreconcilably hostile ones this situation was notably acute. The Hungarian frontier between the Austrian Habsburgs and the Ottoman Empire was the scene of incessant raiding and petty warfare even when the two states were formally at peace, as they were for half a century or more after 1606. More serious, governments might in time of formal peace make deliberately aggressive armed gestures in border areas, sometimes on a dangerously large scale, in an effort to put pressure on a rival and secure strategic advantages and increased influence for themselves. The outbreak of war in 1635 between France and Spain, a striking example, was preceded by a long series of tit-for-tat troop movements of this kind. From 1629 onwards the French were trying to drive Spanish forces from Alsace, then part of the Holy Roman Empire, while early in 1630 troops of the Emperor Ferdinand II, the close ally of Spain, seized fortresses in the Bishopric of Metz, a French protectorate. In 1632 there was really serious fighting between French and Spaniards in the Electorate of Trier and a confused struggle developed for control of the quasi-independent Duchy of Lorraine. Yet all this took place while France and Spain were formally at peace. At sea, moreover, the situation was even less effectively controlled and regulated than on land. Navies evolved more slowly than armies. Ships, because of their greater mobility and the much longer distances over which they operated, were less effectively under central government control than regiments. Privateering, piracy's only slightly more respectable brother, was widespread. Letters of marque or reprisal, which allowed the recipient to recoup some alleged loss by preying on the shipping of the state which he claimed had caused it, were issued much too liberally by many governments. All this meant that at sea the dividing line between peace and war was even more blurred than on land. When two governments were on bad terms it was possible for there to be extended periods of what was in effect undeclared naval warfare between them; the hostilities between England and France in 1649–55 are only one of a number of cases in point.

Armed conflict in early seventeenth-century Europe, therefore, ramified into every aspect of life and was able to do this because it was still in many ways badly defined, because the boundary between peace and war was still fuzzy. But lack of clear definition did nothing to reduce its importance. Most of the governments of Europe were first and foremost, as they had been for generations, machines for waging war. Both the scale on which they fought and the effective control they could exert over their fighting forces were to increase markedly during the seventeenth and early eighteenth centuries, and that increase will make up much of the subject-matter of this book.

Militias

The land forces of the European states in the first years of the seventeenth century presented a picture of marked variety and often of considerable complexity. On the one hand there were professional armies whose development over the previous hundred years or more

16

has been discussed in the preceding volume of this series.[1] Side by side with these could be found a wide range of militia forces, many of them newly created or recently revived; and though these had many weaknesses their potential importance was still considerable. The sixteenth century, at least from the 1530s onwards, had seen an unprecedented growth in the size of armies; and this was to continue throughout the century which followed. The Spanish army, perhaps a mere 20,000 in the 1470s when Spain's rise to the military leadership of Europe was about to begin, had reached 300,000 in the 1630s when it was at its peak (though by then it had become a multinational force and largely lost its Spanish character). France, which was maintaining an army of about 50,000 in the 1550s, had one three times as large in the 1630s, while the emerging Dutch Republic, a very small state in terms of population and territory, had 60,000 men in pay in 1606. Moreover as arms and equipment slowly became more complex and expensive, armies became more costly irrespective of any increase in size. The increasing displacement of the cheap and simple pike by relatively expensive firearms had by itself a considerable effect in raising costs. It has been calculated that in Elizabeth's later years the expense of equipping an English infantry company grew in this way by about half. Bigger and costlier professional armies, which had to be paid with some approach to regularity to keep them reliable, meant unprecedented financial demands on states none of which was equipped administratively, still less psychologically, to meet them. These demands, moreover, were being heightened by the increasing length and intensity of international struggles, by the growing importance, at least in western Europe, of sieges which were often far more expensive than any pitched battle, and by the continuing inflation of all European currencies, a process which was still poorly understood and which made existing tax structures more and more inadequate. The effects of these financial pressures were seen unmistakably during the struggles of England, France and the Dutch against Spanish hegemony which began in the 1580s and ended temporarily with the Dutch-Spanish truce of 1609. The effective bankruptcy of Spain in 1597, the financial prostration of France, the increasing difficulties of Elizabeth and her ministers in the queen's last years, made the point with a force which could not be ignored.

All this increased the attractions, at least for defensive purposes, of

17

militias, much cheaper than full-time professionals, more reliable than footloose mercenaries with no allegiance to anyone but their paymaster for the time being. Moreover almost everywhere there was some surviving traditional obligation, however neglected and ill-observed, for all able-bodied men to serve in time of crisis in defence of their own homes and immediate localities. It is not surprising, therefore, to find during the later sixteenth century and the first years of the seventeenth a series of efforts to create or resurrect substantial militia forces. In the Netherlands the Union of Utrecht of 1579, the most important single step towards the formal emergence of an independent Dutch state, provided for the registration of all the male inhabitants of the rebel provinces for the formation of a militia. In 1600 this was followed by a proposal for universal military training. In neither case was there any practical result. The Dutch, now on the threshold of an age of brilliant economic success, quite correctly judged it more efficient to develop a highly productive agriculture, to become the leaders of Europe in trade and financial techniques, and to hire professional soldiers with the proceeds. Nevertheless the idea of some residual obligation to contribute in person to the defence of the new state was not lost. In 1629, for example, when after the resumption eight years earlier of the struggle for independence there seemed for a moment a real threat of Spanish invasion, orders were given that in the area between the Texel and the Maas one man of every six in the population must appear, equipped with a spade and an axe, to build border defences. In Spain also there was a series of attempts in the later sixteenth century to create some form of effective militia, largely for protection against raids from the Barbary states of North Africa, and perhaps also after 1589 from England. Another was made in 1609; but ten years later its application was limited to areas within twenty leagues of the coast. Though it had its full share of the difficulties which affected most forces of this kind – shortage of money, reluctance to serve, the restricting effects of class and regional privileges – the Spanish militia was by no means completely ineffective. After 1640, in particular, it gave significant help to the army in the unsuccessful attempt which began in that year to repress rebellion in Portugal. Similar efforts at militia-building can be seen almost simultaneously in many other parts of Europe. In Piedmont decrees of 1585 and 1594 provided that all men between eighteen and sixty who were physically fit to bear arms should be enrolled. From this heterogeneous general force it was hoped to raise one of 18,000 picked men which would not be used merely for local defence but would serve wherever it was ordered to; but this interesting early attempt to use a militia systematically as a recruiting ground for the professional army seems to have had little result. In the German states there were a number of efforts to create militias in the later sixteenth century; that in Bavaria in 1596 was the most significant.

In England the importance of professional forces had always been relatively slight and that of the militia correspondingly greater than in most continental states. In 1591 it was calculated that its paper strength was just over 100,000 men, though only 42,000 of these were trained and armed. In the Habsburg territories there had now emerged what was for long to be one of the most effective of all fighting forces of this kind, though a relatively small one. This was the Grenzers, the free peasants settled in Croatia and organized for frontier defence against the Turks. This organization had been taking shape throughout most of the sixteenth century, ever since the Turkish capture of Belgrade in 1521 and conquest of most of Hungary in the years which followed. In 1630 the *Statuta Valachorum* gave it for the first time some clear formal structure and emphasized its overwhelmingly military character. When the alarm of Turkish attack was given all Grenzers were to assemble at fixed muster-points ready for action, while the Habsburg government would supply arms and ammunition. In this way six to seven thousand men could take the field in a few hours. These were to serve not merely against the Turks but against all enemies of the emperor, and as the seventeenth century went on they tended to be used more and more against the largely Protestant Hungarian nobility. They were also to help in building and garrisoning defensive works and field fortifications. Further east, in Poland and Russia, another force of somewhat similar type, much better known than the Grenzers, can be found in the different Cossack groups which were now in full development. Originally the Cossacks were probably renegade Tatars employed by the Grand Dukes of Muscovy from the mid-fifteenth century onwards to guard their southern frontiers against the raids of their fellow-Tatars in the Crimea or the Khanate of Kazan. A century later, by the 1550s and 1560s, these had been outnumbered by Cossacks of Slav descent, runaway peasants and masterless men of different kinds who had taken refuge in the undeveloped wastes of the Ukraine, and had themselves become largely Russianized. By then, moreover, there had emerged the important distinction between 'service' Cossacks, employed by the Russian government as frontier guards and paid by it (normally in land and grain, sometimes also in vodka and saltpetre) and 'free' Cossacks. The latter, though increasingly employed by the tsars in their armies, remained autonomous and outside effective Russian control in their fortified villages beyond the frontiers of the tsardom. By 1614 there were probably about 6500 Cossacks bearing arms on the Don, in the most important of these free communities. Well before then the Polish government had also begun to make use of this source of military manpower. Stephen Batory, the most militarily successful Polish king of the sixteenth century, raised a Cossack regiment in 1572, and by 1625 there were 6000 Cossacks in Polish service.

The Grenzers and Cossacks, however, were special cases which do not fit comfortably into the pattern of militia forces normal in western Europe. Every west-European government had to contend with essentially similar difficulties in creating any effective organization of this sort. Shortage of money was almost always a problem. In Spain the government was more and more forced by sheer poverty to pass on the financial burden to the municipalities and to local magnates and wealthy church dignitaries; but this inevitably weakened its control of its militia. Sometimes efforts to find the money needed could stimulate discontent which was politically dangerous. In England by the 1630s the increasingly heavy rates levied to pay for the militia were a grievance comparable to the much better known Ship Money about which the opponents of Charles I and his ministers complained so strenuously. Nowhere was militia service popular. In Spain town councils were often reclutant to produce, as they were supposed to, lists of men of military age to ease the task of recruiting (largely from fear that this might compromise the cherished exemption of *hidalgos*, the very numerous claimants to noble status, from military service). The result was that in 1625 the government had to agree that in future enlistment should be entirely voluntary. In England too it is clear that there was often a deep reluctance to serve.[2] Standards of training, discipline and equipment were everywhere low. This again was notably the case in England, where geographical isolation and relative immunity to invasion tended to make the militia seem more than elsewhere an expensive and unnecessary imposition. There the only professional soldier associated with it was the muster-master who, in theory, provided basic training for the levies of each county. Yet some counties did not have a muster-master for years at a stretch; and where he existed he was often unpopular and resented, largely because he was a charge, through the rates, on the resources of the county. Also the different English county forces were armed with muskets of varying calibres and pikes of different lengths (the government tried several times, without success, to specify uniform standards for these weapons) while some counties, especially those far from London, found it almost impossible to obtain gunpowder. There were complications also in that the Cinque Ports, the Stannaries in Cornwall and the Isle of Wight had separate militias of their own, as had a number of corporate towns. All this meant inefficiency; and there is little reason to think that England was very much worse off in this respect than most other states in western Europe. Cavalry militia units, in particular, because of their much greater cost, were everywhere more difficult to equip and maintain than the much more numerous infantry ones. Nevertheless the existence of militias of varying kinds, and the attention given them by governments, are an important corrective to any picture of the early seventeenth century which shows its military life as simply a matter of professional armies and mercenary soldiers.

Feudal and quasi-feudal forces

Another such corrective is the fact that social linkages and obligations of the personal and family kind which may be loosely called 'feudal' still played a very significant part in the military life of all European states. It was still possible for feudal levies based on the obligation of the vassal to fight for his lord, that of the nobility to support their overlord the king in time of need and to bring their dependants to uphold his cause, to have some role. Charles Emmanuel I of Savoy called up the feudal levy of his dominions in 1625 (largely because of his hopes in that year of seizing some of the territories of the Genoese republic), while in both Spain and France there were efforts to mobilize the nobility and gentry for the struggle between them which broke out in 1635. In 1637 the nobles of Catalonia were ordered to take their vassals to the war at their own expense, and in France Cardinal Richelieu, the chief minister, had tried in the previous year to raise the *ban* and *arrière-ban*, the traditional feudal levies of the nobility. These efforts had little success. On both sides the nobles willing to fight were usually already serving in the army and the others, if they appeared at all, soon drifted away. In England Charles I tried in 1640, in much the same way and with the same lack of success, to raise an army for use against the rebellious Scots by exploiting the feudal obligations of the English nobility: it is easy to understand why Parliament in 1646 and 1656 should have passed ordinances which in effect abolished feudal tenures, the abolition which was confirmed at the Restoration of 1660. In Poland, again, the poverty of the government and still more its increasing administrative weakness meant that the standing army was always very small in the context of the republic's huge size and long exposed frontiers. There national defence in wartime rested mainly on the General Ban (*Pospolite Ruszenie*), a levy primarily of the privileged landowning class, the nobility and their *szlachta* followers.

A more important illustration than these, however, of the continuing importance of feudal influences was the fact that everywhere noblemen played, and were expected to play, leading and often indispensable roles in military life. Every army was permeated by the assumption that this would and must be so. Everywhere it was taken for granted that hereditary nobility conferred, in some almost mystical way, not merely physical courage but also a superior understanding of warfare and a greater ability to meet its still modest intellectual demands than men of common clay could pretend to. In 1578 one English commentator asserted that 'the knowledge and practise [*sic*] of the arts and feats of arms principally and properly are of the profession of noblemen and gentlemen of great revenues', while two decades later another claimed that 'a nobleman well brought up is able to attain to more knowledge in the art and science military in one year than a private soldier in seven'.[3] Given the structure of society and the unspoken assumptions which underlay it, attitudes of this kind were inevitable. Consciousness of rank, of being part of a fixed and God-given hierarchy, was all-pervasive. Everywhere it was taken for granted that social superiors would and must lead those inferior to them. It seemed entirely natural, therefore, that those who controlled society in peacetime should also command its armies in war. As time went on, the demands of growing professionalism were to weaken and undermine this assumption of the naturalness of aristocratic leadership; ability and experience were inevitably to gain ground against inherited status. But this was a very slow process, one very far from complete even at the outbreak of the French Revolution. It was often, after all, quite realistic to feel that a great noble was the most effective commander of any army. His birth and upbringing gave him the habit of command, self-confidence and the expectation of obedience; where specialized skills were involved, in gunnery and siegecraft, he could call on the advice of low-born professionals. In an age when systematic training for officers was almost non-existent he ought, given reasonable intelligence and strength of character, to make a perfectly competent commander.

Moreover every great nobleman stood at the head of a complex network of social relationships and connexions, those of family, of clientage, of various forms of dependency. He often had enormous influence in his own locality; and this was usually based not merely on the extent of his estates or the number of his tenants (though this was very important) but equally on the assumption that he had a prescriptive right to a leading position in that area. This meant that he could, if he so chose, contribute powerfully to the military strength of the state, most obviously by raising men for its army or militia through the use of his influence. Where local or provincial patriotism was strong and the hold of the central government relatively weak this could be of crucial importance. In Spain, for example, where political unity was still embryonic, in 1634 the Council of State recommended that a young and inexperienced nobleman be appointed to the captaincy-general of the province of Guipúzcoa (a vital post in view of the approaching war with France) because 'his house has a great following in the province and many vassals, and his presence there could be of considerable advantage'. In the same decade a Spanish official admitted quite openly that 'The manner of raising troops, cavalry as well as infantry, must be to entrust it to the grandees and lords of Castile who are most influential in the provincial capitals.'[4] A few years earlier the Duke of Medina-Sidonia, the wealthiest of all these grandees, had been commanded by the king to raise a *tercio* of 3000 infantry at his own expense, while in 1625 another nobleman had been entrusted with the reestablishment of the militia throughout the whole of Jaén province. Spain was an extreme case. The strength of local patriotism, particularly in Catalonia, the Basque provinces and even Valencia, coupled with the increasingly desperate financial position of the government (especially after the great crisis of 1627–9, one of the turning-points in the history of Habsburg Spain) made it exceptionally difficult there to assert effective central control over military affairs or anything else. But the same forced reliance on the goodwill of great families and local notables, especially when it came to raising men, can be seen to varying extents in most European states. This situation was long to continue.

The growth of professionalism

Nevertheless it had become quite clear long before the beginning of the seventeenth century that the future belonged to paid, full-time, centrally controlled professional armies. Against these, neither reluctant and badly trained militias nor feudal levies which were mere embarrassed ghosts of the past could hope to hold their own. Of all the professional armies of the early seventeenth century the most efficient was that of the new Dutch Republic. In large part it was recruited outside the United Provinces, notably in Germany but drawing men also from England, Scotland and elsewhere. But in an age when no one expected armies to be national this did nothing to reduce its efficiency or the impression it made. Under Prince Maurice of Nassau and his cousin John it became for contemporaries a model to be copied and a challenge to be met. The technical and organizational changes which made it so important are well known and have been often described. There was a marked increase in the proportion of musketeers to pikemen in the regiments in Dutch service compared to that seen in sixteenth-century armies. The proportion of officers and NCOs was also much larger than had hitherto been normal; this helped to improve discipline and also opened new opportunities of promotion and of the army acquiring at least some embryonic career structure. Maurice insisted on regular and intensive training: this was the most important factor of all in making the soldier a true professional and, at least in a very simple way, something of a technician. Drill became more elaborate and systematic; in 1597 the words of command used in the Dutch army were given a standard form and in 1607 the *Wapenhandlinghe* of Jacob de Gheyn (116 fine engraved plates with a comprehensive accompanying text), which was intended for use as a drill manual, provided the most detailed work of the kind which Europe had yet seen. In some respects these changes were clearly incomplete. There was no reform of the cavalry comparable to that carried out for the infantry; the lance was abandoned by the Dutch army in 1597 and its cavalry was as far as any in western Europe from being a genuine shock force pressing its charges home. Only the splendid Polish cavalry still acted in this way, and showed the possibilities of these tactics very clearly by destroying a Swedish army at Kirkholm in 1605, the most decisive military victory of the early seventeenth century. Maurice and his cousin also failed to grasp the possibilities which now existed of combining effectively field artillery with both infantry and cavalry units. Nevertheless the Dutch army was an outstanding success. A nation of traders, farmers and fishermen, one in which aristocratic traditions and military influences were weak, had after little more than a generation of warfare produced a force, if a largely non-national one, which could hold its own against Spain, the greatest power of the sixteenth century. At a deeper level it can be argued that the tighter discipline of the Dutch army, its elaborate tactical evolutions, its breaking-down of the processes of loading and firing the musket into a series of simple steps which the soldier could be brought to perform automatically, its emphasis on rationalized routines, marked a step towards the modern world with all its stress on uniformity and organized mass action. One sociologist has gone so far as to speak, surely with a good deal of exaggeration, of 'this earliest of industrial revolutions, the industrialization of military behaviour in the Netherlands'.[5]

On a smaller scale and with less completeness, a growth of professionalism can also be seen, in varying ways and to varying extents, in other European armies of the period. In France tactical innovations similar to some of the Dutch ones, notably the use of smaller and more flexible infantry units, seem to have evolved independently by about 1600.[6] In Sweden regular regiments were established in 1590 for the first time since the deposition of the unbalanced Erik XIV in 1568, while in 1604 Charles IX persuaded the Estates to grant him a special tax to pay for a force of 9000 mercenaries. In Russia the first regular standing force, the *streltsy* (musketeers), had been founded in 1550: by the end of the century they numbered about 25,000 in a total military strength of perhaps 110,000 (the remainder was made up essentially by the cavalry levies provided by the landholding service class which had now emerged as the dominant element in Russian society).

This growth of professional standing forces composed of mercenaries, often foreign and with increasingly elaborate and expensive equipment, was not a uniform process throughout Europe. Forces of this kind were too costly for any but the wealthiest states to afford on any considerable scale. Even Spain, which controlled some of the richest parts of the continent and had the silver she drew from America to back her war effort, was now staggering under the financial burden of her great army. Her most tenacious opponent, the Dutch Republic, in spite of spectacular commercial and financial progress, was also under severe strain. By 1606 its army was costing 9 million guilders a year – an immense commitment for a country whose population was still only about 1½ million. It was largely the financial demands of the war of independence which led the Dutch to agree to the twelve-year truce of 1609. Over the greater part of the continent rulers and governments were simply too poor to put all their military eggs into the single basket of a professional standing force. All over eastern Europe, in Scandinavia, in England, there was still a high degree of reliance on various forms of militia, on what could be made of feudal or quasi-feudal forces, or on the hasty levying of men, by persuasion, chicanery or outright force, to meet some immediate need or imminent crisis.

Moreover even in the greatest states of western Europe and those to which the sea was vitally important, naval forces remained much less professional than land ones: the dividing line between government and private enterprise was more difficult to draw at sea than on land. Every state still relied heavily for its naval strength on ships hired or commandeered from civilian owners and manned by crews who were neither government-recruited nor government-paid. Sometimes the relationships involved were intimate and complex. In 1603, for example, the French government signed a contract with the Genoese financier Ambrogio Lomellini for the building of six galleys for use in the Mediterranean. The voyages they made during part of the year would be as naval vessels and at the expense of the king; but Lomellini was to be allowed to use them for two months in each year for private trading. A number of other French galleys were built in the early years of the century by their captains; but because the government failed to refund the cost of their construction as had been promised, it was agreed that in two cases the captains should keep them as their own property, receiving however an annual government grant to cover the cost of their crews and upkeep.[7] The mingling of private and public enterprise in naval matters could hardly be closer than in these cases. Until the 1660s, indeed, a considerable proportion of the French galley-fleet was provided by private entrepreneurs (often Knights of Malta) who owned the galleys they commanded and served the king under contract for a fixed period in return for a specified sum. In Spain in 1616, when the navy was at a very low ebb, of the seventeen vessels in the fleet five were privately owned, hired merely for the summer (the campaigning season at sea as on land), while in the following year another six or seven had to be hired to provide an escort to bring the silver flotas from America into port. In England, of the twenty-five ships which had made up Drake's expedition to the West Indies in 1585 only two were supplied by the queen; and though he sailed as Elizabeth's admiral and had official instructions, only about a third of the cost of fitting out the expedition was met by the government. Seventy years later Robert Blake, the most successful naval commander of the Commonwealth, still had as his ideal a fleet in which the proportion of hired merchantmen could be reduced to two-fifths. Even in the Dutch Republic, now approaching its peak as a naval as well as an economic power, strength at sea depended very heavily on hired and converted merchantmen. Something like two-thirds of the fleet with which Martin Tromp won his great victory over the Spaniards at the battle of the Downs in 1639 consisted of such ships.

There were thus important obstacles to the growth of professional, permanent and effectively government-controlled armed forces in

27

early seventeenth-century Europe. It is also true that armies at least of this kind, as they developed, were usually to become essential supports of absolutist monarchies. Habsburg dynastic power in central Europe could not have survived the shocks of the seventeenth and still more the eighteenth centuries without the support of its army. The rise of the Hohenzollerns in Brandenburg-Prussia as one of the major ruling families of Europe was bound up indissolubly with the growth of the Prussian army. In the most extreme case of all, the emergence in Russia of a uniquely harsh form of absolute rule and oppressive social structure was conditioned by the need for military power and by the immense demands made on a poor and undeveloped country by a rapidly growing standing army. It is easy to see the new armies therefore as the enemies of free institutions, of individual liberties and of local and regional self-government; and in many cases the charge is justified. Yet it should not be supposed that these growing professional armies were necessarily unpopular with the ordinary citizens who paid for them. They were recruited, after all, largely from elements which society did not want or need and which it feared and rejected – vagrants, the unemployed, the destitute, even criminals. It was people of this stamp who were most likely to be swept up by any form of government levy of men for the army, as in England in the 1580s and 1590s; and although those who volunteered to serve were a very mixed bunch they also included a very significant proportion of those for whom society in general had no use. Armies could thus be seen as removing from it, at least temporarily (and given the mortality rates from which they suffered, very often permanently), elements of which it was glad to rid itself. In Elizabeth's later years 'masterless men' who seemed a constant potential source of danger were taken for the army as far as possible, for reasons of domestic peace and security rather than with any idea of creating an effective fighting force. The local authorities concerned indeed often stressed explicitly the advantages of thus ridding society of vagrants and thieves. It was well realized that men of this kind, recruited in this way, could not provide the basis for an efficient army; but efficiency was unhesitatingly sacrificed to social convenience. To varying extents the same feelings can be seen almost everywhere in western and central Europe. Moreover in poor areas such as Scotland, most of the Swiss cantons and much of Castile, a career as a professional soldier was an important and perhaps essential outlet for young men who would otherwise have found it very difficult to wring a living from the land and who might have become a threat to domestic peace and stability. Military service allowed areas such as this in a sense to export their poverty to wealthier regions more able to cope with it. Sometimes this export was on a truly spectacular scale: it has been calculated that in 1626–32, the most critical and dramatic years of the Thirty Years War in Germany, about 25,000 Scots went to fight there. This meant that something like a tenth of the entire male population of Scotland was given employment in this way.

Professional armies, in other words, acted as a social safety-valve; and this ensured them at least a certain tolerance from the respectable citizens who paid for them. An army recruited largely from the margins of society and often including a significant element of foreigners interfered with normal life, if all went well, only through its financial demands. It was therefore acceptable to the ordinary man, to whom war was a matter for rulers and governments and not one in which, regardless of its causes, he wished or expected to have any sort of direct share. Sir Walter Raleigh's remark that a foreign war was 'like a potion of rhubarb to waste away choler from the body of the realm' was one which many contemporaries would have accepted. The early seventeenth century saw protests, sometimes serious ones, against the increasing cost of armies, but little criticism of the idea of professional and mercenary forces as such.

The state as monopolist of military power

Many governments were now struggling to establish a principle which to us seems obvious and natural, essential to effective administration and social peace. This was in their efforts to assert their right to a monopoly of military power in their own territories. Increasingly they were now claiming that no individual subject or subordinate entity could have significant armed forces of his or its own, at least in circumstances in which these could be used against central authority, or could hold dangerous fortified strongholds or possess large stocks of arms, particularly of artillery. To contemporaries such claims were often far from self-evidently justified. There was no doubt that when

29

public order was seriously threatened, by rebellion or riot, the army must be brought into play to restore peace, often by very brutal means. In an age without any approach to a modern police force this was unavoidable. Until far into the nineteenth century in all European states the policing function of the army was essential: gangs of brigands or smugglers, peasants rioting against the demands of their lords, towns resisting some new tax demand, could be controlled only in this way. Armies were everywhere supports of the existing structure of society. Sometimes resistance to the government or, more serious, attacks on the social order, could be broken before they took organized shape by quartering soldiers on some discontented and potentially rebellious area, as when French troops were billeted on Huguenot families in the years before the revocation of the Edict of Nantes in 1685 as a means of bullying them into conversion to Catholicism. In the extreme case large-scale campaigns might have to be fought to crush large-scale revolt: something like this happened in France in the widespread resistance to increased taxation in the later 1630s, when 10,000 soldiers (mostly foreign mercenaries, regarded as more reliable for this purpose than native Frenchmen) were used to crush the *nu-pieds* rising in Normandy. But it was a long step from this kind of thing, in the early seventeenth century, to agreeing that the central government was the only legitimate holder of any sort of military power.

Over much of western Europe towns still had militia forces of their own, usually commanded, *ex officio*, by municipal officials. (Military rank and authority, with their strong aristocratic overtones, were often greatly prized by status-conscious notabilities of this kind.) The cities also had often their own considerable stocks of arms. Vienna, for example, owned an arsenal, set up in 1547, as well as powder mills and a gun foundry. In France even the little town of St Emilion had in 1620 324 firearms and 158 halberds and pikes, distributed among 216 of its citizens.[8] At moments of crisis forces raised by local initiative and under local rather than central control might be of real significance. Thus in 1636, when for a time Paris seemed threatened by the advance of a Spanish army from the Netherlands, the city, its guilds, the university, the *parlement* and other bodies all recruited companies and even regiments at their own expense and became the proprietors of these new units.[9] The possession of arms was still everywhere widely diffused throughout society; and the greater nobles often retained in their castles veritable arsenals which could well include significant amounts of artillery. To end this situation by concentrating military resources completely in the hands of the ruler and the central government was no easy task. In Spain the results of such efforts were patchy. On the one hand the smaller nobility of the kingdom of Valencia, a province notoriously disorderly and afflicted by feuds among its ruling families, found their little seigneurial armies effectively repressed; they were left largely without leadership by the fact that of the eight great noblemen who dominated the kingdom only two were resident there after the early 1620s. The Duke of Gandía, the greatest of these magnates, who in 1564 was said to have a private arsenal from which 50 men-at-arms and 600 arquebusiers could be equipped at a moment's notice, by the 1630s had been reduced to borrowing arms when he needed them from the standing committee of the Estates. But over much of Spain poverty forced the government to devolve administrative powers, particularly to the cities, and to rely increasingly in military matters on private resources and on contractors as opposed to government officials. The Dukes of Gandía may have seen their arsenal dwindle; but in the south-west of the country the Duke of Medina-Sidonia, who in 1579 had only twenty-six cannon in his main castle, had forty-two two generations later. In England also military resources remained widely diffused throughout the topmost ranks of society. When civil war broke out in 1642 one of the most important supports the royalists could draw on was the private armories and arsenals of their adherents: at least two royalist peers, Lord Paulet and Lord Mohun, were able to supply field-guns to the king's armies in this way.

It is in France, however, that the clearest and most explicit efforts to assert some exclusive central government control of military resources can be seen: this was an understandable reaction to the civil wars which had so weakened the country from the 1560s to the 1590s. In 1604 the Duc de Sully, the chief minister of Henry IV, called for inventories to be made of all firearms and ammunition in the different provinces. In the following year the king told his minister firmly that 'to us alone belongs the right to possess artillery'; and he went on to order the removal of cannon from a number of chateaux.[10] These were little more than gestures, however. Local authorities, particularly in

Protestant areas, were often unwilling to disclose their holdings of military equipment, while the murder of Henry IV in 1610 and his succession by the child Louis XIII was followed by a rapid though temporary weakening of royal authority. Cardinal Richelieu was able in 1626 to secure a decree ordering the destruction of fortresses and castles in the interior of France, privately owned fortifications which played no role in defending the country against foreign attack; but even this had only limited effect. The continuing disruptive potentialities of seigneurial armed forces and to a lesser extent urban militias were to be seen all too clearly in the upheaval of the Fronde rebellions of 1648–53. Not until the second half of the century, in a very different political environment, were such obstacles to untrammelled royal power in France effectively nullified. Even then there was considerable opposition. When attempts were made from the 1660s onwards to list, seize and take to the frontiers for defensive purposes the artillery still possessed by many towns in the interior, these faced much resistance; and though the character of urban militias changed considerably (notably after officer ranks in them were made venal and hereditary in 1694), they continued to exist down to the Revolution. Nevertheless the moves, however halting and ineffective, towards giving governments a monopoly of military power within their own territories which can be seen in the early seventeenth century were a clear pointer to the future. They deserve more attention from historians than they have received.

PART ONE

The Age of the Entrepreneur,
1618–60

The struggles for power

In May 1618, a group of Bohemian noblemen rebelled against the Austrian Habsburgs (partly as Protestants reacting against Catholic pressure, more as nobles resisting the monarchical centralization with which Catholicism in Bohemia was now associated). By so doing they set off an immensely complex sequence of events, the Thirty Years War, which was at different times to involve almost every significant state in Europe and to end in 1648 with much of the German world devastated as never before. It broke upon a continent in which Spain was still beyond doubt the greatest military power and political force. In spite of their failure, in an effort extending over four decades, to subdue their rebellious provinces in the northern Netherlands, in spite of their growing economic difficulties, the Spanish Habsburgs, closely allied with the Austrian branch of the family, seemed almost as much as in the 1580s, when the power of Philip II had been at its zenith, to threaten much of Europe with 'universal monarchy'.

The events of the 1620s made these fears seem only too well justified. The Bohemian rebels were totally defeated at the battle of the White Hill, outside Prague, in 1620; this was followed by severe and successful persecution of all forms of Protestantism in Bohemia and Moravia and by huge transfers of land from the native nobility to a new one, largely foreign, whose entire position was based on loyalty to the emperor in Vienna. The Elector Frederick of the Palatinate, who had become the very ineffective leader of the Bohemian revolt, now found his own territories overrun by a Spanish army and himself a fugitive. When in 1626 Christian IV of Denmark intervened in Germany (largely to secure territory there for one of his sons, an ambition cloaked in the pretext of helping the Protestant states now under heavy Habsburg and Catholic pressure) he was completely

33

defeated. By the end of the 1620s Habsburg power seemed more threatening than ever. Spain now wielded great influence in German affairs; and in the war with the Dutch which had broken out once more in 1621 she was making some headway. The Holy Roman Emperor Ferdinand II seemed about to give the German world effective leadership and central control, something it had lacked for centuries. France, the traditional counterbalance to Habsburg power, was still weakened by the rivalries of noble factions and the autonomy enjoyed by the Huguenots, the French Protestants. Militarily she was still hardly a match for Spain, and though her efforts in 1628–9 to secure the disputed Italian Duchies of Mantua and Montferrat for a French claimant inflicted very severe financial strain on her rival, she could not yet challenge Habsburg power directly on a large scale. The Dutch, the one great Protestant power, had their hands full with their continuing struggle for independence. England, militarily a third-rate state, had squandered her limited resources during the 1620s in brief and completely ineffective hostilities with both Spain and France.

This situation was dramatically changed by the landing of Swedish forces in north Germany in 1630. In 1629 a truce with Poland ended the long and largely unsuccessful war which Gustavus Adolphus, the warlike King of Sweden, had been waging in Livonia since 1621. This allowed him, backed by French money, to give free reign to the alarm which the growth of Habsburg and Catholic power in north Germany had now aroused in Stockholm. In 1631 he inflicted on the army of the Catholic League (an association of German Catholic states) at Breitenfeld, near Leipzig, one of the most decisive military defeats in European history. Gustavus himself was killed in the following year in the indecisive battle of Lützen with a newly raised imperial army commanded by Albrecht von Wallenstein; and the Swedes were very badly beaten two years later at Nördlingen by the Spaniards and the remnants of Wallenstein's forces. Nonetheless the growth of Habsburg power in Germany had been decisively checked. When in 1635 France at last declared war on Spain the way was opened for an eventually successful assault on the position of both the Austrian and the Spanish branches of the family. This took time to develop: Spain, in spite of growing economic exhaustion, was still a very great power capable of remarkable military and financial efforts. Although in 1643 she suffered at Rocroi in the Ardennes a defeat which has often and arbitrarily been taken as marking the end of her period of greatness, she was still capable, helped by the factional conflict and civil war of the period of the Frondes in France (1648–53), of winning important successes. The treaty of 1659 which ended almost a quarter of a century of Franco-Spanish struggle undoubtedly marked a French victory; but Spain's territorial losses in the southern Netherlands and the Pyrenees were relatively light. The failure of the Austrian branch of the dynasty came more quickly. Ferdinand III, who succeeded his father as emperor in 1637, soon found himself deserted by his German allies, while the Swedes now held a dominant position in much of north and central Germany. When in 1648 a series of agreements which made up the Peace of Westphalia at last brought peace to an exhausted central Europe, Swedish forces had briefly held Prague and were threatening Vienna itself. The peace meant that the last real prospect of any effective central control over the heterogeneous mass of states which made up the Holy Roman Empire had vanished. But it had also wider significance; it was far more than a purely German settlement. One of the agreements which composed it recognized at last the independence of the Dutch Republic from Spain, while Sweden gained on the north German coast a number of small but economically and strategically valuable territories, and France strengthened her position on her eastern frontier, notably in Alsace.

Around the Franco-Spanish antagonism and the maelstrom in Germany revolved a series of minor conflicts which often interacted with these great struggles. Short wars between Sweden and Denmark in 1643–5 and 1657–60, expressions of the rivalry between the two Scandinavian states which was to remain a constant feature of European politics until the end of the eighteenth century, ended in Swedish victories: the short but intensely warlike reign of Charles X (1654–60) saw the reputation of the Swedish army carried to perhaps the highest point it was ever to reach. In 1652–4, again, the newly established English republic fought with the Dutch a war which, perhaps more than any previous one in European history on a comparable scale, was inspired by economic rivalries and material ambitions – by struggles for control of the East Indies and their spice trade, by disputes over the North Sea herring fishery, and most of all by a deep underlying envy in England of Dutch efficiency and prosperity. But neither this nor the less important Anglo-Spanish struggle of 1655–9 were fundamental aspects of international conflict. This still centred, as it had done for a century and a half, around the rivalry between Bourbon and Habsburg, between France on the one hand and Spain and Austria on the other. Even more peripheral to most contemporaries was the war between Russia and Poland which broke out in 1654. Antagonism between Orthodox Russia and Catholic Poland, two different traditions and different intellectual worlds, was now more bitter than the Bourbon-Habsburg rivalry. Hitherto the Poles in general had had the upper hand; in 1611–13 Moscow had seen a Polish garrison in the Kremlin. By the mid-century, however, the 'crowned republic' of Poland was in rapid and irretrievable decline. Noble factions and internal divisions, the greed and hostility of Sweden and Brandenburg, a great Cossack revolt in the Ukraine, all drastically reduced its ability to resist a Russia which was now rapidly modernizing its army. When the war ended in 1667 Kiev, all the Ukraine east of the Dnieper and much territory in eastern Poland were surrendered to the tsar. This was a turning-point in the history of eastern Europe, though one little attended to by most contemporaries. Henceforth it was to be Russia, until now little-known, semi-Asiatic and militarily weak, which was to be the greatest expansive force in the eastern half of the continent, and soon arguably the greatest military power of all. This was a break with the past sharper than anything involved in the outcome of the Franco-Spanish struggle and one which was to have consequences at least as great.

Growing forces, growing demands

The growth in the size and cost of armed forces already visible during the sixteenth century continued during the first half of the seventeenth. It is almost as difficult to obtain really reliable figures for this as for most other social indicators of the age; but the direction and magnitude of the movement are beyond question. The French army during the 1620s, for example, when it had already to do a good deal of fighting, cost on average about 16 million livres tournois a year. After 1635, with the declaration of war against Spain, this figure rose sharply to over 33 million. After 1640 it climbed to over 38 million: in two decades it had a good deal more than doubled. In Spain, already much the greatest military power in Europe during the 1620s, the change was less marked. Nevertheless the plans for an attack on France in 1635 drawn up by its chief minister, the Conde-Duque de Olivares, involved coordinated action by two fleets (one from Dunkirk and another in the Mediterranean) and four armies (two from Spain and one each from the Netherlands and Italy). It demanded field forces totalling something like 100,000 effective men and has been described by a recent historian as 'surely the most ambitious military conception of early modern Europe'.[1] The example of increasing military numbers which most impressed contemporaries was probably the startling growth in the forces controlled by Albrecht von Wallenstein, the Bohemian nobleman who in the 1620s became the supreme example of the military entrepreneur. From about 62,000 in 1625 they had risen to perhaps 150,000 at their peak only five years later.[2] Both in its size and still more in its control by a man who was, for all his power and wealth, still a private individual, this great army was something new in the history of Europe. Simultaneously the Dutch commander-in-chief, Prince Frederick Henry, brother of the Prince Maurice who had done so much to remodel the Dutch forces a generation earlier, had at his disposal for the campaign of 1629 an army of 128,000 men, double what it had been when the truce of 1609 was signed. By March 1632, Gustavus Adolphus, then at the height of his successes in Germany, had under his command perhaps 120,000 men (of whom however only 13,000 were native Swedes).[3] In England, a highly unmilitary country, the transformation which came in the 1640s with the civil war and its aftermath was in some ways more striking than any continental development. Before the war there were fewer than 1000 men in the military service of Charles I, including those employed in the Ordnance Office and the Tower of London. Even if English subjects fighting on the continent in foreign armies, and the strengthened army in Ireland (which was largely Welsh and later native Irish), are added, the figure hardly exceeds 10,000. Yet within a year of the beginning of the conflict both sides were actively pressing men into service and there were probably in all over 110,000 under arms in England.[4] This was a ratio of soldiers to civilians, achieved very quickly, substantially higher than anything reached in France under Louis XIV, and a striking illustration of the new scale of military effort which it was now possible to evoke in European societies. In 1652, when internal peace had been restored, there was still an English standing army of 34,000, the first genuine one the country had ever had, and an incomparably larger and more expensive force than she had ever before maintained except very occasionally for large-scale military operations on the continent. Even at the end of 1654 there were estimated by a parliamentary committee to be still 53,000 soldiers in England, Scotland and Ireland combined. Almost two decades earlier, indeed, England had shown that she had the capacity to become a serious military power. Between the middle of 1624 and the beginning of 1628, for the pathetically unsuccessful expeditions to Cadiz in 1625 and La Rochelle in 1627, about 50,000 men, some 2 per cent of the entire male population, had been recruited for the army, often by highly oppressive means.

At the other end of Europe, in Russia, there can be seen during the middle decades of the century a military transformation which, though less sudden than that in England, was more lasting and had far more profound social effects. There the internal collapse and foreign attacks of the Time of Troubles (1605–13) had shown the ineffectiveness of the existing army, made up mainly of quasi-feudal cavalry levies, as a protection against the Polish and Swedish invaders. The result was that from 1631 onwards foreign officers began to be recruited more systematically and on a much larger scale than ever before. Ten regiments 'of the foreign type', with a Russian rank-and-file, were formed in 1630–4; and though they were disbanded in 1634, when a long struggle with Poland ended, renewed attempts to attract foreigners and build up regiments of the west-European kind began once more in the later 1640s. The new struggle with the Poles which began in 1654 produced an unprecedented Russian military effort. In 1658–60 three compulsory levies of recruits (on the basis of one to be supplied by every twenty-five peasant households) produced 51,000 men; and by the end of the war in 1667 over 100,000 had been raised. The social implications of these developments were profound. They accelerated an existing process of change, of growing state power and deepening social degradation for much of the Russian people, which was to gain momentum during the generations to come.

This growth in military numbers was not unbroken or universal. In

Germany the remarkable increase of the 1620s and early 1630s was not maintained. As much of central Europe became increasingly exhausted, it became more and more impossible to feed, clothe and pay forces of the size Wallenstein and Gustavus Adolphus had controlled. At the battle of Wittstock in 1636 the Swedish commander Baner had only 16,000 men, of whom perhaps no more than a third were Swedes. His successor, Lennart Torstensson, had only 15,000 when the campaign of 1642 began, while in 1647 the total strength of the (largely German) Swedish forces in Germany was probably no more than 20,000. In the same year the Bavarian army numbered only about 10,000 and the imperial one had shrunk perhaps to as little as 9000, so weakened were many of the German states after decades of war and destruction. Moreover large armies very often could not be brought to bear as unified forces at any one point, even for a decisive battle. Although there were during most of the English civil war well over 100,000 men in all engaged on the two sides, 5000 constituted a respectable field force and 12,000 was considered an exceptionally large one. It is doubtful whether the royalists, at least, ever had as many as 20,000 operating at any time as a single force.[5] Also the most formidable army, if there were serious difficulties in paying and feeding it, might shrink with disconcerting speed through desertion. It might also find its fighting efficiency sharply reduced as discipline collapsed and starving soldiers became increasingly difficult to control. The armies which fought the Thirty Years War, made up mainly of footloose mercenaries and lacking any kind of national or linguistic unity, were particularly vulnerable in these ways. Thus in May 1631, when Gustavus Adolphus was on the brink of his greatest triumphs, a Swedish official wrote of his army that 'I can give you no adequate idea of our miserable condition. The foot are fifteen pays in arrear, and both officers and men mighty discontented, so that I never heard such grumbling, both public and private. The foot desert by thousands, and some 600 have gone off in this camp alone. The cavalry do as they list; it is not safe to ride a mile outside the camp. They plunder the land to the bare bones, provoking complaints and curses fit to make you shudder.'[6]

Nonetheless, the general picture of Europe during these decades is one of growing military effort, of a remorseless general tendency for armies to become bigger, often much bigger, than ever in the past.

Bigger meant more expensive. More men inevitably meant more money; and the increase in the financial burden was often greater than the mere increase in numbers indicated. This was largely because war as waged by the greatest European armies, the Dutch, the French and the Spanish, was now, as it long continued to be, very much a matter of sieges. This was most strikingly the case in the Netherlands, densely populated and thickly studded with cities whose fortifications had been becoming stronger and more elaborate since at least the 1570s. The predominance of siege warfare there is well illustrated by the fact that the long struggle between Spain and the Dutch in 1621–48 produced only a single pitched battle, which is now almost forgotten (the Spanish victory at Kallo, on the left bank of the Scheldt below Antwerp, in 1638). A long siege ate up money, materials and often men in a way that even the greatest battle hardly ever did. To some observers in western Europe it seemed, indeed, that a predominance of siege warfare was a mark of advanced civilization. It was, after all, a systematic and technologically demanding way of fighting. It called for careful planning and detailed organization. Rapid movement of armies over long distances, on the other hand, a paucity of elaborately fortified cities, a resulting importance of often irregular cavalry and unimportance of artillery and engineers, seemed a badge of backwardness. Thus in 1656 the Dutch statesman John de Witt advised his young cousin to study fortification and siegecraft, which he regarded as the main form of warfare, rather than the 'wild and savage' war of movement between Russians, Poles and Swedes which was then in progress in the Polish Republic.[7] Certainly no state east of the Elbe and probably none east of the Rhine could have borne for long the costs of really large-scale and up-to-date siege warfare. It is true that there were some large-scale fortifications in eastern Europe and that some long and expensive sieges took place there. The defences of Smolensk, built in 1586–1602, have been described as 'probably the largest construction project of the sixteenth century',[8] and in 1633–4 the Poles spent several months in an effort to capture the city. Nevertheless in Russia or Poland fixed fortifications had nothing like the overriding importance they possessed in much of the western part of the continent.

A great siege was, with the possible exception of the building of a great canal, the biggest engineering operation known to the age.

Normally a besieging army protected itself against attack from any relieving force while the siege was in progress by building elaborate defensive lines which often enclosed a very large area. These, coupled with the siege-works proper, the digging of trenches and mounting of batteries or exploding of mines to breach the defences, were an immensely expensive undertaking. In 1602 the French envoy to the Dutch Republic reported of the siege of Grace, a very minor fortress, that 'the works which Prince Maurice has made before this place are truly gigantic. Every redoubt, however small, has its own wet ditch and drawbridge, and the continuous line is so huge and vast that it takes nearly five hours to make the circuit.' In 1629, for the siege of the much greater fortress of s'Hertogenbosch, Prince William Henry built defensive lines which took eleven hours to walk around. They included six separate entrenched camps, nine major forts and a dozen hornworks (a smaller form of fortification). He then used 116 guns, most of them much heavier than would normally have been employed on the battlefield, to attack the walls at four different points. These operations involved the damming of two rivers. War of this sort meant expenditure, of men as well as money, on a potentially crippling scale and one which tended continually to increase. It seems clear, for example, that the number of heavy guns used in sieges was growing, at least in the Netherlands, during the first half of the seventeenth century.[9] Any reliable calculation of the money-cost of a great siege is very hard to make; but that of the Huguenot stronghold of La Rochelle by the French army in 1627–8 (admittedly an unusually long one: it lasted for fifteen months) was believed to have cost 40 million livres. This was at a time when a bushel of wheat cost about a livre and an agricultural worker's daily wage was about 10–12 sous (at 20 sous to the livre). In other words the siege may have cost the equivalent of 40 million bushels of wheat or 70 million or more days of unskilled labour. A siege, particularly a long one, could also be very expensive in men to the besieging army. As it dragged on, supply problems might become acute, the disease fostered by the concentration of large numbers of soldiers for a long period in very poor sanitary conditions might take a heavy toll, boredom and frustration might intensify the ever-present threat of desertion. Thus in 1622 the Spanish commander Spinola lost 9000 men (1900 of whom deserted to the besieged garrison) during his unsuccessful attempt to take Bergen-op-Zoom, while in 1640 the successful Spanish attack on the relatively minor French fortress of Salses in the Pyrenees may have cost 10,000 men – a quarter of the total besieging forces. About the same proportion of the entire Catalan aristocracy died in this siege.[10]

One of these operations, even if successful, could therefore strain the resources of the greatest states so seriously as to make it impossible to accomplish anything more in an entire campaigning season. The nine-month siege of Breda by the Spaniards in 1624–5 made such demands that it forced a purely defensive strategy on the ministers in Madrid for the following year: there was simply no money available to finance any further advance into Dutch territory. In 1636 the capture by the Dutch, after a siege of six months, of the important fort known as the Schenckenschans at the junction of the Waal and Rhine made it impossible for them to attempt anything else of importance for the rest of the year. In 1644 the French army in the southern Netherlands spent the entire campaigning season in taking the minor fortified town of Gravelines, while in the following year the Swedish commander Torstensson lost a whole campaigning season, as well as 8000 men, in an unsuccessful attack on Brünn in Moravia. Very slow and expensive siege warfare in the Netherlands, and to a lesser extent on the Rhine, in northern Italy and in the Pyrenees, meant that in western Europe rapid or easy territorial conquest was impossible. Swift movement of armies over considerable distances, bold strategies, the taking of big risks to secure a decisive victory, were more and more neither practicable nor desired. The existing distribution of territory between the combatants in any west-European struggle became increasingly difficult to alter very much by purely military means. Provinces covered with fortified cities and protected by defensive lines were now prohibitively expensive to conquer. The clearest illustration of this is the survival (with some losses such as Dunkirk, taken by the French in 1658) of Spanish power in the southern Netherlands. Sandwiched after 1635 between the Dutch in the north and an increasingly aggressive France in the south, with Spain herself, by the 1650s if not earlier, in rapid economic and military decline and faced by great difficulties in sending men or money to her Netherlands provinces, the position might have appeared hopeless. Yet Spanish power survived there to the end of the century, and then disappeared for political rather than military reasons, as the result of a change of dynasty and as part of a general European peace settlement in 1713.

Bigger armies and expensive sieges had to be paid for. Every change in the nature of war during this period made it more costly. Every government which tried to carry on a large-scale conflict for any length of time found itself in financial difficulties, usually serious ones. Moreover the great monarchies of western Europe – France, Spain and to a lesser extent England – had all borrowed heavily to finance the struggles of the years 1585–1604. They therefore faced the new cycle of conflicts which began after 1618 already heavily in debt and confronted by the need to maintain interest payments and repay past borrowings. In some cases and up to a point, war might be made to pay for itself. If any army could quickly occupy a large area of enemy or neutral territory it might be able to force the inhabitants to provide it with the food, horses, fodder, even the money which it needed, and thus limit the demands it made on its own government. Sweden employed these methods with remarkable success. Gustavus Adolphus was able to maintain an army quite out of proportion to his country's very limited resources by exploiting in this way the territory it controlled, first in his Polish wars until 1629 and then in Germany after his landing there in July 1630. There were, however, limits to the practicability of a policy of this kind and it made demands which were potentially dangerous. An army, especially if it were concentrated as it needed to be for active operations, was likely soon to exhaust the resources of the territory it controlled. It must then move on to new pastures by making fresh conquests, or risk disintegration through lack of pay and even of food. 'Far more armies in history', noted Richelieu in his *Testament Politique*, 'have been lost from lack of bread and discipline than from the efforts of the enemy.' The only kind of war which could be self-sustaining was one which was continuously and victoriously aggressive. Sweden succeeded in fighting a series of such wars during her three generations of quasi-great power status (c.1630–c.1710); but none of the major west-European states could do so.

This situation could have only one result – a steady and often rapid increase in the demands of rulers and governments for money. This became obvious in the mid-1620s, with the outbreak of short Anglo-Spanish and Anglo-French wars and the emergence in Italy of serious crises over the Valtelline (the strategic Swiss valley through which Spanish forces could be moved from the Duchy of Milan to the Austrian provinces and the Netherlands) and the succession to the Duchies of Mantua and Montferrat. In 1626 the English parliament found itself faced by unprecedented demands of this kind. Simultaneously in Spain Olivares proposed to give the country's war effort a wider and more secure base than ever before by the creation of a Union of Arms. This would have involved the establishment of a reserve of 140,000 paid soldiers supported by all the kingdoms and provinces of the Spanish empire. It was the most far-sighted proposal of its kind made by any statesman of the age; but the *Cortes* of Catalonia, Valencia and Aragon refused to accept it (though Olivares did eventually obtain a little money from Valencia and Aragon). In 1624–5 similar pressures to raise the yield of taxes had already been felt on a much smaller scale in Savoy-Piedmont. Neither the institutions nor the political traditions and psychology of any state favoured demands of this kind. Everywhere local or at most regional and provincial interests rather than national ones were uppermost in the minds of almost everyone. Members of parliaments and assemblies thought in terms of their responsibility to the areas they represented and their local communities, not in those of high policy or national need. The extreme example of this is once again Spain, still a bundle of separate kingdoms loosely tied together and hardly at all a state. The men who rejected Olivares's proposals thought of themselves as Catalans, Valencians or Aragonese, felt no obligation to pay attention to the interests of the Spanish empire as a whole and had little or no interest in events in Naples, Milan and perhaps even the Netherlands. Everywhere custom and precedent were immensely powerful barriers to change. The fact that Europe was moving into an age of new and much greater military needs and pressures, that grants of revenue which might have been more or less adequate in the past were now quite inadequate, was little understood. The result was that where representative bodies remained significant, as in England, parts of Spain, or Denmark, there was serious friction between them and their increasingly demanding governments. In the most disastrous case, that of Spain, her multinational empire in Europe was eventually disrupted by rebellions in Catalonia and Portugal in 1640 and Naples in 1647; and these were partly a result of unprecedented war-generated financial demands. The Catalan revolt, a particularly clear case, was finally triggered off largely by the strains imposed on the province by the siege of Salses at the beginning of 1640.

Yet for all the difficulties governments encountered, the frustrations they faced at the hands of recalcitrant parliaments and assemblies, the debts they were forced to pile up, the dishonesties they were driven to at the expense both of their creditors and of the ordinary serving soldier, somehow the greater armies and the more costly wars were paid for. In Denmark Christian IV, after his unsuccessful intervention in the German struggle in 1625–9, was able in spite of considerable difficulties and a good deal of friction with the *Rigsrad* to obtain a large increase in spending on his armed forces. In the peaceful years 1629–43 the amount taken in taxes from the Danish people was more than twice as great as in the period 1600–14; and of this money nearly two-thirds was spent on the army and a good deal more on a large and expensive navy.[11] Sweden was able to maintain for long periods during the 1630s armies which were enormous in terms of her very limited population and resources; though this was possible only because she was receiving substantial French subsidies and still more because supplies and large numbers of recruits for her forces could be extorted from the areas she controlled in Germany. Equally impressive was the ability of the Habsburg emperors to keep on foot for almost two decades from the mid-1620s onwards armies which often totalled over 50,000 men. This too was achieved in part by raising forced contributions in Germany; but it also involved heavy taxation in the Habsburg hereditary lands which met with no organized resistance after the rising of 1635 in the Inner Austrian provinces. The lesson was clear and in some ways ominous. A determined government could successfully demand from its subjects, in the interests of military strength, sacrifices greater than had hitherto seemed possible.

Entrepreneurs and governments: recruitment, pay and plunder

Armies were still far from being completely reliable or well-disciplined forces. The effective control which governments had over them was often slight and on occasion it could disappear completely. Several factors contributed to this situation. In the first place it was still the exception for recruiting to be under direct government control. When men were needed the most common procedure was for commissions to be issued, normally to noblemen or high-ranking and experienced officers, for the raising of new regiments of which they would be the colonels. They in turn would commission more junior officers, the captains, to raise companies in these regiments: often the captain was also a member of a noble or gentry family and would try as far as possible to recruit his men in the area from which he came, using his family name and influence for this purpose.[12] Men enlisted for a variety of reasons. Some were fleeing from some personal difficulty – an intolerable family situation, a girl made pregnant, perhaps criminal proceedings and a prison sentence or worse. Some were attracted by the opportunity to break out of the narrow horizons and dreary routine of life on the farm or in the workshop. In an age when travel was difficult and expensive and the man seeking work outside his own immediate environment an object of suspicion, military service was one of the few ways in which the poor could hope to see something of the world. Most of all, however, men were driven to enlist by poverty, the best of all recruiting-sergeants. As a soldier, after all, the peasant or artisan would have some entitlement to pay, however scanty and difficult to enforce in practice, and there would be someone who, at least in theory, was responsible for his basic welfare. A bad harvest and the hunger which followed invariably made recruiting easier. The terms in which a very experienced Italian soldier summed up in 1572 the reasons why his fellow-countrymen became soldiers were to apply for generations to come: 'To escape from being craftsmen working in a shop; to avoid a criminal sentence; to see new things; to pursue honour (but these last are very few). The rest join in the hope of having enough to live on and a bit over for shoes and some other trifle to make life supportable.'[13] Whatever his motives, however, the soldier was recruited by an individual officer of a specific regiment rather than by the state, an entity still unknown and incomprehensible to the ordinary man. The colonels were the proprietors of their regiments and the captains of their companies; these commands could more and more be sold or otherwise transferred like any other kind of property, though this process of privatization did not reach its fullest development until the second half of the century. It has been estimated that during the Thirty Years War there were in the different German armies in all close to 1500 'military-enterpriser' commanders, colonels and generals who owned regiments,[14] and in the great majority of seventeenth-century armies (though there were some exceptions to this) regiments were known, quite logically, by the names of their colonels.

The recruit when he enlisted was given a down-payment (in Spain normally ten days' pay) which sealed the contract, and this *Handgeld*, as it was known in the German world where this form of recruiting was perhaps more highly developed than anywhere else, was normally supplied by the government he was to serve. So was the conduct money which maintained him on the way to the depot where he would be formally enrolled in his company. But the ordinary soldier had hardly any direct contact with the government and state for which he fought: what mattered to him was his officers, their efficiency and the degree of care they took of him. His clothing and weapons were supplied by them; very often the colonel bought in bulk for his regiment and made a profit, frequently a considerable one, in the process. The soldiers' pay, almost always in arrears and often grossly so, reached him through his officers. It was therefore possible for unscrupulous colonels or captains to profit by delaying still further payment of what was owed to their men; on the other hand there are recorded cases of officers using their own money to keep in being regiments or companies which threatened to disintegrate through lack of pay. The officer, then, both in recruiting and in the day-to-day work of the regiment, was also a businessman. He traded in weapons, clothing and often food, and on occasion he acted also as a moneylender. At this level war was a private rather than a state enterprise.

The potential defects of this system, which in essentials continued in many parts of Europe far into the eighteenth century, are all too easy to see. It meant a likelihood, almost a certainty, that governments would often be cheated by being called on to pay for soldiers who had died, or deserted, or perhaps never existed, but whose pay was still pocketed by dishonest officers. When the Venetian Senate in 1616 spoke of 'our armed forces, so many fewer when called to fight than they are when they are paid' it was voicing a complaint which was to be heard for generations to come.[15] Much later, in 1693, the great French soldier Marshal Vauban claimed that Louis XIV would save 12 million livres a year if his government assumed control of recruiting and took it out of the hands of colonels and captains. But to do this would have placed too much strain on most seventeenth-century administrative systems, and would have threatened too many vested interests, for it to be practicable. Such a reform was not in fact carried out in France until 1762.

Private-enterprise warfare was carried to its highest pitch in the 1620s and 1630s by a series of commanders who raised on their own account, in the service of some ruler who employed them, not merely regiments but entire and sometimes very large armies. Count Ernst von Mansfeld until his death in 1626, Duke Bernhard of Saxe-Weimar in the 1630s, most spectacularly of all Wallenstein, who was commander-in-chief of the imperial forces in 1628–9 and again from 1632 until his assassination in 1634, are outstanding illustrations of this. Mansfeld in 1621–4 negotiated with a series of possible employers – the Dutch, the French, the Spanish government in the southern Netherlands. In 1624 he proposed to Richelieu that he should raise 24,000 infantry and 7000 cavalry which might be used to support French policy in Germany, and in the following year he raised substantial forces for Christian IV of Denmark. In 1625 and 1631 Wallenstein signed contracts with the Emperor Ferdinand II by which he undertook to provide armies (24,000 in the agreement of 1625) for the latter; he even issued recruiting-patents to colonels in his own name, not in that of his employer. In 1635 Bernhard of Saxe-Weimar agreed in a similar way with the French government to recruit 12,000 foot and 6000 cavalry in return for a payment of 4 million livres a year. This was making war a private and profit-making enterprise on a scale never seen before and never to be repeated. Wallenstein's army was the greatest business enterprise of the age. He was able to raise such forces only because of the immense wealth he had acquired in the early 1620s in estates confiscated from the defeated Protestant rebels in his native Bohemia, and to a lesser extent from the profits he made when the currency in the Habsburg lands was devalued in 1622–3.

All these military entrepreneurs, to varying extents, were the centres of complex webs of credit and financial dealings. Wallenstein both lent to and borrowed from the colonels who raised regiments for him; in 1627 they owed him 600,000 florins. In 1621–8 he may have lent as much as 8 million florins to his employer, Ferdinand II; and the grant to him of the Duchy of Mecklenburg in north Germany in 1628 was largely a payment for these advances. He also made great profits by supplying his army from his own resources with arms, food and clothing. On his estates he produced gunpowder, cannonballs, small arms and saltpetre, while in 1632 20,000 loaves were being sent each day to his regiments from his Duchy of Friedland in Bohemia, as well as supplies of rye, barley, hay and beer. For a short period in the early 1630s, when the whole structure of imperial power seemed on the point of collapse before the Swedish onslaught, his position was extraordinary. In his contract of 1631 with the emperor it was hinted that he might be given the Electorate of Brandenburg if he could conquer it. If this had happened it would, with his other holdings, have made him the greatest territorial ruler in the entire Holy Roman Empire. The same agreement gave him the right to confiscate property anywhere in the empire and even, astonishingly, to veto any pardon granted by the emperor. Such power was certain to arouse jealousy and distrust in Vienna; and it was these fears, intensified by Wallenstein's own ambitions and intrigues, which led to his murder. Bernhard of Saxe-Weimar, though he never achieved the same overwhelming position, nevertheless also showed what a great military entrepreneur might hope to achieve. In 1633 he was given by the Swedish government a newly created Duchy of Franconia which included most of the conquered Catholic bishoprics of Würzburg and Bamberg; and in his agreement with Louis XIII two years later he was recognized as ruler of the former Habsburg lands in Alsace, though he was never in fact formally invested with them. When he died in 1639 he left a large personal fortune (including very substantial legacies to the men he had commanded). Military entrepreneurship on this scale was a short-lived phenomenon. It developed to its fullest extent only in the German world, an area of increasing political weakness and disintegration. Nevertheless it was essentially a large-scale version of methods and attitudes which were very widespread over most of western and central Europe. The captain who recruited a company or the colonel who raised a regiment hoped to profit and eventually, if all went well, to be rewarded for his services with an estate or a pension. The great entrepreneur who raised an army hoped for bigger profits and to become ruler of a principality. The scale was different but the ambitions were at bottom the same.

There were of course other methods of recruiting. When men were needed quickly and in considerable numbers they could be raised by various forms of conscription, all of them in varying degrees primitive and inequitable. Thus in England 10,000 men were pressed for the expedition to Cadiz in 1625 and 6000 for the unsuccessful effort to relieve La Rochelle two years later. This was done on the authority of letters from the Privy Council to the lords-lieutenant in the counties, from whom orders descended to the justices of the peace and eventually the constable at village level. During the civil war two decades later, both sides pressed men energetically into service in the areas they controlled. In March 1644, for example, the royalist parliament in Oxford voted the immediate raising in this way of 6000 recruits to strengthen its field army. Sometimes militias could be made to provide recruits for the regular forces: the urban militias in France were used to some extent in this way in the difficult years of the late 1630s, when the war with Spain was straining severely the country's still inadequately mobilized resources. Sometimes *ad hoc* expedients were resorted to, as when in the crisis year of 1636 master-craftsmen in Paris were forbidden to keep more than one apprentice each and ordered to send any others at once for service in the army. Every attempt to raise men by compulsion was unpopular. All of them produced strenuous efforts to avoid service, which were reflected in high rates of desertion. All of them opened a wide field to corruption of various kinds, such as the acceptance of bribes from those seeking to avoid service or the taking of boys in place of grown men. They also gave much scope for the exercise of personal vindictiveness and malevolence by the minor functionaries who effectively chose at the grassroots level those to be taken for service. In one state, however, there was a form of conscription which was not grossly inequitable and which produced a steady stream of good-quality recruits. This was Sweden. There the arrangements systematized in 1620 (they had roots going back far into the sixteenth century) divided the conscriptable male population (sons of widows, priests, nobles and their servants, and workers in the mines and the arms-producing industries were exempted) into groups of ten. Each of these had to produce one recruit whose equipment was paid for by the other nine. In peacetime the ordinary soldier, if as was normal he did not own a farm of his own, was billeted on one whose owner deducted an appropriate amount from the rent or taxes he owed to the crown and paid it to the soldier, who was also bound to help with the routine work of the farm to pay for his board and lodging. This system was often burdensome, and even in the 1620s there were complaints that it was leading to farms being abandoned for lack of labour. Nevertheless it gave Sweden for many years perhaps the best and most reliable of the major armies of Europe. Moreover it was a system uniquely uniform and centrally controlled, and in these ways something of a pointer to what was still a distant future.[16]

In addition to the men they obtained from their own territories by inducement or compulsion every government was willing, and often anxious, to recruit others abroad. The foreign mercenary with little in the way of national or religious loyalties, faithful only to his paymaster and usually reliable so long as he was paid, was an important element in every major army of the period. Often, it could be argued, he was the most desirable type of soldier. If he could be obtained cheaply, it might well make sense to hire him rather than take from civilian life a peasant or artisan who was contributing to the wealth of the state. In the richer parts of Europe this was an argument of some force: the heavy reliance of the United Netherlands, the most economically advanced part of the continent, on foreign mercenaries is to be explained largely in these terms. Furthermore this sort of soldier, when he was discharged, was unlikely to present the same problems as a native recruit who might well return to his village, unemployed and perhaps unemployable, a potential criminal and drain on parish funds. Often, moreover, to hire mercenaries abroad was the easiest and perhaps the only possible way to raise large forces quickly. When a government wished to make some particular and immediate military effort, therefore, its first reaction was frequently to try to recruit in a foreign country. Thus in 1629, when Gustavus Adolphus was preparing for his landing of the following year in north Germany, he sent agents to England, France and the Netherlands in an effort to raise men there. A decade later, in 1640, confronted by revolt in Catalonia and Portugal and a threatened collapse of the Spanish monarchy, Olivares considered recruiting in Ireland and the Ukraine; an offer of 10,000 Cossacks from the King of Poland was in fact accepted by the government in Madrid, though little came of this. The later stages of the Thirty Years War saw the armies involved become more and more heterogeneous as the endless struggle seemed to acquire a momentum of its own: by 1644 one Bavarian regiment is known to have included men of sixteen different nationalities. This heterogeneity was aided, moreover, by the abandonment even of the pretence that religious allegiances counted for much in this context. In 1647 Spain, the most ostentatiously Catholic of all the great powers, was openly recruiting in Lutheran Hamburg: two years later it was even trying to raise men in the largely Calvinist Dutch Republic.

The ease with which foreign mercenaries could be raised varied sharply at different times. The market for their services was an international one; and if wars were being fought simultaneously in several parts of the continent the demand for soldiers grew and they became more expensive and more difficult to obtain. It was the conflicts in the Netherlands, in Italy, and on a smaller scale between England and France, which partly stultified the Swedish efforts to raise men in western Europe in the later 1620s. In an age so dominated by war, the market was often a good one for those selling their services. Men discharged by one ruler were very often immediately re-engaged by another: in 1636, for example, eight regiments in the Habsburg army were formed from soldiers who had just been disbanded by the Polish government. In the same way, when Bernhard of Saxe-Weimar died in 1639 there was considerable competition to take over his army: though France was successful, both Sweden and the Emperor Ferdinand III had hoped to acquire it. The end of the Thirty Years War inevitably threw on the market a large number of professional soldiers in search of new employers; and though some of these were forced to go as far as Russia to find them, others were more lucky. The Swedish units now disbanded in particular benefited from the very high reputation they had acquired over the last two decades. France, Spain, Poland, Venice and even some of the leaders of the Fronde rebellions in France all showed interest in recruiting from them.

An army in the field was effective and reliable only insofar as it was paid with some regularity. Nothing weakened a government's control over military operations so much as inability to provide at least some minimum and token amount of money to satisfy the demands of its soldiers. The history of these decades, during which almost every major government tottered continually on the verge of bankruptcy, is full of examples of this sort of difficulty. These took the form of 'mutinies' which were in effect strikes in which the armies concerned 'withdrew their labour' and refused to fight or even to move until they had received some satisfaction. Action of this kind can be seen as a form of popular revolt, perhaps in this period the most typical of all. The most spectacular example came in 1635, when the German officers of the Swedish army in Germany held the Swedish chancellor, Axel Oxenstierna, for some time in their camp near Magdeburg as a hostage for the arrears of pay owed them. Before he was released he had to promise that if, when a final peace was signed, their claims were still unsatisfied, they could come to Sweden to collect the money they claimed. Six years later, in May 1641, the same army was once more paralysed by mutiny over arrears of pay; and in this case the Swedish government could obtain the money it needed only by undertaking, in return for an increased French subsidy, to fight with the French against the Habsburgs until the end of the war in Germany and not, as hitherto, for a limited period. This is a good illustration of the political importance crises of this kind could sometimes have. Payment of these arrears, 'the contentment of the soldiery', was therefore for Sweden a very important element in the final peace in Germany. In at least one remarkable case the claims of a high-ranking officer were met by a payment in kind. When the Scottish soldier of fortune Alexander Leslie left Swedish service after a highly successful career in it he was given his arrears of pay in the form of two field-guns and two thousand muskets which he took home with him.[17] (An example of the way in which private individuals could still have at their disposal very large stocks of arms.) A congress at Nürnberg to organize the paying-off of the different armies which had fought in Germany began its work after the peace of 1648 had been signed and did not break up until July 1651; while the last Swedish garrisons in the German states, which had been maintained to enforce payment of the 5 million thalers for which the soldiers had eventually agreed to settle, were not withdrawn until 1654. The Swedish forces were in no way unique, moreover, in their demands or their efforts to enforce them. In 1638 the French army refused to cross the Rhine into Germany until it had received at least some of the arrears owed it. In 1647 the parliamentary army in England mutinied mainly because of lack of pay – not surprisingly since it was owed the then gigantic sum of almost £3 million and Parliament was mean enough to propose disbanding the New Model Army infantry regiments with a mere six weeks' wages.[18]

A soldier whose pay was months and sometimes years overdue was driven to look elsewhere for money. This he must have because normally he had to find much or all of his own food, buying it from the regimental sutlers and butchers, all civilians, and from the traders, often women, who brought it to camps and garrisons for sale. All these were part of the network of ancillaries – dealers, prostitutes and hangers-on generally – which accumulated around every army. Without money the soldier might be hard-pressed to live even if food itself were in good supply. One of the many Scottish officers in the Swedish army recalled that during the long siege of Hameln in 1633, 'my best entertainment was bread and water, abundance of the last, but not so of the first; but this proceeded from want of money, for the leager [i.e. the camp] was plentiful enough.'[19] To unpaid men the main alternative source of money was some form of plunder. Even if they had been paid much more regularly, many of them would still have been strongly attracted by possibilities of this kind, for the chance of at least temporary and relative wealth through looting, or through the capture of a prisoner who could be made to pay a substantial ransom for his release, was sometimes a substantial inducement to enlist. The Thirty Years War in Germany, because of the anarchy it produced over much of the country and the increasing poverty of many of the governments whose forces fought there, saw plundering carried to a pitch unique in the history of modern Europe. From the highest ranking commanders to the humblest private soldier armies were involved in the seizure or extortion of money and goods from the civilian population. New recruits, at first too ignorant or burdened by scruples to take advantage of their opportunities, soon learned the facts of this aspect of military life. After the first stages of his service, wrote one of them, 'I had learnd so much cunning, and become so vigilant to lay hold on opportunities, that I wanted for nothing, horses, clothes, meats, nor moneys; and made so good use of what I had learned, that the whole time I served in Germanie, I suffered no such miserie as I had done in the first yeare and a halfe that I came to it.'[20] In the highest ranks looting was possible on a much greater scale and could be correspondingly more profitable. An outstanding example is the capture of Mantua by the Habsburg commanders Gallas and Aldringen in 1630: the contents of the ducal castle taken on that occasion were estimated to be worth 18 million scudi, the greater part of which went to the victorious generals. Another is the capture in 1648 of part of Prague, a great city still little touched by the war, by the Swedish commander Count Königsmarck. Some contemporaries argued that too successful looting was bad for an army, not so much because of its effects on discipline as because men would fight well only under the spur of want. One claimed that the disastrous defeat of the Catholic League commander Tilly by the Swedes at Breitenfeld in September 1631 was caused partly by the 'richesse of his souldiers', especially the cavalry, from the booty taken when they captured Leipzig only two days before. The result was that 'loth to loose so soon their richesse with their lives, many Troops of horse went from hym, even when they were to goe to fight: wich is a maxime "A rich souldier will never fight well" '.[21]

Plundering and extortion were not the only means by which impoverished armies could maintain themselves and soldiers hope to grow rich. A wealthy or important prisoner could be made to pay a ransom or have one paid for him by his superiors. The ransoming of prisoners was a practice as old as recorded history, and the right to a ransom a well-established form of property: there are cases of their being paid to children, the heirs of the original captor, after his death. In practice a valuable prisoner taken by a common soldier was usually sold at once to a superior, often to the colonel of the regiment, who might in turn sell him to someone still higher in the hierarchy. It was, therefore, again a practice which tended to benefit officers, particularly high-ranking ones, rather than privates or NCOs (though of course it was also high-ranking officers who might, if taken, find themselves in their turn compelled to pay heavily for their freedom). By the 1630s efforts were being made to assert the principle that prisoners were the property of an army as a whole rather than of the individuals who had taken them; but until the second half of the century ransoms remained an element in the maintenance of armies which, although secondary, was occasionally significant. The Swedes, for example, are said to have made 120,000 thalers from the prisoners taken when they defeated the imperial and Bavarian forces at Jankau in 1645.

There were more direct means, and very important ones, by which soldiers made demands on civilian society. Every army demanded 'contributions' from the population of the areas through which it marched and in which it fought, payments in money and kind, in food, fodder, clothing etc., which were enforced by the threat of burning villages and seizing livestock. These gave scope for a great deal of extortion, corruption and dishonesty. A district might pay in order not to have troops quartered on it, or to have them marched through it as quickly as possible, or merely for a promise that good discipline would be observed when the army was on the march. Towns and villages regularly offered bribes to have the amount of the contribution demanded from them reduced. Nürnberg, a good case in point, paid out large sums in the 1620s in efforts to avoid the depredations of the competing armies in south Germany. A neutral area unable to defend its neutrality by force might pay to have it observed or at least infringed in a not too destructive and expensive way. All these devices were seen in their most developed and widespread form in Germany in the terrible generation from the 1620s onwards; but all of them were prevalent and taken for granted throughout Europe. For the areas affected by them they were a greater burden, and one imposed more ruthlessly, than even the heaviest normal taxation.

The limits of government control

In these armies the most basic forms of professionalism were still far from complete. Hardly anywhere could there be found any real effort to train officers, while for the rank and file training was still elementary. Officers were still, by the standards of later ages, scandalously lax in the performance of their duties. In France an ordinance of 1629 commanded colonels to spend at least three months of the year with their regiments, captains four months, and lieutenants and ensigns eight; but this was never enforced, and when the war with Spain began in 1635 it was found that in one of the French field armies no less than 144 officers were absent without leave. Eight years later a French commander in the southern Netherlands suddenly abandoned his army, virtually in the face of the enemy, and retired to his estates. A year or two later again, in 1650, it was complained that the army in France was still 'a real republic' and that the lieutenants-general considered their brigades (groups of two or more regiments) 'as so many cantons'.[22] Even the distinction between military and naval commands was still blurred. The Earl of Essex who served as vice-admiral in the Cadiz campaign of 1625 was also second-in-command of the army raised in 1639 for use against the rebellious Scots; and more than a generation later John Churchill, later the great Duke of Marlborough, first saw service as a volunteer in the navy in 1672 at the battle of Solebay against the Dutch. Claude de Razilly, the most successful French naval commander of the age of Richelieu, had earlier commanded a regiment, as had Robert Blake, the outstanding English admiral of the 1650s.

At sea the lack of discipline, of effective organization and real government control, was even more obvious than on land. No state as yet had a corps of professional naval officers with a clear hierarchy and some approach to a recognized career structure. Even in the United Netherlands, the greatest maritime power of the age, the efforts of the Stadtholder Frederick Henry to create one had little success. The more or less indiscriminate issuing of letters of marque by the combatants in every naval war meant that the seas swarmed, in peace as well as in wartime, with actual or potential corsairs, many of whom were hardly distinguishable from outright pirates, and that the shipping of neutral states was plundered with complete contempt for embryonic international law. The way in which the remains of the English royalist fleet degenerated from the later 1640s into little more than a gang of pirates is a good illustration of what could happen in a situation still so chaotic and uncontrolled. The treaty of 1632 by which the English and French governments undertook to restrict in future the issue of letters of marque showed some grasp of the problem; but it had little practical effect.

The extent to which an older annd quite unprofessional ethos still lingered is clearly visible in other ways. There were still commanders who treated war as a sporting contest in which personal honour was the real stake; and occasionally this attitude was pushed to almost ridiculous lengths. During the Franco-Spanish war which began in 1635 the French naval commander in the Mediterranean, Sourdis, when offering battle to a Spanish admiral whose forces were a good deal smaller, suggested that to produce a more equal contest he should send some of his ships into port in Genoa in order not to take an unfair advantage of his adversary.[23] Almost everywhere, moreover, there could be found, side by side with gross brutality and uncontrolled violence, a taste for ceremonial, a stress on appearances and conspicuous consumption, which was an inheritance from the knightly past and which did not easily fit a future which was slowly to become more rigorously professional. This can be seen, for example, in an almost universal passion for the unnecessary and sometimes inconvenient display of flags. The largest English warship of the early seventeenth century, the *Prince Royal*, was issued with no less than seventy flags of different sizes, while in 1626, when the navy in England was desperately short of money to pay its sailors and buy essential supplies, it still spent £1280 on flags of various sorts.[24] In a somewhat similar way French infantry regiments had flags which were so large that they could rarely be unfurled and had usually to be carried with a large part of them held under the arm of the standard-bearer. The same taste for show can be seen in the widespread liking, particularly in navies, for firing salutes. The English squadron at Plymouth was said by a witness in 1628 to have 'shot away £100 of powder [which in England was sometimes quite hard to come by] in one day in drinking healths'; and when a French squadron arrived in the Tagus in 1641 it was saluted by over a thousand shots from other ships and the forts on shore.[25] The ludicrously disproportionate sums which were sometimes spent on decorating warships with carving, gilding and other luxury embellishments show the same attitude. As late as 1676 one of the galleys in the French Mediterranean fleet was being lavishly decorated with red velvet, gold fringes, embroideries and gold brocades. The estimated cost of the cloth alone was 109,000 livres; and this was at a time when the whole cost of building an ordinary galley was only 28,000.[26]

Some efforts were made during these decades to increase the control of governments over their armed forces; but they did not go far. Standardization of weapons and equipment was one of the most obvious benefits of such control. However the organization of armies, and to a lesser extent of navies, made this difficult to achieve. Colonels who were the proprietors of their regiments expected to make money from supplying them; and this clearly became much more difficult if they had to accept weapons and clothing of a standard pattern. The complete indifference of most governments to the origins of the soldiers they employed meant that not only armies but single regiments were often very mixed in nationality and language: the whole concept of system and uniformity, so familiar to the mind of the twentieth century, was much weaker in the age of Richelieu and Olivares. A certain amount was beginning to be achieved by the adoption of approved patterns for weapons. A factory was established in Sweden, for example, to produce sword-blades to a single official design. But this process, and any general acceptance by governments of responsibility for supplying their forces, had still far to go. In France the government sometimes tried to compel the towns to produce clothing and shoes for the army. In 1628 Paris provided 2500 suits of clothes, and other cities over 2800; and there were a number of other such demands in 1635 and 1646–59. But it was only slowly that it became at all usual for the French government to supply its soldiers directly in this way. When in the later 1620s it sent consignments of clothing to the regiments in the Valtelline this seemed so extraordinary a proceeding to its customs officers at Valence in southeastern France that the supplies were held up by them en route.[27]

If governments could not introduce uniformity into the arming and clothing of their regiments it was still more difficult for them to shoulder the greater burden of feeding and supplying them. Very often a government did not aspire to provide its soldiers with any food except a ration of bread, the basic foodstuff: for anything more, meat, wine etc., they were frequently expected to fend for themselves. In western Europe at least the task of supplying armies on a large scale with such things as bread, horses and fodder was usually undertaken not by the still small and inefficient central administrations of the day but by businessmen and entrepreneurs. These contracted with a government for the supply of specified quantities of these things and had their own distribution networks through which the goods reached regiments and companies. From this process they hoped and expected to make a profit, sometimes, if they were lucky, a disgracefully large one. In France, the country where it has been most intensively studied, groups of *munitionnaires* of this kind had for long been essential to the functioning of the army, and the age of Richelieu saw the rise of true dynasties among them. Often, significantly, these originated from the eastern and north-eastern frontier provinces where the movements and demands of armies were a matter of great economic importance; the Jacquier family in Champagne and the Berthelots in Picardy are good examples. Some of these entrepreneurs went on to hold very high office in the French financial system; indeed Cardinal Mazarin, who was chief minister from the death of Richelieu in 1642 to his own death in 1661, himself made money as a *munitionnaire.* The Spanish armies, notably in the Netherlands, were supplied in essentially the same way, as were those of many other states, and supply mechanisms of this kind continued to function over much of Europe throughout the seventeenth and eighteenth centuries.

The relationship between governments and their armed forces was thus still in many ways an arms-length one and was long to remain so. Nonetheless, some progress was made towards increasing effective central control. In France this was largely the work of the great military administrator Michel Le Tellier, who from 1643 onwards began a struggle to introduce some order and method into what had hitherto been a chaotic picture. New officials, the *commissaires des guerres*, were stationed in the French armies with powers to scrutinize muster-rolls (to guard against the ever-present danger of paying for soldiers who existed only on paper) and to oversee the billeting and supply of the troops. They were responsible to the *intendants d'armée*, who were normally members of the *noblesse da la robe*, the caste of holders of great administrative posts which was now becoming one of the most important elements in the whole French nobility. These *intendants* had police and disciplinary powers extensive enough to control even very high-ranking officers, but in their turn they were supervised by inspectors sent periodically from Paris to ferret out and report irregularities of any kind. The whole of this complex hierarchy was overseen by the secretary of state for war. It was not easily or quickly constructed. Much of Le Tellier's work was accomplished only in the last years of his period in office, after the coming of peace with Spain in 1659. Nevertheless he had laid the foundations on which his more famous son, the Marquis de Louvois, was in the 1670s and 1680s to raise a structure of French military power which made Louis XIV feared as no ruler of France before him.

Mercenary forces or levies raised by fraud and coercion were unlikely to feel any deep loyalty to their employers, especially if these proved, as they so often did, negligent or inadequate paymasters. Rulers often treated those who fought for them with disgraceful meanness. In 1658, for example, the Dutch government, generally regarded as the best of all paymasters, was in process of raising a number of regiments to support Denmark, then at war with Sweden. When the Danes unexpectedly made peace with Charles X, to the annoyance of the Dutch, the newly raised recruits found themselves reduced overnight to destitution. When news of the peace arrived, wrote the commander of one of the regiments concerned, 'they discharge our leavies under paine of death, arrests our ships, sets our men ashoare, and giving each of them halfe a dollar, bad them goe where they pleased.'[28] For generations to come, this sort of casual cruelty was to be the lot of soldiers and sailors whose services were no longer needed. It is a striking fact, however, that with one significant exception no government during this period was ever overthrown or even seriously threatened by its army. That exception was England. There, after royal power had been temporarily destroyed by civil war, the years 1647–60 saw a series of military coups which made and unmade successive regimes. The Self-Denying Ordinance passed by Parliament in 1645, which disqualified MPs from holding military commands, helped to make the group of army officers which had by then emerged on the parliamentary side an independent political force. In the decade or more which followed they were able to draft constitutions, reduce Parliament to a puppet, take over the chief functions of government and eventually set up what was in essentials a military dictatorship. It is a paradox that this sort of instability, reminiscent of many underdeveloped countries today, should have emerged in perhaps the most constitutionally minded of all the major states. But nothing comparable was to be seen anywhere else in western Europe until the 1790s, when legitimate authority had been disrupted in France even more completely than in England in the

1640s. Elsewhere royal power might be threatened in the mid-seventeenth century by the irresponsible ambitions of great nobles. In Spain the efforts of the Duke of Medina-Sidonia and the Marquis of Ayamonte to create a separate kingdom of Andalusia in 1641, or those of the Duke of Hijar in 1648 to make himself ruler of an independent Aragon, are good cases in point. In France the disruption of the Frondes in 1648–53 is another. But from military conspiracies rulers in general had little to fear.

There were signs, though as yet faint ones, that a service psychology of a more modern kind was developing. The most obvious of these can be seen in the first moves towards the introduction of uniforms which proclaimed to the world at large that the soldier wearing one belonged to a particular regiment or even a particular army. The eventual significance of these in developing *esprit de corps* and a sense of belonging to a great impersonal organization was to be immense. However uniforms were still very much an innovation and moves to introduce them hesitant and tentative. Men of the same army had for long identified themselves on the battlefield by wearing distinctively coloured armbands or shoulder-knots, green branches in their hats, or some similar token. Soldiers in the Austrian and Spanish armies, for example, wore red symbols of this kind, most usually a sash or a feather in the hat; and in 1632 Wallenstein ordered that no other colour should be used for this purpose. From this to genuine uniforms, however, was a considerable step. There was still a feeling, at least in some countries, that a soldier's morale and fighting qualities would be impaired if he were not allowed to indulge himself and advertise his aggressive masculinity by wearing fine clothes: for this reason luxury articles worn by soldiers were specifically exempted from the scope of the sumptuary laws passed in Spain in 1623 and later.[29] It was easier, for obvious reasons, to introduce uniforms in small and coherent forces than in larger ones. Members of the municipal guard raised by the city of Nürnberg in 1619 were all to be dressed alike; and in the same year the Duke of Brunswick-Wolfen-büttel ordered two of his regiments to be clothed in blue. A few years later Wallenstein's personal bodyguard was wearing uniform. In big armies, less homogeneous in their composition and often suffering from more difficult supply problems, the innovation was harder to achieve. By the 1620s, however, the Swedish army was beginning to adopt a number of standard forms of dress, though these varied from one regiment to another, while at the same time both Christian IV in Denmark and the Elector Maximilian in Bavaria tried to clothe their soldiers in distinctive uniforms. By the end of the Thirty Years War the imperial forces were beginning to take as their own the pearl-grey colour which they had adopted fully by the early years of the following century, while in England the New Model Army had red prescribed as its uniform colour in 1645. By the 1650s or soon after, moreover, colour symbolism was being extended to flags. These, when they were more than merely regimental, were still dynastic and not yet national. However particular colours and symbols were now becoming clearly associated with different countries – red with Spain, orange with the Dutch Republic, white with France, the black double-headed eagle with the Austrian Habsburgs and their mainly German territories. Here another focus for collective loyalty can be seen emerging, though again slowly. Even without these stimuli, moreover, *esprit de corps* may well have been strengthened by the sheer duration of so many of the wars of this period. Men who had fought and suffered side by side for years began, in some cases at least, to develop a common outlook and objectives: the demands of the Swedish army in Germany for the pay owed it may be a case in point. Certainly it seems that in England the fact that during the civil war, and the struggles with the Dutch and Spain which followed, many sailors served for long periods on naval vessels, and captains and other officers were almost constantly employed on them, did something to generate for the first time a feeling of belonging to a distinct service with its own needs and traditions.[30]

The impact on society

The destructive effects of war in this period were all too evident. At the most obvious level there is the direct loss of life, the men who were killed on the battlefield or died of their wounds. One statistician has put these, in an inevitably very arbitrary calculation, at 800,000 for the entire continent during the whole of the seventeenth century.[31] Certainly some of the battles of these decades were very bloody. At Breitenfeld in 1631 7–8000 of the 31,000 imperial troops involved were killed, while at Nördlingen three years later the fatal casualties on the Swedish side were even heavier, perhaps close to half of the 25,000 engaged. At Wittstock in 1636 the defeated imperial and Saxon armies may have lost 60 per cent of their strength; even the victorious Swedes had a third of their men killed or wounded. A difficult and painful retreat across country already stripped of supplies by earlier exactions usually damaged an army far more seriously than any battle, however, as hunger, demoralization, desertion and often attacks from peasants infuriated by forced contributions, pillaging and destruction took their toll. Any commander who could manoeuvre his opponent into such a retreat had won an overwhelming military success. Thus in 1644 the Swedes under Torstensson forced the imperialists under Gallas (probably the most incompetent commander of the Thirty Years War) to retreat from north Germany to Bohemia through areas for the most part already devastated, and by so doing destroyed them completely as a fighting force. According to one contemporary, of the 18,000 men who began the retreat barely a thousand finished it. Nine years earlier the same unfortunate general had lost between 10,000 and 20,000 men in a few weeks during his retreat from the French frontier into Germany. Even under better campaigning conditions poor commanders and inept organization could devastate an army; in the campaign of 1635 in the Low Countries, without any big battle being fought, the French forces were reduced, according to another contemporary observer, 'from 20,000 soldiers to 6000 beggars'.[32] Armies moreover were peculiarly susceptible to epidemic diseases. Large bodies of poorly disciplined and badly fed men, frequently irresponsible and even desperate, often crowded together in grossly unhealthy conditions, were more exposed to infection than was the population in general. In 1620 the army of the Catholic League lost 24,000 men in this way during its campaigns in the Austrian provinces and Bohemia, while in 1633 in Silesia 8000 died of disease in Wallenstein's army and 12,000 in the Swedish and Saxon ones.

These risks of a soldier's life were increased by occasional ferocious punishments meted out to men who had misbehaved in some way, and by the brutality with which the wounded and prisoners were treated. It was by no means unknown for units to be decimated (i.e. to have every tenth man put to death) after showing cowardice in battle: this happened to one regiment of the imperial army after the battle of

Lützen in 1632 and to another after that of Leipzig ten years later. Wounded men left on the battlefield, many of whom would of course have died in any case, were routinely slaughtered by looting soldiers of the victorious army, and very often also by its civilian hangers-on and local peasants. There were many instances in the Thirty Years War of the killing of prisoners in cold blood and on a considerable scale, most usually after the surrender of some fortress (for example the massacre of the garrison of Ingolstadt in 1633). When part of the garrison of Turin was slaughtered by the besieging French army in 1640 the French commander, the Comte d'Harcourt, himself pursued and struck down one of them as he tried to escape (though this earned him some strongly unfavourable comment from those who saw the incident). Even in unmilitary England the civil war as it progressed saw some very nasty, though usually small-scale, incidents of this kind. When Hopton Castle in Shropshire was taken by the royalists in 1644 the men of the garrison were bound and then had their throats cut one by one as they lay helpless, while a year later when the royalist stronghold of Basing House was stormed in October 1645, many of the garrison were massacred.[33] When prisoners were spared they were often simply incorporated into the forces which had captured them; in armies so mercenary and non-national this transition was an easy one. But if they were not needed to increase the numbers of the victor, were unwilling to take service with him and were not ransomed, their fate could be harsh. During sieges when food ran short, enemy prisoners held by the garrison sometimes starved to death, while in 1635 1400 taken by the French from the army of the Duke of Lorraine were condemned to serve as slaves in the galleys at Marseilles (though only 150 of them seem actually to have been used in this way).[34]

This was, then, a period in which armies often suffered crippling losses, casualties much higher than were soon to become the norm in the second half of the seventeenth century. Yet this was only a minor part of the whole story. Between the 1620s and the 1650s the fabric of society in many parts of Europe was severely damaged by war and in some areas the effects of the damage lingered long. Destructive epidemic disease was a very important part of this damage. In Germany typhus in particular down to about 1630, and after that bubonic plague as well, together with dysentery and smallpox, carried off many more people than died as a direct result of the fighting. But epidemics, though the movements of armies helped to spread them and their effects were increased by the disruption which war caused, were regular occurrences after all even in time of peace. The damage in terms of lost production and population growth inflicted by the sucking of so many young men into the competing armies and by the deaths of a high proportion of them is impossible to estimate; but sometimes at least it was severe. Sweden is a good example. Her ruthless exploitation of the parts of Germany which she controlled meant that the money cost to her of her share in the Thirty Years War was surprisingly small: by its closing years only 4 per cent of the Swedish budget went to pay for the struggle in Germany. But she paid a high price in blood. The total Swedish losses in the fighting in Poland and Germany in 1621–32 have been estimated at 50–55,000, and those of 1633–48 may have been twice as high – enormous figures for so small a country. A recent study has shown that in one village in northern Sweden 230 men were recruited for military service in 1621–39 and that of these 215 died. During these years the number of adult males in the parish fell catastrophically from 468 to 288. No society could withstand for very long depopulation on this scale.[35] In England, of twenty men who are known to have joined the royalist forces from three Shropshire villages in 1642 thirteen died in action – a rate of loss higher than that suffered by the same villages in the First World War.[36] Given the much shorter duration of the English civil war as compared with the struggles of Gustavus Adolphus and his successor, these figures tell the same story as the Swedish ones. But war did not impede population growth simply by depriving society of many young men. It also tended to raise food prices in the areas it affected, often to disastrous levels; and in many cases this led not merely to hunger and increased vulnerability to disease but also to a marked fall in the number of conceptions. It seems clear that this happened in parts of the Spanish Netherlands in the early and middle 1620s, for example.[37]

Most important of all, war during this period profoundly dislocated society over wide areas by causing enormous physical destruction and loss, by disrupting industry, trade and even agriculture, and sometimes by generating a mood of pessimism and despair which was hostile to any kind of risk-taking and hence to economic development. The need to provide billets, fodder and sometimes horses and money for armies on campaign was a heavy burden on parts of Europe where fighting was frequent – Lorraine, Catalonia in the 1640s and early 1650s, large parts of Germany during the Thirty Years War – especially since these demands were enforced almost as a matter of routine by carrying off livestock and burning villages. One French duchess left in her will sums of money to villages through which troops commanded by her son had passed, 'to avert from her the wrath of God, which she feared so much cruelty and so many extortions might attract'.[38] Much depended on the frequency with which armies visited any particular area and the length of time they stayed there. The occasional appearance of soldiers demanding food, forage and money could be borne. Regular and incessant demands, or worse still a prolonged occupation, were likely to be disastrous. When, after the cession to Sweden by Poland in 1629 of the area around Memel, it was occupied for a year by seventeen Swedish cavalry companies the results were devastating. Before the occupation there had been counted in the district 154 horses, 236 oxen, 103 cows, 190 pigs and 810 sheep. After it there remained only 26 oxen and one cow; all the rest had been seized or slaughtered by the soldiers.[39] It was easy to slip into a vicious circle in which looting and destruction made it impossible for the countryside to produce the contributions on which the feeding of an army depended, so that lack of food in its turn drove the soldiers to further looting. Quite often the occupation and devastation of an area made it impossible to plough and sow in the normal way, so that the following year's harvest was lost. This happened, for example, in Burgundy as a result of the invasion by imperial forces in 1636. The hatred of the civilian for the soldier, and especially the hatred of the peasant, usually more vulnerable and defenceless than the townsman, is the background to every war of this period. Usually the peasant had to suffer in silence or to evade the demands made on him by bribery or flight, so far as he could. Sometimes, however, goaded beyond endurance, he might react violently; and he could then become on occasion a factor of some military significance. A defeated army might well find itself under attack by embittered peasants, as happened to the remnants of Tilly's forces after his disaster at Breitenfeld. In 1632 the Swedes found themselves faced in south Germany by peasant guerrillas as well as the Bavarian and imperial armies. Gallas during his disastrous retreat in

1636 had his army mercilessly harassed by ruined and desperate peasants who massacred without distinction men from both the imperial forces and their Swedish opponents. In England the growth during the civil war of considerable armies on both sides and of corresponding demands on the civil population produced similar reactions. The violence of the peasant movement known as the Clubmen, which affected the west midlands and parts of the west country in 1645, was inspired mainly by a bitter dislike of soldiers of all kinds, whatever the cause for which they professed to be fighting. Moreover just as peasants hated soldiers indiscriminately, so soldiers despised all peasants. French soldiers defending Burgundy against attack from the Spanish forces in neighbouring Franche-Comté often showed more fellow-feeling with the enemy than with the French peasants they were allegedly protecting.[40]

The towns, though less exposed than the villages, also often suffered severely. Sometimes their capture by a besieging army produced an orgy of murder, looting and devastation. The outstanding case of this is the complete destruction of Magdeburg by Tilly's army in 1631, an event which shocked even so hardened an age and generated a huge pamphlet literature of condemnation; but even in England, Bristol was looted for two days after it was taken by the royalists in 1643, and two-thirds of Taunton was destroyed in the siege of 1645. Even without any spectacular catastrophe many towns were seriously affected by the devastation of the surrounding countryside which provided their food supply and a market for their products: good examples are Berlin, which had 12,000 inhabitants in 1618 and only 7500 two decades later, or more impressively Tarragona, which within two years of the outbreak of the Catalan revolt in 1640 may have seen its population drop from 7000 to little more than 2000. The most comprehensive recent survey of the economic and social effects of the Thirty Years War in Germany concludes that although the countryside as a whole may have lost about 40 per cent of its population the towns lost not much less, perhaps as much as a third (though these figures are speculative and probably too high).[41]

Some qualifications must be made to this gloomy picture. The experience of different parts of Europe varied enormously. Large parts of the continent – most of France, Spain apart from Catalonia in 1640–52, Sweden, England except for a few years in the 1640s – felt the effects of war only indirectly. They had to pay additional taxes and provide recruits; and these burdens were sometimes very heavy. But they did not have to face the demands of armies in the field for quarters and supplies and the disruption these entailed. Their towns and villages were not burnt and sacked. Even in Germany, which as a whole suffered more and longer than any other part of Europe, the picture is far from simple. There was not a single German economy but several 'in which different regions suffered different disasters at different times'.[42] The population of the country as a whole fell by at least 15 per cent, from about 20 million in 1618 to about 16–17 million in 1648 (though some estimates put the loss much higher); but this fall was very unevenly spread. Pomerania, Württemberg and Mecklenburg may have lost half their inhabitants. Bavaria, Brandenburg and Franconia were only a little less badly affected. But on the other hand the cities of north-west Germany – Hamburg, Lübeck and Bremen – even prospered during the struggles of these years and gained population by absorbing refugees from less favoured areas. Within regions and provinces again there were great variations. Towns and villages which were easily accessible, particularly those which stood on or near traditional military routes and were therefore frequently occupied by bodies of soldiers on the march, often suffered severely. Others geographically quite close by, but in less exposed positions, usually escaped more lightly. Even within a town or village war and its demands might affect individuals in markedly different ways. Some groups such as innkeepers and shoemakers could, under favourable conditions, benefit at least for a time from a strong demand for what they sold and from resulting higher prices, even when those around them were suffering badly. It must be remembered that much of the money extracted by soldiers from civilian society was returned to it very quickly in payment for such goods and services. One group in particular benefited markedly from the Thirty Years War. This was the Jewish communities of central Europe, whose numbers appear to have grown quite sharply. Vienna, a striking case, where there were only 50 or so Jewish families in 1625, had about 2000 Jews by 1650, while the Jewish colonies in Prague, Hamburg and other cities also increased. All the major belligerents in Germany made use of the Jews as a source of money and resources, often selling them protection from a potentially hostile population in exchange, while a considerable number of Jewish traders rose to leading positions in their communities by selling food and other supplies to the competing armies. By the 1640s there were signs of the emergence of a number of Jewish army contractors able to work on a very large scale, though this was a development which did not come to full fruition until a generation later.[43] This rise in the position of a marginal and often persecuted group is a striking illustration of the way in which war could sometimes open doors and offer opportunities as well as wreaking havoc. It is also true that recovery, even from severe devastation, may sometimes have been surprisingly rapid. The French commander Grammont, who had served in Westphalia in 1646, when the area was suffering the cumulative effects of many years of warfare, claimed that he could find no trace of them when he revisited it in 1658.

Undoubtedly there was serious and lasting economic decline in some parts of Germany during the first half of the seventeenth century. Old and famous trading cities such as Nürnberg, Augsburg and Cologne suffered particularly from this and never recovered their former importance. But it is clear that this decline had begun earlier and that though the long series of upheavals after 1618 accelerated and deepened it, they were not its cause. It was the product of other and more deep-rooted factors – the movement of economic activity to the Atlantic seaboard which followed, after some time-lag, the discovery of the new transoceanic trade routes to America and the East; the emergence of new competitors for the great German cities (notably the Dutch); and the political weakness and division of Germany and the way this increasingly hampered trade within it.

It is often difficult, moreover, to distinguish absolute losses of population in these years from mere population movements. Fortified towns, the castles of nobles, sometimes mere fortified houses, were recognized places of refuge for countrymen when the hated soldiers threatened. The shoemaker Hans Heberle of the village of Neestetten recorded in his diary thirty separate occasions during the Thirty Years War when he and his family fled for safety to the nearby city of Ulm, while in the years 1634–48 2000 peasants from the surrounding districts are recorded as having taken refuge at various times in the small west-German town of Heilbronn. It was not unknown for peasants to enter into contracts by which they were promised refuge in some nearby stronghold in case of danger in return for a money payment, in effect a kind of insurance premium. Thus in 1617 the seigneur who owned the chateau of Tumejus in Lorraine (a border area continually invaded and fought over throughout the seventeenth century) promised the inhabitants of the neighbouring village of Crézilles, in return for 500 francs to be paid over three years, 'to receive their persons and goods in times of trouble and threat of war in his said chateau of Tumejus and to keep and defend them there'.[44] Sometimes also leases of town houses stipulated that a room should be reserved for the lessors in case they wished to take refuge there in time of war. Very often, therefore, what appears at first sight a horrifying absolute decline in population turns out to be merely a displacement and often a temporary one. Such displacements reflected fear, deep insecurity and much human suffering; but they did not mean death on the scale which leaps to the uninformed eye.

The financing of war during this period had also considerable social implications, though no government foresaw or expected these. Few aspects of the seventeenth century, indeed, are more striking than the willingness of rulers and ministers to embark on increasingly expensive conflicts without the slightest realistic consideration of their cost. Nowhere outside the Dutch Republic, and possibly England in the second half of the century, did costs play a serious role in decisions on peace or war. Very often, highly destructive struggles were begun with almost criminal irresponsibility: both the French and Spanish governments in 1635, for example, grossly underestimated the demands which would be made by the long war which broke out in that year. Struggles between states were paid for in the main in two ways – by increased taxation or by borrowing. Both diverted scarce liquid resources away from more productive uses. Taxation meant a transfer of resources from agriculture (which still bore virtually everywhere the brunt of the taxes levied) to soldiers and army contractors. Borrowing made the same transfer with state creditors as the beneficiaries. Taxation in particular was a rapidly growing burden and one which sometimes weighed heavily on economic activity in general. In Spain this can be very clearly seen. The *millones* (indirect taxes on foodstuffs) paid by Castile doubled in the later 1620s, while in 1631 a tax on salt was introduced and in the following years new duties were levied on tobacco, meat, wine and other widely consumed commodities. The same process can be seen in the Spanish Netherlands. Flanders paid the Spanish crown 1,680,000 florins in 1629 as against 660,000 ten years earlier, while Artois in 1630 was paying 500,000 – two and a half times what it had done in 1620. In the Kingdom of Naples the *servicio* paid to the Spanish crown trebled between the late 1620s and the late 1630s. In spite of all this, however, Philip IV had to finance the exhausting struggles of 1621–59 in part by selling regalian and feudal rights and alienating royal estates in a way which seriously undermined the position of the monarchy. In France there was a similar progression. It has been calculated that there in the first decade of the seventeenth century 'the annual effort a hypothetical average worker put in for the state' amounted to the equivalent of only two to three days' wages, whereas by the 1690s it had grown to between ten and fourteen. Allowing for the costs of collecting taxes and exacting services, the total burden on the peasant may have increased tenfold.[45]

At a deeper level, war in these decades often meant lasting social change for the worse. Very often the position of the peasantry, and sometimes also that of the towns, was permanently weakened, usually to the advantage of landed nobilities. In Bohemia the vast confiscations of estates of Protestant rebels after 1620, and of Wallenstein's lands in 1635, helped to create a new group of great nobles of very diverse origins, often with no local roots whatever. Their emergence helped to pave the way for the great peasant revolt of 1680. This was a special case; but in Germany in general, nobles often profited by buying very cheaply land abandoned by its former peasant owners and thus building up large estates. This seems to have been particularly marked in Pomerania and Mecklenburg. In one district in the latter where in 1606 there had been 194 peasant holdings there were only 59 left in 1666. In another with 423 such holdings before the Thirty Years War this number had fallen to 115 by 1670.[46] Quite often it was not even necessary to buy, for normally land leased by a peasant from a lord reverted to the latter if it was abandoned. Even the shortage of labour caused by the war damaged the position of the German peasant, at least in many eastern parts of the country. Far from being able to profit from it, he often found himself compelled by new legislation, in Saxony and the Mark of Brandenburg in 1651, for instance, to perform a period of compulsory service to his lord (*Gesindedienst* or *Gesindezwangsdienst*) before he could take up his father's holding. Sometimes again village communities, their resources overtaxed by war demands, contracted debts which were difficult to pay off; this further weakened their position vis-à-vis neighbouring nobles and landlords. This change can be seen in the middle decades of the century not merely in Germany, above all east of the Elbe, but in many areas affected by prolonged military operations. The cumulative result of all these pressures is illustrated in microcosm in the case of the community of Noiron-les-Cîteaux in Burgundy, a province where the effects of war were relatively severe. In the 1550s this community was well off. It had extensive and fertile common lands and paid only a small amount in *taille* (land-tax). By the 1660s, however, this situation had changed drastically for the worse. The common lands had been alienated, the *taille* had markedly increased, and to it had been added various payments in kind and compulsory services.[47] Moreover while the towns in general suffered less than badly hit rural areas, the need to buy off the competing armies meant that in Germany at least many cities, like village communities, fell into debt; the municipal borrowing of Nürnberg rose during the Thirty Years War from 1.8 million gulden to 7.4 million.

But the contrasts are striking. In the most developed part of Europe, the United Provinces, the long struggle of 1621–48 with Spain had remarkably little damaging effect. There the outbreak of war in 1621 had been widely welcomed by many who argued that Dutch trade had grown more rapidly before the truce of 1609 than after it. On land the struggle was remarkably static, and indeed from the early 1630s strikingly inactive. There was little of the movement of troops over substantial distances which was so destructive elsewhere. This was a war of fortresses whose garrisons, on the Dutch side at least, paid cash for what they took from the surrounding population and thus often had a stimulating rather than a retarding effect on the local economy. From the early 1620s privateers from Dunkirk took a great many Dutch ships – probably about 2500 in the decade 1629–38 – but even this did not succeed in reducing Dutch trade. On the contrary, it grew steadily and showed signs of decline only after the middle of the century when the threat from Dunkirk had, for the time being at least, receded. Sometimes also war brought a temporary benefit to industry in a belligerent country by freeing it while the conflict lasted from enemy competition. Thus the sustained attempts of the Spanish government after 1621 to cut off all trade with the Dutch (the most genuine effort at economic warfare hitherto seen anywhere in Europe) did much to protect the textile industries of such towns as Toledo and Segovia. In a rather similar way, by diverting trade from its normal channels, war might bring windfall benefits to neutrals. These same Spanish embargoes on Dutch trade meant that the Hanse towns of northern Germany, and to some extent England, played for a quarter of a century a more prominent role than they otherwise would have done in the great carrying trade between the Baltic and the Mediterranean. Occasionally also it is possible to point to industrial growth which was the result of war demands or preparations. The arms production of Liège benefited from the long struggle in the Netherlands. In Spain a *junta* was set up in 1623 to stimulate the production of gunpowder, though it seems to have had little effect. More strikingly, the 1630s saw the creation of a substantial armaments industry in the Tula area of Russia, the work of the Dutchman Andries Vinius and his associates. In 1636 this was already able to export 600 cannon to the United Provinces, surely one of the most remarkable industrial triumphs of the seventeenth century.

It is also true that in a very limited and haphazard way war might be an engine of social mobility. It could offer opportunities for exceptionally able or lucky men of obscure birth to rise to positions which in peacetime would have been beyond their reach. This is most obvious in Germany during the Thirty Years War. The duration and savagery of the conflict, the dislocation of normal life which it produced, the competition between the belligerents for commanders of proven ability, gave openings of which new men with sufficient ruthlessness and energy might sometimes take advantage. An outstanding example is Peter Melander, the son of peasants, who after commanding the Hessian army became one of the leaders of the imperial one. He also became a count holding directly from the emperor and thus entitled to attend the Reichstag in person, while his daughter married the reigning prince of Nassau-Dillenburg: the descendants of the marriage included crowned heads. This was an extraordinary achievement in an age so dominated by inherited status. In more normal times it would have been an impossible one. There are other striking examples – Johann von Werth, also of peasant stock, who became a colonel in the Bavarian army in 1633, a baron in the following year and finally a field-marshal; or Georg Derfflinger, who rose to high rank in the Swedish army, gained fame as a Brandenburg cavalry commander after 1648 and, in spite of his humble origins, twice married into noble families. On a slightly lower level there were the son of a bricklayer who became a colonel in the imperial army, or the converted Jew who reached the same rank in the little force maintained by the Elector of Cologne. The ennoblement of commoners on the battlefield after conspicuous displays of courage, moreover, was quite common. After Lützen, in one imperial cavalry regiment, a major, a captain, an ensign and eight common soldiers achieved noble status in this way. In Russia, though in the wars of the 1650s and 1660s the very highest commands were still invariably reserved for members of great families, there was a tendency for the most important secondary ones to be given to a new group of specialists of lower birth who led regiments of the new European type. There were even a very small number of new men who rose to membership of the *Boyarskaya Duma*, the council of great aristocrats which advised the tsar, through their military abilities.[48] In England too the upheavals of the civil war were, up to a point, favourable to this sort of achievement. They allowed one or two generals on the parliamentary side to rise to positions of power from humble origins, like Skippon, or from minor gentry ones, like Lambert.

Not too much should be made of all this, however. It was still very much the exception for a commoner to rise to a really high military post. Of the 107 colonels in the imperial army in 1633 only 13 were commoners (though a few of the others may have been only recently ennobled). In the Swedish army the proportion of non-nobles was probably rather higher; in the French one it was certainly much lower. War occasionally opened doors to social advancement; but few and narrow ones. And with the coming from the 1650s onwards of more effective bureaucratic control of armies, careers of this kind became much more rare.

All these positive features – localized stimuli to industry, windfall profits to a few types of trade, a small number of spectacular individual careers – were however almost trivial when compared with the loss which war brought. Even the Dutch-Spanish struggle, the most moderate and civilized of this period, almost certainly on balance retarded rather than helped economic development. A leading authority on the subject has concluded that 'most of the money and resources which the various combatants poured into the war in the Netherlands were, in economic terms, entirely unproductive. . . . The war was, in many ways, conspicuous expenditure on a monstrous scale by the various government of Europe.'[49] If the verdict on the Netherlands struggle has to be so unfavourable then that on the far more destructive and uncontrolled fighting which went on in northern Italy, in Catalonia and most of all in Germany must be even more so.

PART TWO

Old-regime Warfare at its Height, 1660–1740

The struggles for power

The half-century which began in the later 1660s saw inter-state struggles which changed the political face of Europe more, and more lastingly, than any since the reign of the Emperor Charles V five generations earlier. Those of the two decades 1700–20 in particular laid the foundations for much of the structure of international relations down to the French Revolution. The diplomacy and warfare of this half-century were in their detail immensely complex; but most of the major changes can be grouped around three great lines of development.

The first of these is the rise, though by no means a continuous and uninterrupted one, in the power of France. When the peace of 1659 was signed with Spain it was already clear that she was the greatest military power in Europe and the most potentially expansionist of the major states. Her young ruler Louis XIV, almost from the moment he assumed clear personal control of the government in 1661, showed himself eager for new territorial gains. His motives have been debated at length and inconclusively by historians. To some extent they were essentially defensive. He clearly hoped to build up for France, by expansion into the Netherlands, west Germany and north-west Italy, an outer protective ring of fortresses and subject-territories, a glacis to aid in the defence of French territory proper. Whether he was driven even more by the appetite for personal reputation and prestige which was undoubtedly strong in him, and the exact place in his thinking and feeling of dynastic influences, are still open questions. The outcome, however, was a series of increasingly long and expensive struggles against increasingly powerful hostile coalitions. A brief war with Spain in 1665–7 won small but significant gains in the southern Netherlands. A sudden and at first apparently overwhelming attack on the Dutch Republic in 1672 produced a wide-ranging but incoherent alliance against him which came to include Spain, the Austrian Habsburgs and a number of smaller states. Against this he more than held his own militarily, and the peace of 1678–9, though a compromise, brought him new territorial gains, notably that of Franche-Comté, the old free county of Burgundy. Further seizures of territory in the years which followed, most importantly of Strasbourg in 1681 and Luxembourg in 1684, intensified the fear and hostility which France now more and more aroused in her neighbours; and the war which broke out in 1689 faced Louis with opposition more formidable than any he had hitherto seen.

Of the members of the Grand Alliance formed against him in that year Spain was now at the nadir of her fortunes, too weak and decrepit to count for much. Moreover the Dutch Republic was beginning to feel the impossibility, given her small territory and population, of playing the role of a true great power, while the Austrian Habsburgs, in spite of impressive territorial gains in the Danube valley, were still much weaker than France, most of all in their financial resources. England, however, ruled since the revolution of 1688–9 by William III, who as leader of the Dutch Republic had already for close on two decades been Louis's most persistent and tenacious enemy, was now for the first time actively on the anti-French side. Militarily far inferior to France, her growing naval and financial strength made her nonetheless a far from negligible opponent, and the anti-French coalition was able to strain Louis's resources as never before. The peace of 1697 was hardly a defeat; but it was bought at the cost of significant concessions by him, though in the main not territorial ones. The last and greatest of his wars, that over the Spanish Succession, the fate of the unwieldy Spanish empire in Europe after the death in 1700 of its last Habsburg ruler, Charles II, saw France almost from its outbreak in 1701–2 suffer a series of unprecedented military defeats of which Blenheim (1704) and Ramillies (1706) were the most important. The most successful allied commanders, Prince Eugene for the Habsburgs and the Duke of Marlborough for England, established an ascendancy on the battlefield which none of their predecessors had been able to achieve. The terrible winter of 1709 inflicted on France suffering unparalleled since the grim years of the early 1650s. Yet all was not lost. She was successful in a long and fluctuating struggle for control of Spain itself from 1704 onwards. An outstanding commander, Marshal Villars, did much to restore her military reputation and self-confidence in the last stages of the war. Her enemies were, as always, deeply disunited: the British government in particular from 1711 onwards showed a brutal indifference to the interests of its Dutch and Austrian allies. The result was that the peace settlement of 1713–14 was far from being the total victory over Louis of which his enemies had for a time dreamed. Little French territory was lost: his grandson was established on the Spanish throne.

The king, however, was well aware in his last years that he had strained France's resources and his subjects' loyalty almost beyond bearing, that as he himself said, he had 'loved war too well'. His death in 1715 ushered in two decades during which the expansionism of the last half-century was notably absent from French foreign policy. Even the brief War of the Polish Succession in 1733–5 (from the French standpoint really another struggle with the Austrian Habsburgs for territory and influence in Italy and the Rhineland) hardly disturbs this generalization; but by the later 1730s the tradition of French advance in the southern Netherlands, towards the Rhine and into northern Italy, was preparing to reassert itself.

The growth of Russian power, the second of the great developments of this period, followed a quite different course. France in the 1660s had for centuries been recognized as the greatest state in western Europe in population, wealth and at least potential military strength. Though Spain had for a century or more, until the 1640s or even later, been able to appear a still greater power, she had achieved this only by becoming the centre of a multinational empire, not through purely Spanish resources. Russia, by contrast, remained until the end of the seventeenth century relatively ignored and disregarded. She was poor, backward, confined to the periphery of European politics, indeed barely regarded as part of Europe at all. The war which she waged against the Ottoman Empire in the 1680s and 1690s, together with Poland, the Austrian Habsburgs and Venice, ended in 1699–1700 with complete disregard of her interests by her allies and disappointingly little gain to her. Yet within a decade she had risen with unprecedented speed to a totally new level of importance. The war on which she embarked in 1700, together with

Denmark and Saxony-Poland, in an effort to partition the Swedish Baltic empire, for many years strained her resources to the limit. Her allies were defeated and compelled to make peace (Frederick IV of Denmark in 1700, Augustus II of Saxony-Poland in 1708). Her armies suffered severe, even humiliating, setbacks. Yet in 1709 at Poltava in the Ukraine she inflicted on the warrior-king of Sweden, Charles XII, a crushing defeat which transformed the situation. A Swedish invasion of Russia which had at first seemed to have hopes of success collapsed in total failure. The Tsar Peter I found himself almost overnight able to dominate Poland, to complete the conquest of the Swedish Baltic provinces, to become a power in the German world and a factor of growing importance in the calculations of the statesmen of western Europe. This was a true political and military revolution, one of the greatest in all European history. The end of the Great Northern War was slow in coming. Not until 1721 was the seal of a peace treaty placed upon Russia's new status. But she was now permanently one of the great military powers of Europe, potentially, at least, the greatest of all. Against the Ottoman Empire in the Balkans and the Black Sea her success was much less complete than against Sweden in the Baltic. Peter I failed spectacularly in a Balkan campaign of 1711; and a Russo-Turkish war in 1736–9 proved difficult and expensive. But neither this nor the weakness and mediocrity of Peter's immediate successors could tarnish his achievement in the eyes of contemporaries. His personal prestige remained enormous; and military victory rather than his efforts at internal change and modernization in Russia was the foundation of that prestige.

The third great developing military power of these decades, though one whose growth rested on narrower foundations than that of France and was less spectacular than that of Russia, was the Habsburg territories in central Europe. These played an important role in the struggles to restrain French expansion from the 1670s onwards. The Holy Roman Emperor, always a Habsburg, was still seen, and saw himself, as the chief protector of the German world against the threat from across the Rhine. But it was the dramatic victories won against the Turks in the 1680s and 1690s which made the Austrian Habsburgs a greater force than ever before in European politics and raised the reputation of their army to the highest point it was ever to reach. The failure of the great Turkish attack on Vienna in 1683 was followed, in spite of the difficulties of campaigning in the unhealthy Danube valley and the thinly populated Hungarian plain, by remarkable successes for what was in many ways the last crusading effort of Christian Europe. When peace was made in 1699 at Karlowitz the Habsburgs had made territorial gains which in geographical extent dwarfed anything achieved by Louis XIV. A shorter but equally successful struggle in 1716–18 gave them much of Serbia with the great fortress of Belgrade: their southern frontier had now been pushed forward into the Balkans as far as it was ever to be. Austrian Habsburg great-power status, however, was a much more tender plant than that of France or Russia. The Habsburg territories still notably lacked any sort of administrative unity. They were an accumulation of provinces (Upper and Lower Austria, Styria, Carinthia, the Tyrol) and kingdoms (Bohemia, Hungary) with separate institutions, interests and outlooks. There was no Habsburg state. Also the acquisition in 1713, with the breakup of the Spanish empire in Europe, of new territories quite separate from the central-European core of the monarchy, in the Spanish Netherlands, Milan and Naples, increased the complications and obligations which the dynasty had to face without any corresponding increase in its ability to meet the challenge. Worst of all, the Habsburg monarchy, even at the height of its military success, was poor. The poverty of almost all the hereditary provinces, the difficulty of raising the money needed to sustain a great army, was a weakness which it never overcame. The strikingly weak performance of its armies in a new war with the Ottoman Empire in 1737–9 and the resulting loss of the Balkan gains made only two decades earlier showed that the foundations of its success were far from completely secure.

The changes in the military balance within Europe which had become clear by the early eighteenth century inevitably meant losers as well as gainers. Spain emerged from the succession struggle shorn of her European possessions. Though she was able to remain a significant military force, and indeed to make a remarkable recovery from the weakness and decrepitude of the later seventeenth century, she had lost for ever the primacy she had enjoyed under Philip II and Olivares. Sweden also was hardly a negligible force, even after the disasters of the long struggle with Russia; but her days of greatness were even more clearly in the past. The Dutch Republic now lacked both the resources and increasingly even the will to maintain the military and naval status it had won in the seventeenth century. England had been driven by the demands of the struggle with France from 1689 onwards to become a significant military force; Blenheim was the first major victory won in continental Europe for almost three centuries by an even partly English army. But most Englishmen still hoped devoutly that their country could avoid becoming a major military power with all the expense and apparent danger to political liberty at home which this involved, and indeed that she could avoid all European entanglements as far as possible. In the wings the most successful of all eighteenth-century armies, that of Brandenburg-Prussia, was taking shape; but the stage was still held by France, Russia and the Austrian Habsburgs. More than ever before, the military destinies of the continent were in the hands of a small group of great powers; the medium-sized ones which in the past had sometimes had an important influence – Sweden, the Dutch Republic, perhaps Denmark, earlier Venice – had now at best secondary significance. Within the great states, moreover, autonomous or semi-autonomous entities which had been important in the past were now being swept away in a process of usually forcible assimilation. The Russian victory at Poltava made possible greater central control of the Ukraine whose hetman, Mazepa, had taken the Swedish side. The Habsburg victories in Hungary meant the end of the sometimes almost independent status of Transylvania, while the succession struggle in Spain ended with the destruction in 1714 of the jealously guarded privileges of Catalonia. In Great Britain, in a rather different way, the defeat of the Jacobite rebellion of 1715 began the assimilation of the Highlands of Scotland, hitherto an almost separate world, to the rest of the country. By 1740 the future of Europe rested more clearly than ever before with a number of great states which could maintain great armies and whose governments were increasingly intolerant of any obstacle to the free exercise of their power within their own territories.

The scale of warfare: armies

In the second half of the seventeenth century many European armies became bigger than ever before. In this respect they were not to be outdone, and in some cases not equalled, until the wars of the French Revolution had transformed the situation. The great struggles of the first decades of the eighteenth century thus saw the culmination, at least for three generations or so to come, of that process of increasing military effort and intensifying military demands on society which had begun at least two centuries earlier. The most striking case, and the best-documented one, is that of France. In 1661, when it had been drastically reduced after the end of the war with Spain two years earlier, the French army numbered, at least on paper, nearly 32,000 infantry (19,000 Frenchmen and 12,600 in foreign regiments), another 8400 in 'free' companies which had no regimental organization, and about 8500 cavalry – a total of 48,900. By 1678, at the end of the first of his really demanding wars, Louis XIV had at his disposal 220,000 infantry, 60,000 cavalry and 10,000 of the élite force of the *Maison du Roi*; and even after the army had been reduced once more with the coming of peace, it still numbered in the following year 130,000 – more than two and a half times what it had been in the early 1660s. By 1690, when France was engaged in a still more exacting and expensive conflict, its total paper strength was 388,000. If the different militia forces (local ones in some cities and frontier provinces and the *milices garde-côtes* in maritime areas as well as the militia proper) are included, as well as the navy, the total number of men who were in some sense under arms reached 600,000.[1] By 1691 73 per cent of all government revenue was being spent on the army and fortifications and 16 per cent on the fleet. This was national mobilization for war of a kind scarcely seen even in the Spain of Olivares; and the critical years of the Spanish Succession struggle saw an at least comparable and probably even greater effort. In 1710 the regular army's paper strength was about 360,000, while militiamen were being forcibly drafted into regular regiments in a way never seen before. The years 1701–13 saw 455,000 men recruited by one means or another into the French army – an average of 35,000 a year. In 1702, when it was completing the move from a peace to a war footing, an astonishing 107 new regiments were created. In 1717 the peacetime establishment, excluding the foreign regiments, was still 110,000 and in 1738 115,000, while in the wars of 1741–8 and 1756–63 France maintained military forces almost comparable to those of the last years of Louis XIV.[2]

Elsewhere lesser powers with smaller resources struggled to make comparable increases in their military strength. The achievements of Russia in particular, given the poverty of the country and the enormous obstacles which distance and poor communications placed in the way of effective central administration, were even more impressive than those of France. By 1680 the Russian army already numbered about 200,000; and though a quarter of these were still in old *streltsy* units, whose military effectiveness was now declining sharply, it was already becoming a modern force. In the unsuccessful campaign of 1689 against the Tatars of the Crimea only 19,000 of the soldiers involved were in traditional Russian-style regiments as against almost 79,000 in the new foreign-model ones. Peter I, from the beginning of his great struggle with Sweden in 1700, made immense efforts to strengthen his army. He raised twenty-nine new regiments in 1699-1700 and introduced a new and more effective (and therefore more burdensome) system of recruiting in 1705 (see pages 113-14 below). During his reign these levies raised about 284,000 men in all. However even at his death in 1725 the Russian army, at about 215,000 men, was hardly bigger than it had been in the early 1680s. Historians have, at least until recently, paid much more attention to the military ambitions and innovations of Peter than to those of his predecessors; but it is a mistake to believe that Russia acquired what was, in proportion to her resources, a very large and expensive army only under his rule.

A comparable growth of military strength, though one very different in its nature, was also to be seen in the last decades of the seventeenth century in Sweden, soon to be locked in a life-and-death struggle with her great eastern neighbour. There in the 1680s Charles XI, essentially for financial reasons, changed the basis on which the army had been recruited, making it almost as national as the Russian one (see page 120 below). When he died in 1697 he left to his son a force of 90,000 men, well-organized, well-armed and well-trained, a very remarkable achievement for so small and poor a country. During the Great Northern War Sweden and Finland made a military effort which probably surpassed any other of this period. By 1710, according to one calculation, they had provided for it 110,000 men –

about 5 per cent of their entire population.[3] In England experience in 1655–7 of the system of rule by major-generals, based on a 'new militia' which was in some ways very close to a standing army, had given more strength to already strong anti-militarist feeling. Yet even she saw herself compelled to admit the need for considerable permanent military forces. The Act of Parliament of 1660 which disbanded the Cromwellian forces specifically allowed the king to raise as many soldiers as he wished so long as he could pay them from the resources allotted him; and though in 1678 Parliament voted the disbandment of the entire standing army, nothing of the sort happened. On the contrary, by 1688 James II had managed to build up a peacetime force of 53,000 men, by far the largest the country had ever seen. By 1697, at the end of eight years of unprecedentedly large-scale and expensive war, there were just over 90,000 men, exclusive of officers, in pay; and though in that year Parliament insisted on reducing this to a mere 10,000 with the coming of peace, it was now increasingly accepted that some sort of standing army could not be dispensed with. The War of the Spanish Succession saw it rise to new levels of strength annd cost, and in the relatively peaceful quarter-century 1714–39 it averaged about 35,000 men. This was no great force (about the same number as was maintained by the Kingdom of Sardinia) and at any moment an appreciable fraction of it was in America, the Caribbean, Minorca or Gibraltar. But by contrast with the situation under Charles II, it meant a true revolution in attitudes.

The armies of this period remained, at least in western Europe, as cosmopolitan in their makeup and as willing to recruit foreigners if they could afford them as their predecessors in the age of Wallenstein and Richelieu. They still served monarchs rather than nations or even governments, and monarchs who often ruled multinational states. Even in its sharply reduced state of 1661 the French army included eleven regiments of foreigners – four Irish, three German, two Scottish and one each from Catalonia and the Bishopric of Liège. In the decades which followed, its net was cast still wider. It had, to take only two somewhat exotic cases, a regiment of Hungarians later in the century and acquired one of Corsicans in 1739, when Corsica was still a Genoese possession, while agreements of 1671 and 1702 confirmed its right to recruit, as it had done for generations, in the Swiss cantons.

As late as 1751, 28 of the 133 batallions of infantry in the Spanish army were made up of foreigners; and in that year it was proposed to recruit twenty more in Italy and the German states. Spain was not an entirely typical case, for there the social prestige of the army was exceptionally low; but in other instances the proportion of foreigners, at least at officer level, was just as great. In the later years of the seventeenth century, for example, nearly a third of the officers in the army of Brandenburg-Prussia were French Huguenot refugees, while the Danish army drew a very high proportion of its officers from north Germany, notably from Mecklenburg. Nor were religious differences normally of any more significance than national or linguistic ones. In 1690, at a time when Louis XIV was savagely persecuting the Huguenots in France and being execrated for it throughout Protestant Europe, more than a tenth of the French army was made up of Protestant (mainly German) soldiers. Even the recruiting of subjects of an enemy ruler in wartime was not necessarily difficult. As late as 1745, when Britain and France were at war, a Jacobite clan chief was actively recruiting in Scotland for the French regiment of which he was colonel.[4] In this situation it was possible for individuals, and occasionally even entire regiments, to move with relative ease from one employer to another. Thus the Hepburn regiment, first recruited in Scotland in 1633 by Sir James Hepburn to fight for Gustavus Adolphus in Germany, five years later entered French service as the Douglas regiment and in the later decades of the century alternated between the French and English ones. A high proportion of the leading commanders of the age served in at least two armies and some in many more. Marlborough began his military career as an ensign in a French regiment and Villars, later to be his ablest opponent, served as a young man in the Habsburg army against the Turks. (Campaigning against the Turks, which had still some of the aura of a crusade, was particularly attractive as a school of warfare to young officers from many parts of Europe.) Perhaps the most striking individual case of all is that of Ulric-Frédéric-Woldemar, Comte de Lowendahl. Born in Hamburg in 1700, he served first in Poland at the age of only thirteen. A year later he was a captain in the Danish army, and then served in that of the Habsburgs. At twenty he was back in Poland as a colonel, and a decade later passed with that rank into Prussian service. He then served in the Saxon and Russian armies before entering the French one as a lieutenant-general in 1747. Four years later he crowned his career by becoming a marshal of France. There are also some striking examples of cosmopolitan dynasties of professional soldiers. The Irishman Peter Lacy, for instance, by the early 1740s a field-marshal in Russian service, had then a brother, Guillermo de Lacy, who was colonel of a Spanish regiment, and a son, Franz Moritz Lacy, on the point of entering the Habsburg army in which he later rose to very high rank.

Besides these mercenaries and soldiers of fortune, recruited in one country to serve in the army of another, there were foreign auxiliary forces which in wartime were often more important. These were regiments raised by one ruler as part of his own army and then hired by him to another for use in the latter's quarrels. This was a device very useful to states which had relatively small armies of their own but also relatively plentiful supplies of ready cash. Of these England had become by the early eighteenth century the outstanding example; and she now made increasingly free use of auxiliary forces of this kind. Thus when the Grand Alliance was formed against France in 1702 she agreed to contribute to the joint war effort only 40,000 soldiers (against 90,000 from the Emperor Leopold I and 102,000 from the Dutch) and of these a mere 18,000 were to be English. The other 22,000 were provided by auxiliary regiments hired in Denmark, Prussia and Hesse. As the war went on, others were obtained in the same way from Hanover, Saxony and other German states. Since it was more difficult and expensive to raise regiments in England than to hire them from some impecunious foreign ruler, this was a perfectly rational policy and one Britain was to follow in every major war she fought during the eighteenth century; but it underlines once more the extent to which armies were still thought of as state or dynastic instruments rather than repositories of national pride.

Bigger armies, as in the first half of the seventeenth century, made greater demands on society. But these demands were not merely a matter of increasing size. They were made heavier by two other factors – the continued growth, at least in western Europe and until the early eighteenth century, of very large-scale and expensive siege operations; and the efforts now being made in many states to make militias larger and more effective. Of both these trends France is once more the best, and certainly the most intensively studied, example.

Louis XIV himself was clearly attracted by the systematic and predictable character of sieges carried out by techniques which had now become an established orthodoxy. 'Great sieges', he wrote, 'please me more than any other action.'[5] Moreover he was excessively conscious of the continuing vulnerability of France's eastern and north-eastern frontiers: memories of the crisis year 1636 still lingered in Paris. The result was a sustained effort from the 1670s to the 1690s, led by the greatest military engineer of the age, Marshal Vauban, to stud these frontiers with powerful fortresses which would not merely deter foreign attack but also provide in some cases jumping-off points for French invasion of neighbouring states. This was inevitably expensive. In 1682–91 France spent on average 8.5 million livres each year on fortifications (though after the early 1690s, as Vauban's work drew to a close, the cost fell rapidly to an average of less than 3 million in 1692–1707). The wars which Louis fought in 1672–8, 1689–97 and 1701–13 were all marked by significant, in some cases great, battles. But all of them, at least in the Spanish Netherlands and west Germany, were at least as much wars of sieges (notably Luxemburg in 1684 and Namur in 1692, culminating in the immensely complex and costly, though ultimately successful, allied assault on Lille in 1708). Even Marlborough after his second great victory over the French at Ramillies in 1706 spent most of his time on sieges. As in earlier generations, operations of this kind, through their great cost and complexity, added significantly to the burdens which war imposed on society.

It can be argued strongly that this prominence of sieges was and always had been a rational response to conditions in the Netherlands, the Rhineland or northern Italy, the great traditional fields of combat for west-European armies. It was in fortified cities that were assembled the magazines of food and stores on which these armies increasingly depended. To capture one was therefore to deprive the enemy of an important asset. Even a successful battle was often a less genuine victory, since it could so seldom be followed up effectively. The difficulty of moving guns and wagons over bad roads with often inefficiently harnessed horses or slow and lumbering oxen, and the dangers inherent in dividing an army into smaller units, moving it over a number of different roads and thus exposing it to sudden enemy attack, meant that an average speed of about ten miles a day was as much as could be hoped for. Sometimes much higher speeds could be achieved: in August 1694, a French army in the southern Netherlands marched a hundred miles in four days, crossing five rivers on the way. But anything approaching this was very exceptional. Also the normal compaigning season was short. An army could hardly move before the spring growth of grass began to provide forage for its horses (which were usually harder to feed than the men) and it was difficult to carry on large-scale operations after autumn rains began to turn unpaved roads to mud. When even moderately rapid movement was so difficult and there might well not be time enough in the summer months to take full advantage of a victory it was not unreasonable for many commanders to feel that battles were hardly worth fighting.[6]

This continuing importance of sieges was reflected in the increasing indispensability of engineers and artillerymen and the way in which they were now for the first time clearly becoming integral parts of any well-organized army. Hitherto, even in the most powerful and forward-looking forces, they had had an ambiguous and peripheral status. They had been important, indeed essential, but still semi-civilians, experts recruited for a specific and limited expertise rather than true soldiers. Skilled engineers, without whom successful sieges were impossible, were particularly valuable and sometimes particularly difficult. 'Good engineers are so scarce', wrote Lord Galway, the British commander in Portugal in 1704, 'that one must bear with their humours and forgive them because we can't be without them.'[7] Now this situation was changing. The French army had five times as many guns at the battle of Neerwinden in 1693 as at Rocroi fifty years earlier; and this transformation explains why the great war minister Louvois created six companies of gunners in 1679 and another six ten years later, as well as two companies of sappers in 1673 and 1679 and a regiment of bombardiers in 1684. Across the Channel, Charles II in 1683 issued the first 'Instructions for the Government of our Office of Ordnance'. This was followed more than a generation later by the establishment in 1716 of a distinct corps of engineers and four permanent artillery companies and by the creation of the Royal Regiment of Artillery in 1727 (though artillery officers did not in fact hold British army rank until 1751). During the half-century from 1660 to the end of the War of the Spanish Succession, therefore, the growth of armies in western Europe was not merely a matter of increasing numbers. They were also becoming steadily more complex organizations and more expensive ones.

This was, however, less completely true of eastern Europe. East of the Elbe, as in the past, smaller armies more able to live off the country and a greater rarity of substantial towns meant that sieges continued to be much less significant than in the west. The long Baltic struggle of 1699–1721 saw only three really big ones (of Thorn by the Swedes in 1703, of Riga by the Russians in 1710 and of Stralsund by the Danes, Prussians and Russians in 1715). The Turkish failure to take Vienna in 1683 was the most widely commented-on military event of the age, and the Habsburg capture of Belgrade in 1717 one of the greatest successes the Austrian ruling house ever won; but both of these were battles as well as sieges. Moreover by the 1730s the siege warfare which had bulked so large for a century and a half was losing its former importance even in western Europe. Fortresses continued to be significant and much time and energy to be spent in attacking them; but more and more clearly it was now field armies, their movements and the clashes between them, which were decisive. Frederick the Great of Prussia made his perhaps exaggerated reputation as a commander in the 1740s and 1750s by fighting battles. He disliked siege warfare and was admitted even by some of his greatest admirers to have no talent for it. But in western Europe and in the age of Louis XIV it was in sieges rather than in battles that the demands of war on society made themselves felt.

Side by side with this growing size and cost of armies went efforts in some parts of Europe to strengthen militias, to make them more efficient and sometimes to use them as a source of recruits for the regular army. This was, however, most marked in a number of west-European countries where the demands of war were being felt with particular acuteness. In other states it was weaker or completely lacking. In Russia there had in the past been a considerable tradition of popular participation in defensive military activity.[8] But by the second half of the seventeenth century this had been undermined by the growth of a powerful regular army; and under Peter I the gulf between army and society became sharper than ever before. The whole governmental structure of imperial Russia was now unsympathetic to the creation of a western-type militia and little effort was made in that direction during the later seventeenth or eighteenth centuries. Some militia regiments were formed in the Ukraine in 1712–13 in response to the war of these years with the Turks: but these were never important, and at the end of Peter's reign they amounted to only about 6000 men. The Cossack groups on the Dnieper and Don, too, were now rapidly losing what remained of their autonomy, and also some at least of their military importance. Already in the second half of the seventeenth century there had developed a marked tendency for poor Cossacks, unable to afford a horse and reduced to the indignity of fighting on foot, to lose their special status and be incorporated into the new western-style regiments as ordinary infantrymen. Moreover Cossack autonomy now seemed a clear threat to Russian unity and security. In 1708 Mazepa, the Ukrainian hetman, sided openly with Charles XII of Sweden against Peter I at a moment when a Swedish victory in the Great Northern War seemed very much on the cards; and in the same year there was a serious rising among the Cossacks on the Don. The result was a determined attack on Cossack autonomy and the deportation of tens of thousands of Cossacks to forced labour elsewhere in Russia. In 1716–22 40,000 were conscripted for canal-building (one of Peter's favourite forms of material improvement) and of these a third and possibly a half died as a result. The Grenzers in Croatia suffered no such fate; but their military importance, always less than that of the Cossacks, declined much more rapidly. As the Habsburg boundaries were pushed rapidly southwards in the 1680s and 1690s and the Turks ceased to be a threat to central Europe, the whole argument for the existence of a military border with its special organization and privileges became much weaker. More and more, with the Turkish danger at an end, it became merely 'a dumping-place for the unemployable nobility of Inner Austria'.[9] Though there were some efforts to make it more of a military reality in the early eighteenth century, these had little result; and in 1747 the Grenzer units were incorporated into the Habsburg regular army. Henceforth the border retained some importance as the source of many of the best and most loyal of the soldiers upon whom Habsburg power ultimately depended; but its special military status had gone.

In Sweden the *Indelningswerk* system of recruiting introduced during the 1670s and 1680s (see page 120 below) meant that the gap between militia and regular army, so clear in many other parts of Europe, largely ceased to exist. The army was settled on the land and an integral part of society. To an extent unequalled elsewhere, Sweden was in time of war a nation in arms, one for which a militia organization of the usual kind was largely superfluous. In England, whose position was totally different, anti-militarist tradition and intense popular dislike of any form of military service ensured as in the past (see pages 20–1 above) that no effective militia could be developed. It was re-established in more or less its Elizabethan form by legislation of 1661–3; and in the later decades of the century it had still a paper strength of perhaps as many as 90,000. But as a fighting force it remained a nullity. The musters which were supposed to take place at regular intervals (annually for each regiment and up to four times a year for each company) often were not held for years on end, while lack of money and widespread reluctance to serve weakened it as they had done its predecessors.

Across the Channel the situation was very different. In 1688 Louvois, in one of the most important of all his innovations, overhauled completely the provincial militia and its organization. Men between the ages of twenty and forty, chosen by their parishes and officered by local gentry, were to be trained on Sundays and other holidays. They were to serve, it was promised, for only two years; but this concession was at once disregarded. Fairly soon, moreover, recruits began to be chosen by lot rather than by their parish authorities, and married as well as unmarried men became liable for service. During the War of the Spanish Succession well over a quarter of a million militiamen were recruited, and many of these were then drafted into the regular army. In 1702–3 alone, as it grew rapidly, sixty-six battalions of militia were incorporated into regular regiments. This inevitably increased the reluctance to serve which was always present; and in 1715, in the reaction which followed the death of Louis XIV, the militia was abolished. But it was re-established in 1726 and then did not change in essentials until the Revolution. It was always an unpopular institution. When the time approached for the drawing of lots to decide who should serve, many peasants tried to escape by marrying (since unmarried men were taken in preference to married ones as far as possible) or by becoming the servants of clerics or noblemen (since these often tried to protect their dependants against militia service) or by raising the money to buy a substitute if the lot fell on them. In more extreme cases men might mutilate themselves to escape service; there were many such cases during the War of the Spanish Succession, and memories of the suffering endured during that struggle strengthened for decades the general dislike of the militia and its demands. It is significant of its deep unpopularity that until far into the eighteenth century recruiting for it was confined to the countryside. To extend it to the towns (which, it will be remembered, often had long-standing militias of their own distinct from the system set up in 1688) seemed to invite serious disorder, whereas peasants, scattered in thousands of small village communities, offered a much lesser threat. No levy of recruits for the militia was carried out in the French cities until 1742, and none in Paris until 1745.

There were other examples in the later seventeenth and early eighteenth centuries of militias playing roles of active military importance. In Piedmont militia units were called out en masse in 1690 and 1693, and again in 1705, to resist French invasion, and were reorganized in 1714. During these turbulent decades there was, in effect, a system of conscription for the Piedmontese militia in some ways similar to that which operated in France. In the Electorate of Brandenburg unmarried peasants between eighteen and forty years old were ordered in 1703 to join local militia units for home defence: this allowed its ruler, Frederick I, to use most of his regular forces against Louis XIV in the Spanish Succession war. In Denmark a substantial militia force was organized from 1701 onwards, again to free the regular army for expansionist adventures outside the country; and in 1710 the Danish government followed French example by drafting militiamen on a large scale into regular regiments. In Spain there were ineffective efforts in the 1690s to raise a large militia force and to recruit men for the regular army by conscription, while in 1705 Philip V decreed that 100 new regiments should be raised in Castile, drawn from men between twenty and fifty who were to be chosen by lot; but poverty and administrative weakness made ambitious plans of this kind quite ineffective.[10] Sometimes urban patriotism made municipal militia forces of very real local significance: the desperate last-ditch resistance of Barcelona to Philip V in 1714 was largely the work of such a body, the *coronels*, recruited in the main from the guilds of the city. But as armies became better organized and more effective it was more and more difficult for forces of this kind to face regular troops. In time of war they were still useful in guarding prisoners and even in garrisoning fortresses and thus freeing regular units for use in the field; but the gap between trained regulars and militiamen was tending to widen. Nevertheless throughout the eighteenth century substantial militias continued, in at least some parts of the continent, to be a significant aspect of the impact which war and preparations for war made on society.

The scale of warfare: navies

The navies of Europe as well as its armies grew during the decades 1660–1740: but their growth was markedly less general and less sustained. It was much more likely to be interrupted by sharp fluctuations and declines. This was because to nearly all European states military strength was much more important than naval strength. The primacy of land over sea warfare was clearly reflected in the frequency with which navies were used to protect the movements of armies rather than as fighting forces in their own right. The efforts to use a British squadron in support of the Austrian attack on Toulon in 1707 or a French one to cover a projected Jacobite invasion of Scotland in the following year are good examples of this. A belief that naval power was something secondary and auxiliary was also given colour by the extreme rarity of decisive battles at sea. Changing weather, the virtual impossibility of any commander controlling effectively a large fleet once battle had been joined (because of the lack of reliable systems of signalling and the clouds of black powder-smoke which made it very hard even to see what was going on), the difficulty of following up any success once achieved; all these made clear-cut naval victories much rarer than those on land. This period saw only four important ones – the French success at Beachy Head in 1690 and defeat at La Hogue in 1692, the British victory over a Spanish fleet at Cape Passaro in 1719, and possibly the success won by the Danes against a Swedish squadron in the Baltic in 1715.

To almost all states, security against invasion conferred by a powerful army was an essential. But for most, seapower, however desirable, was a luxury, or at least something they could at a pinch dispense with. Navies, like armies, were becoming more expensive. From soon after the middle of the seventeenth century hired or conscripted merchantmen no longer figured in any significant naval force. Such vessels were still used as fireships, usually to attack an enemy fleet caught at anchor in confined waters; but they could no longer hope to face in battle heavily armed and purpose-built warships. Probably the last occasion on which any admiral thought of taking merchantmen into his line of battle was in 1693, during the devastating French attack on the 'Smyrna convoy' of English trading vessels bound for the Levant: and this was in a situation of extreme emergency. Warships, moreover, were very costly. A man-of-war demanded capital investment in a way which a regiment did not (see below, pages 141–2). When a choice had to be made, therefore, it was inevitable that seapower should normally be sacrificed to strength on land.

To this rule, as to so many others, England was the great exception. She alone among the powers of Europe both needed a strong navy more than a powerful army and had the resources to maintain permanently a truly great fleet. In 1688 she had 173 warships of all sizes armed with 6930 guns: by 1697 this had grown to 323 ships with 9912 guns and by 1714 to 247 with 10,603 guns (these figures bring out well the enormous concentration of artillery which a first-class navy involved). The Dutch Republic, still the greatest trading state in the world, also remained, at least until the end of the seventeenth century, a leading naval power. But the imminent threat from France which hung over her for two generations from the middle 1660s forced her to concentrate more and more on strengthening her army and defending her land frontiers. In the 1670s and 1680s she did a good deal to modernize her sea forces by building more of the large ships of the line (in effect those mounting fifty or more guns) which were now the backbone of every significant navy. The 10,000 sailors who manned her warships at the beginning of the struggle of 1689–97 had increased to 24,000 at its end. Nevertheless by the end of the century she had fallen well behind England as a naval power; and in 1710 she had to admit that she could no longer afford to maintain a North Sea squadron at all. Spain, still the greatest colonial power, also had an obvious need for naval strength. But in the later decades of the seventeenth century her economic weakness was so crippling that it was beyond her to support even a second-rate fleet; and by the end of the Spanish Succession struggle she had hardly any navy left. After 1713, however, she showed marked powers of recovery in this as in other respects; by 1737 she had a very respectable fleet of thirty-three ships of the line. Sweden's Baltic empire was also in a very real sense a maritime one. The ability to move men and supplies freely from Sweden itself to northern Germany and the Swedish Baltic provinces was essential to it. Yet her fleet never attracted the attention and resources which were expended on the army. Though during this period she was always a naval power of some significance (in the 1690s she had almost forty ships of the line), by the second decade of the eighteenth century it was clear that her position in this respect was under very serious threat, in part from her old rival Denmark, but much more from the entirely new challenge now being offered by Russia. Sharp fluctuations in strength at sea were almost as marked in France as in Spain. By the end of the 1670s the work of Colbert, the great finance minister of Louis XIV, had given France a navy of over two hundred ships of all sizes, one which inspired admiration and fear in both England and the Dutch Republic. Yet from the early 1690s onwards, as the strains imposed by long and increasingly expensive wars began to tell, resources were increasingly and deliberately devoted to the French army at the expense of the navy. In 1695–8, when England launched forty-four new ships of the line and the Dutch twenty-four, France was able to add only nineteen to her navy. In the War of the Spanish Succession, when the military situation became much more threatening and the shortage of money more acute, the navy suffered correspondingly more severely. After 1707 virtually all building for the French fleet came to an end. A real recovery in France's naval strength did not come until the 1730s; but her productive resources, the length of her coastline and her growing overseas trade meant that she was always potentially a great naval power.

However French strength at sea was more than merely naval. In this period she came to rely more heavily than any other state on privateers as a weapon in maritime war, and developed the strongest privateering tradition in Europe. To many Frenchmen this seemed an ideal form of war at sea. It would be cheap, since most of the cost would be borne by speculators in search of profits from captured English and Dutch ships. It would be carried on by relatively small though often heavily armed vessels, not by the large and expensive men-of-war which France now had such difficulty in affording. It would do maximum damage to enemy trade and thus produce pressures in favour of peace from influential merchant circles in London and Amsterdam. In 1693 Vauban argued that this was 'the only naval warfare that can be of any use to us' and proposed that to reduce the financial difficulties of the government and provide crews for privateers only forty-five to fifty French ships of the line should be used in that year's campaign as opposed to the ninety which had been at sea in the previous one.[11] The 1690s saw a remarkable growth of French privateering, most of all from Dunkirk, where this sort of warfare had deep historical roots. French warships were hired to individuals on a considerable scale for use as privateers and often manned by sailors recruited by the official machinery of the *inscription maritime*. Privateer captains were encouraged by gifts of money and such symbolic recognitions as swords of honour and gold chains. Successful ones were admitted to the navy and the most successful of all, the Dunkirk captain Jean Bart, a common sailor by origin, was ennobled in 1694. The same years also saw much privateering on the English and Dutch side; but whereas in France recources were transferred from the navy to the privateers, among her enemies the movement was rather in the other direction. In 1692 English privateers were ordered to hand over half their men to the navy, and two years later men-of-war were commanded to take for their own use half the crews of any privateers they should meet at sea. The Dutch made similar efforts: in 1692–3, when the shortage of men for their navy was acute, efforts were made to recall all privateers at sea so that the men on them could be used to make up naval crews.

The privateering which reached its climax around the turn of the seventeenth and eighteenth centuries was the most colourful aspect of naval warfare under the old regime. A few ports made in this way profits which were short-lived and unstable but sometimes large – Dunkirk, St Malo and Brest on the French side, Flushing and Middleburg in the Netherlands, in England the Channel Islands (where there was an explosive growth of privateering in the Spanish Succession struggle). Jean Bart has achieved in French naval history something of the status of Drake in that of England. For a few years privateering acquired such social cachet in France that several duchesses and at least one bishop were involved in fitting out vessels to prey on enemy shipping. But French reliance on a *guerre de course* of this kind during these years was the clearest of all signs of weakness at sea. In the middle 1690s this weakness arose largely because France lacked any clear strategy in the use of her still great fleet. Soon, however, it became a growing inability to meet her enemies there on equal terms.

The most striking bid during this period for naval strength, though one which was not sustained, was that of Russia. This was entirely the work of a single man, the Tsar Peter I. From his first sight of the sea when he visited Archangel in 1693 as a young man of barely twenty, the building of a navy was of all his ambitions the most personal and deeply felt. The difficulties were enormous. Russia had no naval tradition or experience whatever. Two frigates, the *Apostle Peter* and *Apostle Paul*, launched on the River Don in 1696, were the very first warships of any significance to be built in the country; and the host of barges and small craft also built on the Don in that year had a purely military function – to help in the capture from the Turks of the fortress of Azov at the mouth of the river. Shipbuilders, sailors and experts of all kinds did not exist in Russia and had to be attracted from abroad. Many came from the Netherlands, others from England, Scotland and Denmark and, for the building of galleys, from Venice. About fifty foreign shipwrights arrived for work at Voronezh, the main centre of this early building on the Don, in the first half of 1697 alone, while of the thousand or so foreign technicians and experts brought to Russia as a result of Peter's famous journey to western Europe in 1697–8 the majority were concerned in some way with the growth of the navy. Many of the ships left much to be desired. The squadron constructed with great expense and difficulty on the Sea of Azov from 1697 onwards was of such poor quality that in 1701 ten of the ships launched only a year or two earlier had to be completely rebuilt. Not until 1703, when the building of the new capital of St Petersburg got under way, did Russia have an outlet to the Baltic. In 1711, after a disastrous campaign against the Turks, the Azov squadron created with so much effort had to be destroyed. Yet when the tsar died, in January 1725, the Baltic squadron numbered thirty-four ships of the line and fifteen frigates, together with a very large galley-fleet: this made Russia a decisively greater naval power than either Sweden or Denmark.

Yet the purely personal character, and indeed the wastefulness, of this Russian naval power was marked. It had no real roots in the country and was always unpopular with the ordinary Russian. It never threw off its reliance on foreign expertise obtained either by importing foreign officers and technicians or by sending young Russians to serve in foreign navies and study shipbuilding and navigation abroad. The nascent Russian navy needed foreigners in a way that the army never had. It depended entirely on the personal ambition of Peter, to whom it was a kind of gigantic toy. Of his deep and abiding interest in it there is no doubt. An acute foreign observer in the later years of his reign noted that 'no victory could bring him so much pleasure as the slightest success which his ships and galleys gained' and that 'the passion for the navy triumphed in him over all other desires and preferences'. But if the navy was a fascinating toy it was also an expensive one. Annual expenditure on it of 81,000 roubles in 1701 had grown to 1,200,000 by 1724; and it is very questionable whether Russia got good value for most of this money. The galleys built in 1696 played a significant role in the capture of Azov in that year. The Baltic galley-fleet was very useful in the last stages of the Great Northern War: its raids did much damage to Sweden in 1719–20. But the much more expensive men-of-war of the Baltic fleet were a poor investment. During the entire war they captured only a single Swedish ship of the line, while the Danish navy took four in 1715 alone. The result of all this was that as soon as Peter died the fleet entered a long period of neglect. Under his successors its strength and efficiency fell sharply; and from this decline it did not recover for the next four decades.

The grip of the state: government control and provision

These decades saw a continuation of the process of extending more effective and detailed state control over armed forces which had been visible in the first half of the seventeenth century. Slowly, and with very varying effect, central governments increased their attention to the day-to-day running of their armies and navies, struggling to increase their effectiveness, to reduce inefficiency and waste and to enforce greater uniformity in organization, tactics and armament. This was an aspect, though an extremely important one, of the pressure for greater efficiency in every aspect of government which marked these decades in many European states, a pressure which was itself generated largely by the demands of growing armed forces and the escalating costs of waging war.

France is once more the most important and best-studied example. There, in spite of the efforts of Le Tellier, the need for more effective central control was marked. By the 1660s, however, his initiatives, built on by his son and successor Louvois, were bearing substantial fruit. By then there was in effect a war ministry in Paris, perhaps the first genuine one in any European state; by the mid-1660s it included five subdivisions, each handling a particular aspect of its business. By 1680 there were seven of them; and in 1688 there began the systematic accumulation of a war ministry archive. In the field this central organization was supplemented by an elaborate structure of royal officials. The *intendants d'armée*, often appointed for only a single campaign or for a single army or province, supervised the supply and payment of the troops, fortifications, military hospitals and a range of other issues. They were supplemented by the *commissaires des guerres*, attached to armies or regiments, who had important functions in recruiting and in organizing troop movements, and by the *contrôleurs des guerres* who were concerned with the essential task of keeping accurate registers of the men actually serving and thus preventing the fraudulent padding of muster-rolls which was still so prevalent. Louvois, though much better known to history than his father, in many ways added little to the fundamentals of his work. He rather expanded and developed the organization he had inherited and used it in a more uncompromising and even brutal manner than his father. This spirit of strict regulation bore fruit notably in an order of 1675 which for the first time laid down clearly a hierarchy of military ranks in France, detailing the powers and privileges of officers in each rank and the requirements for promotion. Clear-cut specifications of this kind were obviously an essential of any effective bureaucratic control of armed forces. In one respect, however, the French army remained highly conservative and backward-looking. In it more completely than in many others regiments and companies were still the property of their colonels and captains and could be bought and sold like other sorts of property. Colonelcies were not cheap. By the 1730s and 1740s prices of 20–50,000 livres for infantry regiments were normal, though one at least fetched as much as 100,000. Not until 1762 did the government lay down maximum prices which could be charged for them. They could also, however, be extremely profitable: in 1741 a French guards regiment (admittedly not a typical case) yielded its owner an income of 120,000 livres. Parallel with the efforts of Louvois to reform army administration went comparable efforts to tighten the hitherto very loose control of the government over the French navy. In 1670 the provisioning of warships was taken over for the first time by the government, and in the same year its agents began to pay sailors directly: the chaotic earlier arrangement by which the captains provided the food and drink for their own ships and themselves paid off the crew when a ship was decommissioned now came to an end. In 1689 a clear hierarchy of naval ranks, comparable to that laid down for the army fourteen years earlier, was issued.

A little later, efforts were made to introduce greater order and efficiency into the still chaotic system of Habsburg military organization. The *Hofkriegsrath* (Council of War) in Vienna was able from the first years of the eighteenth century to increase its control over the autonomous provincial military authorities at Graz and Innsbruck, while other bodies concerned with the fundamental task of supply, the War-Commissariat (*Generalkriegskommissariat*) and General Supply Department (*Generalproviantamt*), saw their importance grow. Prince Euguene, the outstanding Habsburg commander of the period, struggled with some success to rationalize the very cumbersome traditional machinery of military control. It was he who in 1705 abolished the branch of the *Hofkriegsrath* sitting in Graz which had hitherto controlled the armies fighting against the Turks. Something, then, was achieved. Nevertheless the whole nature of the Habsburg territories, a mere bundle of provinces markedly lacking in any sort of unity, was deeply hostile to effective central control and rationalization. Eugene was able to do little more than dent the surface of a very intractable problem. The regiments of the Habsburgs, more than any others in Europe except perhaps in France, still remained the property of their colonels, virtually feudal seigneuries, and as in France sometimes very profitable ones. An Austrian regiment was calculated in 1690 to bring its commander, through the profit he made on supplying and equipping it, what he received by the sale of commissions in it and other miscellaneous fees and perquisites, an income of 10–12,000 florins a year, while in 1704 a French officer pressed to accept such a colonelcy was told it would yield an annual return of 20,000 crowns.[12] The first decades of the eighteenth century saw the selling of commissions in the Habsburg army reach its highest point, while the defects of both military administration and of the higher officer-corps, aristocratic and cosmopolitan, were to be painfully shown up by the Polish Succession war of 1733–5 and that of 1737–9 against the Ottoman Empire.

Elsewhere the same striving for greater order and regularity to be enforced through an extension of central control achieved varying results. In Piedmont an embryonic war ministry had come into existence by 1692: until then the officials charged with the different aspects of military administration – financial control, the inspection of troops, etc. – had been directly and personally responsible to the ruler.[13] In Russia Peter I inherited a system which was complex and confused, with control divided between a number of different departments (*prikazy*); and for much of his reign this complexity persisted. It proved easier to raise large numbers of recruits and increase the production of arms than to give all this effort stable and efficient administrative backing. The *Prikaz Voennykh Del'* (Department of Military Affairs) set up in 1701 lasted for only five years and was then replaced by the *Voennaya Kantselyariya* (War Chancery), while the *Pushkarskii Prikaz* (Gun Department) was replaced in 1701 by the *Prikaz Artillerii* and this in its turn in 1714 by the *Artilleriiskaya Kantselyariya*. The new navy was controlled by a Navy Department (*Voennyi Morskoi Prikaz*) created at the end of 1698, while three years later the Admiralty Prikaz was set up to supervise shipbuilding for it. It was only with the establishment in 1718–19 of the War and Navy Colleges, small administrative committees of a kind already common in many parts of Europe, notably Sweden and the German world, that some real stability was brought into the picture. The War College in particular was to remain for the rest of the eighteenth century one of the most important elements in the whole

Russian administrative machine. However the most significant effort at increased central control of the Russian army was not the creation of any new institution but rather the drawing-up in 1716, with the participation of the tsar himself and under his strict personal control, of the *Ustav Voinskii* (Military Regulation). This was a very elaborate specification of all Russian military organization, replacing and codifying a series of more limited efforts of the same kind issued from 1699 onwards: it was the most impressive thing of its kind attempted by any government during this period. A corresponding detailed scheme for the navy, the *Morskoi Ustav*, on which Peter also worked in person for several months, was issued in 1720.

The relative unimportance of the army in England, and the deep suspicion with which any standing force in peacetime continued to be regarded, meant that there no such thoroughgoing effort at rationalization was attempted. Military administration remained traditional and markedly lacking in unity by comparison with that in most other states. The Secretary at War, the Master-General of the Ordnance and the Board of Ordnance, the Paymaster-General, the Commissioners for Sick and Wounded, all had a finger in the pie. Even here, however, there was progress. In 1703 an effort was made to improve the paying and supplying of the troops by the creation of the new post of Comptroller of Army and Accounts; and by the end of the Spanish Succession struggle it had been established that many aspects of army administration, notably the prickly one of promotions, were under the control of the Secretary at War, who was a civilian and a politician, though usually not one of the first rank. 'Our armies here,' wrote one commander, 'know no other power but that of the Secretary-at-War, who directs all their motions and fills up all vacancies without opposition and without appeal.[14] George I and George II both made serious efforts to improve the army and the way it was administered. In 1720 George I was able to ensure that though most commissions remained open to purchase this would at least be regulated by an official tariff of prices: both he and his successor disliked the whole system of purchase, which they saw as an obstacle in the path of the poor but deserving professional officer, and ensured that they retained some right of veto over clearly unsuitable appointments. However the weight of conservatism and vested interests, and more fundamentally a feeling that an efficient army was not really necessary and might even be dangerous, made progress very difficult.

Naval administration in Britain, in spite of the far greater popularity of the navy, remained almost as unsatisfactory as that of the army. Nonetheless, here there were some real successes. The Navy Board emerged as, for most purposes, the most important controlling organ, as the Board of Admiralty became more and more a formal body, while the long tenure of office by many of the ablest administrators concerned was a significant force making for continuity of policy. (The best-known of them, the diarist Samuel Pepys, was Admiralty Secretary in 1673–9 and 1684–90, while Josiah Burchett held the same post from 1694 to 1742.) The last decades of the seventeenth century witnessed, therefore, the emergence of what was, at least in some respects, a modern navy. The reign of Charles II saw the drawing-up of Instructions, which were to remain unaltered in essentials for more than a century, specifying the duties of naval officers of different ranks and penalties for neglect of them. They also established something not paralleled in any army of the period, examinations for promotion to the rank of lieutenant and appointment to the very important post of master. (The master, responsible for the sailing and handling of a man-of-war, was often a more significant figure than the captain.) No attempt was made, however, to set up training schools for young naval officers, as Colbert did in France in 1669: this omission reflected the very heavy emphasis on practical experience and the low regard for theory and book-learning which was to distinguish the British navy for generations to come. Nevertheless a genuine corps of naval officers was now emerging. By 1692 the Navy Board had for the first time a single table of seniority for all the captains, lieutenants, warrant-officers and masters, and length of service was beginning to be accepted as the most important criterion in making promotions. This was a significant move towards giving officers greater *esprit de corps* and a more distinctive and clearly marked status. The first Navy List, another step along this road, appeared in 1700. In some respects English naval administration was still very poor. In particular the way in which sailors were recruited and paid left a great deal to be desired (see pages 127–8 below). Yet it was also during these years that the Admiralty scored what was arguably the greatest administrative success of any government of the age. This was the refitting of the main English fleet at Cadiz in the winter of 1694–5, an undertaking which involved the setting-up at short notice of all the essential services of a great dockyard 1100 miles from England and on foreign (and uncooperative) territory.[15]

More effective central administration meant in practice a number of things; but it showed itself most clearly in a search for greater rationality. This in its turn usually meant greater uniformity. One aspect of this was the specification of the ranks and duties of officers and the drawing-up of schemes of organization such as the *Ustav Voinskii* and *Morskoi Ustav* in Russia. Another was a widespread effort to achieve uniformity in the arming and supplying of armies and navies. Almost everywhere there was considerable scope for this, since in so many armies the equipment, supply and pay of a regiment remained firmly in the hands of its colonel. So far as its relations with the central government were concerned, indeed, very often in effect the regiment was still simply its colonel, and dynasties of colonels were far from unknown – in France one regiment was commanded in 1612–76 by five successive members of the same family.[16] It was not until the 1680s that French regiments began to be usually referred to by provincial or regional titles rather than by the names of their colonels, and not until 1712 that British ones began to be designated by numbers; until then they also were normally identified merely by the names of their commanders. In Britain, indeed, the colonel's complete personal control of his regiment, and the personal obligations which went with it, were emphasized at the beginning of the eighteenth century almost as heavily as anywhere in Europe. 'The sole responsibility of the colonel for the pay and equipment of his regiment,' stated a regulation of 1707, 'is the principle of military finance, who [*sic*] is held responsible in his fortune and in his character for the discharge of his duty in providing the supplies of his regiment.'[17] Such a situation had, as in the past, obvious potential dangers. Most serious from an operational point of view, a colonel might have personal idiosyncrasies about arms, uniforms, drill or even tactics. In England in the 1680s fourteen different varieties of musket were in use in different regiments, while the Board of Ordnance complained in 1706 that 'Few of the officers agree in the sort of bayonets to be used or in the manner of fixing them, as may appear by the various sorts there are of them in the army.'[18] A French officer in 1727 lamented that it was impossible 'to make several regiments drill together, there being not one who does it in a uniform manner', since every colonel preferred his own drill and his own words of command.[19] In the Habsburg forces, an extreme case, there was no unified system of tactics until as late as 1749, after the experience of the War of the Austrian Succession had finally driven home the need for one. In Russia, on the other hand, the sort of state control and state-enforced uniformity achieved under Peter I gave much less scope for this sort of variation: in this respect the Russian army was more modern than those of most of the wealthier and more developed states of western Europe. For a few years, indeed, Peter did try to feed and clothe his army indirectly rather than through direct government action. Each soldier in the new regiments raised in the first years of the Great Northern War would, it was hoped, be supplied by the landowner who had sent him to the army with a kaftan each year, a sheepskin coat every second year, a rouble each year to buy other clothing and an annual allowance of rye-flour. But this soon proved quite unworkable; and in 1704 the feeding and clothing of the army was taken over by the government.

But even where the proprietary powers of colonels were deeply entrenched, the movement towards uniformity, though slow, was unmistakable. This was notably so in the supply of arms, uniforms and equipment. In France the government began to provide the soldier's weapons from 1727 onwards without his having to pay for them; they were no longer a charge, as hitherto, against his wages or the account of his colonel. This helped the process of standardization; and at the same time uniforms ceased to vary in accordance with the whims of regimental commanders as they had done in the past. Even in the Habsburg army an order of 1707 provided that henceforth all infantrymen should be dressed in the same light-grey colour; and a few years later there was similar standardization in Brandenburg-Prussia, whose colonels ceased to be responsible after 1713 for clothing their men. In Britain from the end of the Spanish Succession war the Board of Ordnance was increasingly able to enforce the use in the manufacture of muskets and most other arms of official sealed patterns. From 1722 colonels had to buy arms made to these patterns, though these did not have to be supplied by the Board of Ordnance if a colonel could buy them more cheaply elsewhere. On a different level the same impetus towards centrally set standards can be seen in the growing practice of regular official inspections of regiments. Here France led the way. The post of inspector-general of infantry was created by Louvois in 1667 and the name of its first holder, Martinet, became a byword for insistence on the rigid observance of official norms. In England a similar system did not begin until 1716; but in both countries regular inspections of this sort had real importance in enforcing basic uniformity in the drill and parade-ground discipline which was seen, on the whole correctly, as the key to success on the battlefield. It is probable also that rationalization and more effective central government control were helped a good deal by the growth of more systematic and accurate accounting procedures. By the eighteenth century it was becoming common to issue soldiers with paybooks in which payments in cash or kind could be recorded: this in itself did a good deal to check embezzlement and peculation and to introduce greater system and uniformity into military life.

This increased control by governments aimed at greater efficiency and better value for money. It was not inspired by any humanitarian considerations. Nevertheless it had some humanitarian implications. The later seventeenth and early eighteenth centuries saw in western Europe the first real efforts to develop some system of military and naval hospitals, and to give better care to sick and wounded servicemen. Hitherto what facilities of this kind had existed had been provided, at least in Catholic Europe, by the church – by religious orders or charities. Now these were beginning to be supplemented by government action. Here again France was prominent. Many French fortresses already had some rudimentary hospital provision in the later seventeenth century and in 1708, in response to the pressures of the war then raging, fifty new military hospitals were set up. The eighteenth century saw an increase in the number of army surgeons in France, an improvement in their training and a quite marked rise in their salaries and social standing.[20] In England too there were some efforts in this direction. The navy had five hospital-ships in use by 1705 (there had been experiments with these in several European fleets during the seventeenth century) though Plymouth was still the only naval base with its own hospital. What could be done to relieve wounds and sickness depended very much, of course, on the resources available; and in eastern Europe, relatively poor and undeveloped, hospital provision was even less adequate than in the west. In seventeenth-century Russia a certain number of doctors from western Europe were attracted by relatively generous salaries, and there was some effort to train young Russians for medical work with the army. But this could have little impact on the needs of armed forces which were growing rapidly and fighting longer and more demanding wars. During the unsuccessful Russian invasion of the Crimea in 1689, for example, sixty-five carts were made available for the evacuation of wounded men; but this was in the context of operations in which 20,000 are said to have been killed. Peter I aimed to have a doctor in every regiment and to provide several military hospitals as well; but the incurable shortage of men fit to fill such posts meant that this remained no more than a pious hope. Even as late as 1776 the entire Russian army, the largest in the world, apparently contained less than 450 men with any sort of medical qualification, and most of these were far from highly trained or highly skilled.[21]

In the more expensive business of caring for old and crippled soldiers France once more set the pace with the building of the *Hôtel Royal des Invalides* in 1670, while in Prussia a fund for disabled soldiers, the *Invalidenkasse*, began to function in 1705 and in 1722 there began the building of the military orphanage at Potsdam, the most impressive in Europe. In England Chelsea Hospital was completed in 1690 and Greenwich Hospital for disabled seamen begun in 1694, while the Chatham Chest fund had existed since the reign of Elizabeth to pay pensions to disabled sailors or the widows of those who died in service. In Piedmont the first organized attempt to provide for old soldiers came in 1710. But all this merely touched the fringes of the problem. No government was as yet willing, or indeed able, to provide generously for those who had suffered in its service. In the eighteenth century the *Invalides*, the largest institution of its kind, housed about 7000 men in all; but this was far from enough to provide for the demand for places (though entry seems to have become somewhat easier as the century went on), while the Piedmontese initiative could cope with a mere 400 and Chelsea Hospital with only 472. Pensions to wounded soldiers or sailors or to the widows of those killed in action were a rare privilege even in the wealthier states; and when they were granted they were often paid in a very irregular and unreliable way (this was true of Chatham Chest payments, for example). Moreover what provision was made was very often financed by enforced payments from those who might hope eventually to benefit, not out of government revenue. Thus in England, Chelsea Hospital was paid for partly by a deduction of eightpence from every pound of soldiers' pay, and the Chatham Chest fund was made up partly by a contribution of sixpence a month from the scanty wages of sailors. In the eighteenth century both Prussia and Bavaria also financed what help they gave to old soldiers by small deductions from the wages of those still serving.

Many states also organized disabled soldiers in special companies to be used in garrisons or for other relatively light duties. Brandenburg had such a company as early as 1675, while in France from early in the following century men admitted to the *Invalides* were often sent on leave for up to three years so that they could re-enter civilian life, earn their own living and thus cease to burden the institution. Some even re-enlisted in the army, though in peacetime this was taken, reasonably enough, as an indication that they should never have been admitted in the first place. The cheapest way of providing for the old soldier who was not completely incapacitated was to give him some not too demanding government post; and this was widely done in several parts of Europe. In the German states particularly, and notably in Brandenburg-Prussia, former soldiers were widely employed in tax-collecting, the customs and the postal services; but even at a low level, administrative work was suitable only for veterans who were literate, and was therefore a refuge for former NCOs rather than for the rank-and-file. Provision for the ex-serviceman was therefore, inevitably, far from generous. Yet again progress is visible. There was now a greater readiness than ever before, at least in the more developed parts of the continent, to recognize some obligation towards men who had fought and suffered for their country.

But increased administrative activity did little to alleviate the most basic of all servicemen's grievances – pay which was inadequate, irregular and often long delayed, and sometimes not received at all. In poor countries with correspondingly penniless governments difficulties of this kind were almost unavoidable. The acute economic weakness of Spain in the second half of the seventeenth century was reflected in the appalling state of her regiments, poorly supplied and often left for long periods completely unpaid. 'I have seen a whole regiment who changed their garrison carried in one waggon,' wrote an

English traveller in the Spanish Netherlands. 'The soldiers hold out their hats to you to beg, whilst they are mounting the guard, and the officers are reduced to live among the Capuchins, on the charity which the good Fathers have mumpt [i.e. begged] for their own subsistence.'[22] The inevitable result was acute military weakness. A fairly reliable estimate of 1703 was that in the whole of Spain there then remained only 13,000 infantry and 5000 cavalry – an extraordinary comedown since the days of Olivares.[23] Russia was also a very poor country, and her soldiers were also badly and irregularly paid. The men raised in 1699 were promised 11 roubles a year but received much less. Some apparently received nothing at all, and in 1710 Peter himself complained that his forces in West Prussia 'last drew pay half a year ago' and were 'extremely poor and lacking uniforms'. Moreover the deductions from pay to cover the cost of uniforms and equipment from which soldiers suffered in many armies seem to have been particularly heavy in Russia – close to half the total. Another observer in 1739 thought that a Russian soldier received in cash only a third as much as one in France or the German states.[24] It is a tribute to the qualities of Peter's soldiers that he was able to maintain so great an army over so long a period and achieve so much with it in spite of the hardships it had to endure.

Nor should it be thought that poor and irregular pay or inadequate supply were in any way peculiar to the less wealthy parts of Europe. Many states, at least in wartime, were almost as bad in these respects as Spain or Russia. In some of the smaller ones the situation could easily become critical. In 1699 a Bavarian colonel reported that thirty of his men had to stay in bed day and night because they had no clothes at all; and in 1716 sixty-nine children of soldiers in a single Bavarian company are said to have died of hunger because their fathers had gone so long without pay.[25] Even in the richest states there could be great difficulties. In France Vauban complained in 1675 that 'in most fortified cities the soldiers are housed like pigs, half-naked and half-dying of hunger'. Thirty years later one of the three treasurers of the French navy complained that 'Here we are in March 1705 and I've still to pay about 12 millions [of livres] for 1704' and that he was being blamed for holding back the salaries of the officers and the wages of the seamen.[26] Even England during the great wars of 1689–1713 often tried her soldiers and sailors to the limit. One colonel in the 1690s apparently failed to pay his men at all for four years; and a regiment at the death of Queen Anne in 1713 (when its colonel was himself in prison for debt) had still £198,000 owed it since the siege of Londonderry in 1689. The situation was even worse in the navy. Movement of men from one ship to another and long absences on distant stations in America or the West Indies meant that delays in the payment of seamen's wages could be enormous. One luckless sailor received in June 1695 money owed him since January 1681. At the same time another, even more unfortunate, was paid wages earned in January 1678. These cases were quite exceptional; but the average delay in payment of arrears during 'King William's War' was about a year, and there were a fair number of cases of men who received nothing for three or four years on end. Moreover seamen and to a lesser extent soldiers suffered from being paid, not in cash, but in tallies or tickets which had then to be exchanged for cash at a heavy discount. The end of the war in 1713 saw an improvement in the situation on both sides of the Channel. Armies and navies dramatically reduced in size were easier to pay and maintain. But no government during this period, however wealthy, was ever in wartime able to pay promptly and regularly all its armed forces.

The grip of the state: recruiting and desertion

The later seventeenth century and the first decades of the eighteenth saw important changes in methods of recruiting in many European states. The assumption by governments of new rights and duties was nowhere more significant than here. In many countries in which he had hitherto played a significant role the military entrepreneur, the man who raised a regiment or a company on his own account as a kind of private enterprise, was now pushed into the background if not eliminated altogether. Recruiting became something which the state sought more and more to control and regulate, or at least to have an increasing say in. Substantial vestiges of the old state of affairs still lingered, notably in central Europe where the first half of the seventeenth century had seen its fullest development. As late as the 1740s there are instances of individuals, usually great nobles, raising regiments on their own account for the Habsburg and Bavarian

111

armies. But in all the major states of western Europe the old methods and assumptions were disappearing, though at widely differing speeds in different countries; and in Russia they had never really operated.

Probably the most important reason for the change was simply that the administrative capacities of governments were growing, sometimes quite rapidly. Now many of them were able, often for the first time, to control recruiting effectively and to operate some form of conscription if necessary, more effectively than in the past, by forcing their non-privileged male subjects to serve or by drafting men from the militia into the regular army. Though none of them ever had anything like all the money it wanted, most of them were now financially much stronger than in the first half of the seventeenth century. They still depended heavily on civilian contractors for the supply of their armies and navies. Such entrepreneurs, often united by close family ties (and, in the case of the Jewish ones who were important from the 1670s until the end of the Spanish Succession war, by religious loyalties) could still powerfully influence by their efficiency or lack of it the progress of a war. Sometimes, as in the past, they made their role as suppliers of the armed forces a stepping-stone to positions of great power. The outstanding example of this is the rise of the Paris family in France. Paris la Masse, originally a mere innkeeper in Dauphiné, began in 1690 to supply the French army in northern Italy. Two decades or less later his family, with enormous resources behind it, was becoming a dominant influence in French public finance: in the 1720s one of its members, Paris-Duverney, was for several years in effect, though not in name, *Contrôleur-Général des Finances* and thus one of the most powerful men in the country. In a less spectacular way Jews such as Samuel Oppenheimer, who supplied the Habsburg army on the Rhine in the war of 1673–9 with France, or Solomon de Medina, who supplied the army of William III in the 1690s and in 1700 became the first professing Jew in England to be knighted, found in war and war demands opportunities of breaking through at least some of the restrictions from which their community had so long suffered and achieving positions of real influence. On this level, then, the private-enterprise element in warfare was still strong. But as governments slowly became more efficient, self-confident and ambitious the balance was very gradually tilting in their favour and their dependence on the *munitionnaire* and the goodwill of a few wealthy financiers being reduced. Bigger and more efficient administrative machines meant higher tax revenues. The regime of Louis XIV was sometimes critically short of money; but French finances were never under him so chaotic and disorganized as in the decade or more after the death of Henry IV or the disturbed years of the later 1640s and early 1650s. England by the 1690s had left behind for ever the financial weakness which had crippled her feeble military initiatives in the 1620s and later her naval effort against the Dutch in 1665–7. Even in the German world governments were less financially weak than in the past. In Brandenburg-Prussia the 'Great Elector' Frederick William (1640–88) began the building up of a large war treasury. This, added to by the careful housekeeping of his grandson, King Frederick William I (1713–40), was to be for generations a central element in the political as well as the military calculations of Prussia's rulers. The Habsburg territories remained of all the major states except Spain the one whose war effort was most likely to be impeded or even brought to a complete standstill (as happened in 1703, for example) by lack of money. But even there the situation was to some extent eased in the great conflicts of the mid-eighteenth century by foreign subsidies – from Britain in the Austrian Succession struggle of 1740–8 and from France in the Seven Years War of 1756–63.

States and rulers therefore were now increasingly able to do their own recruiting and to bypass the intermediaries – colonels recruiting for their own regiments, captains for their own companies – who had been so often important in the past. The extent to which they used this power varied widely. At one extreme were Russia and Brandenburg-Prussia, the two states whose rapidly growing military strength was to transform the political balance of eighteenth-century Europe. In these, more notably in the former, government initiatives and controls were paramount. Of the 32,000 men produced by Peter I's first effort to raise forces for the approaching war with Sweden, probably a quarter or even a third were volunteers; but very soon the Russian army became one of conscripts. The older forces raised in different ways – the quasi-feudal levy of landowners, the *streltsy*, the regiments 'of the foreign model' so important in the previous decades – were never formally abolished; but they rapidly faded away. From 1705 onwards there were frequent levies of peasants at widely varying rates – from one man from each ten households in 1711 (a year of exceptional difficulty, when war with Turkey was superimposed on that with Sweden) to a mere one from eighty-three in 1721, the last year of the struggle with the Swedes. In Peter's reign there were twenty-one of these general levies, as well as thirty-two others limited geographically or otherwise, while there were similar though much smaller demands for men for the new navy. The Petrine recruiting system, once established, remained a permanent feature of Russian rural society, helping to shape it and to give it a distinctive tone and atmosphere. In the three-quarters of a century after his death in 1725 about 2¼ million men were raised in this way for the Russian army.

The Prussian army differed from the Russian in at least one very important way. Unlike that built up by Peter and his successors, it always contained a very large foreign element. These non-Prussians, who were predominantly German, were officially volunteers, though many of them were recruited by methods which amounted virtually to kidnapping, and were regarded as more desirable recruits than conscripted Prussian subjects. In the early eighteenth century they received a *Handgeld* of fifteen thalers as against the single thaler given to Prussian peasants enlisted under the scheme of cantonal organization introduced in the 1730s. But there was an increasingly important element in the Prussian army of conscripted peasants, though these were still chosen for the most part by the captains of the companies in which they were to serve. In an order of 1713 and an edict of the following year Frederick William I asserted more clearly than ever before the principle of the lifelong obligation of the peasant to perform military service. An effort was made to give these demands legitimacy by reference to the medieval obligations of *Heerfolge* and *Landfolge*; but these had long ago lapsed. In reality Frederick William, like Peter, represented a relatively new and very powerful form of military autocracy, one in which the army dominated society and to a large extent moulded it for its own purposes. In 1733 three cabinet orders gave recruiting in Prussia a form which, in essentials, it was to retain for years to come; but these merely completed a process which had been going on for decades. The system established in that year meant that each of the 'cantons' of about 5000 households into which Brandenburg-Prussia was divided was made responsible for producing recruits for a particular regiment, which was normally stationed in that area in time of peace. The cantonists, as the recruits were called, were given a training period of eighteen months or two years; but after that they were usually with their regiment for only two or three months in each year and were thus free to work on the land or elsewhere for the rest of it. This system was a compromise, essential in a poor country, between the claims of the army and the competing ones of agriculture. Indeed, already in 1721–2 Frederick William, for all his passion for the army, had been forced to set limits to the demands which his recruiters were making on the peasants and which threatened to make their position impossible and therefore to undermine that of the junkers whose estates they worked.

Nevertheless in both Russia and Prussia these intensified state demands bore harshly on those subject to them. In both they had results which were not foreseen when the new recruiting systems were created; and in neither was the government able to prevent abuses. In both the officer-corps was drawn overwhelmingly from the land-owning class, the holders of estates (though often very small ones) worked by peasant labour. In both, therefore, the relationship between lord and peasant in the countryside was reflected and closely paralleled by that between officer and soldier in the army. Peter I believed firmly that any male landowner who did not serve the state in the armed forces or the bureaucracy had lost all right to his privileged status and was no better than a parasite. His reign therefore saw a series of attempts, often drastic and brutal ones, to force every eligible member of this group into service. From 1710 onwards increasing efforts were made to search out and round up young men of the landlord class: these culminated in a decree of 1722 ordering that any who concealed themselves and avoided service should be outlawed and treated as bandits. Under his successors the obligation to serve was made, by a number of devices, less onerous. In 1736 the period of service for officers was reduced to twenty-five years (hitherto it had been unlimited, as it remained for peasant recruits), and one male member of each family was allowed to remain at home to manage the family estate; though these concessions did not in fact become effective for several years. In 1762 the obligation of the landowning class to serve was formally abolished. But the experience of preceding generations had gone deep. Far into the nineteenth century the outlook of the Russian landlord class remained that of a caste of hereditary state servants and army officers.

In Prussia as in Russia it was the early decades of the eighteenth century which saw the forging of a very strong link between army and landowning class, a link produced by the creation of an enlarged and permanent officer-corps. Until then many Prussian junkers had served in foreign armies; but Frederick William was as insistent as Peter on the obligation of the landowner to serve him and no one else. He forbade young men from landowning families to enter foreign service or even travel abroad without permission, on pain of losing their estates, while they were also forbidden to attend foreign schools or universities. Each year the *Landrat*, the chief official in each country district, was to send to Berlin a list of young junkers who were of an age to enter the army, so that none should escape the government's grasp. 'My successor,' wrote the king in an instruction of 1722, 'must have as one of his policies . . . to employ the nobles and counts in the army and compel their children to join the cadet units (i.e. the four training schools for officers which he had set up at Berlin, Potsdam, Stolpe and Kulm).'[27] There were thus many essential similarities between the situations in Russia and Prussia. In both, a determined and even ruthless ruler made increased military strength his supreme objective. In both, the landowners, accustomed to control and direct the work of their estates, were the only group available to command an army of conscripted peasants.

In both, moreover, there was now becoming established the assumption that an officer, simply because he was an officer, was inherently superior to a civilian official, largely irrespective of his social origin. In 1712 Peter explicitly ordered that officers were to take precedence over civilians from the same gentry class on all occasions. A decade later the application of this principle was seen at its most extreme in the last years of his reign, when the new poll-tax introduced in 1718 (which produced about half of all government income and was spent almost entirely on the army) was collected by the wholesale use of soldiers to supervise, threaten and if necessary arrest the civilian officials concerned. Very significantly, the decree ordering the census on which the assessment of the new tax was based was entitled 'On the carrying-out of a revision and on the distribution of the maintenance of the army in accordance with the number of revisionary souls'. In other words, this great innovation, which had immense results in extending and consolidating serfdom in Russia and in worsening the position of a great proportion of the peasantry, was from the first explicitly linked with the needs of the army. In particular the guards regiments, the nucleus and training school of Peter's new army, were used on a large scale in the taking of the census; and not merely officers from them but also NCOs and even ordinary soldiers were able to terrorize high-ranking officials with impunity. The deputy-governor of Moscow, for example, had to bow to the demands of a sergeant of the Preobrazhensky guards regiment; and for a time the city and the surrounding area found themselves under a kind of military dictatorship.[28] Simultaneously, with the ending of the war with Sweden, the army was quartered on the countryside in what one great Russian historian has called 'a regular assault on their fellow-subjects by over one hundred regiments'.[29] In effect, the new army had now taken over much of the running of the country; and this situation continued for more than a generation. Only in 1764 did the collection of the poll-tax begin to be controlled by civilian officials. Until the reign of Catherine II Russia had to be administered largely by the army because there was no other way of doing the job. In Prussia, though the civilian bureaucracy was far larger in proportion to the population than in Russia, and also much better educated and more efficient, the precedence of the army over civilian administrators was equally taken for granted. There too officers, though usually high-ranking ones, were used to investigate and report on the alleged failings of bureaucrats, while it was officers, not civilian officials, who regulated the price of necessities in garrison towns. In mixed courts made up of civilians and military men an officer was always chairman, while in wartime officers were normally exempt from all legal proceedings.

The impact of compulsory service on the peasant varied a good deal as between the two countries. In Russia, where service in the ranks was for life (a twenty-five-year term was introduced only in 1793) and where, in an enormous empire, the recruit would almost certainly be sent hundreds or thousands of miles from his home village, enlistment was in effect a kind of death sentence. A recruit was very unlikely to see his village or his family again. Inevitably those liable to serve made great efforts to avoid such a fate, by procuring substitutes or by the use of any influence they possessed at the village level where the fatal choice of recruits was often made. Thus in time a complex system of substitution and commutation of service for money payments grew up, while landlords and merchants were able to trade in recruits and even to build up reserves of them for use when needed. The effect of all this at the grassroots was to increase the powers of village elders and heads of households, who could decide who was taken and who spared; to keep households large, since this made the loss of a male member less economically devastating; to generate a good deal of corruption and peasant indebtedness through the procuring of substitutes; and to foment tensions within and between families.[30] In Prussia the implications of army service for the individual, though serious enough, were less overwhelming than in Russia. However the identification of the landowner with the officer and of the peasant with the common soldier, so that army discipline mirrored the social relations of the countryside, was pushed further and made more explicit in Prussia. The duties of the Prussian peasant to the army and to his lord were thought of as similar, even identical. The peasant who fled from his holding on the lord's estate was a deserter just as much as the soldier who tried to escape from the army; the term *Soldaten-und Bauerndeserteuren* was quite frequently used. Soldiers on leave had to wear full uniform in church on Sundays, while peasants working in the fields were often dressed in old army uniforms. Relations between lord and peasant on many estates were governed by military-style punishments which the former could inflict on the latter. In a wide variety of ways, therefore, the military functions and duties of the peasant were continually brought home to him. This situation might, up to a point, safeguard his position. If the army must have a steady supply of suitable recruits it followed that unbearable exploitation of the peasant, extreme misery and large-scale flight from the junker estates, which would dry up this essential flow, must be prevented. The result was a long series of decrees, in 1709, 1714, 1739, 1749 and 1764, by which the rulers of Prussia tried to protect the peasant against excessive seigneurial demands, so that the supply of soldiers could be maintained. This legislation was not easy to make effective in practice; but these efforts in Prussia contrast sharply with the absence of anything of the kind in Russia, where the position of the peasant vis-à-vis his lord deteriorated steadily throughout the eighteenth century.

In both the Russian and the Prussian armies the helplessness and lack of rights of the soldier, once recruited, were marked. In both, particularly in Russia where the grip of the government was in practice much looser, officers frequently used soldiers as workers on their own estates. Frederick II forbade this by an order of 1748 and strictly instructed company commanders not to treat soldiers 'like serfs' or to 'illtreat, sell, exchange, or give away people in the Kantons'; but he could not enforce these prohibitions any more effectively than his father had. It seems also to have been fairly common for Russian commanding officers to give men from their regiments unofficial leave in exchange for money or, more often, labour-services; and the same thing happened in Prussia. In both countries the process of recruiting gave scope for extortion. A Prussian order of 1739 and many later ones forbade officers to use it as a means of extracting money from the peasants. All this, allied to the ferocious discipline to which the soldier was subjected (worse in the Russian than even in the Prussian service) paints a grim picture of the human suffering which was the foundation of these great armies.

Nor were peasants and common soldiers the only sufferers. The drive towards greater military strength begun by Peter I and Frederick William I imposed severe sacrifices also upon those who officered the new armies. In both Russia and Prussia, the son of a small landowning family normally found himself living in poverty during his first years as an officer: in Prussia at least it was often only when he obtained a company of his own that he could pay off the debts he had accumulated as a lieutenant. Even on the eve of the French Revolution an expert observer was struck by the poverty of Prussian subalterns, though he thought that captains made more, mainly from the profits they drew from soldiers released for long periods for civilian work, than in any other European army.[31] In both countries, again, the obligation to serve was very onerous. In Russia even after 1736 it lasted for a quarter of a century, and in Prussia an officer was usually about fifty before he could return to his estates as a retired captain or colonel. In both, therefore, many landowners during their long years of service were forced to leave the running of their estates in the hands of bailiffs, sometimes even of one of their tenants. What all this could mean is well illustrated by the petition of a Russian officer asking for promotion in 1727. 'I have served Your Imperial Majesty from the year 1700, first in the Swedish war in the regular army and in combat . . . and in 1722 I was taken out of the regiment as a major and assigned to the College of Justice as procurator, and from that time on I have been in this office without interruption and without home leave. And in 1705 my father was killed in Astrakhan, and the few miserable villages I inherited and those I owned have deteriorated completely as I could not supervise them, and from this I have been ruined and fallen ill.'[32] Neither Peter nor Frederick William had any wish to weaken the landowning class on which they depended so heavily. Yet their quest for military power, by its very success, tended in some ways at least to undermine its economic position. The result was that the second half of the eighteenth century saw a series of efforts in both countries to bolster up the landlord-officer class – in Prussia by prohibitions of the sale of 'noble' land to commoners, and in Russia by the creation in 1754 of a Noble Bank which by the end of the century had lent to landowners a sum greater than the government's entire annual revenue.

In Sweden also a system of conscription can be seen, but one very different from those of Russia and Prussia. By the *Indelningsverket* or 'allocation system' introduced in the 1680s, essentially a development of that of Gustavus Adolphus, each province agreed to maintain a regiment, using for this purpose the land which had been recovered by the monarchy from the nobility in the 'Reduction' of the previous decade or more. This was divided into 'files' of two farms each; each file was to provide one soldier. In peacetime he would work as a labourer for one of the peasants in the file and would be given somewhere to live, usually a cottage of his own. This meant that the army was recruited largely from landless peasants; but the system succeeded well in achieving its main objective – the reduction of reliance on expensive foreign mercenaries and the use of very limited resources to produce an army which was almost uniquely national and very well trained (regiments from different provinces were called up in rotation for periods of training). The quality of the forces which it produced was to be shown to great effect in the long struggle with Russia after 1700.

In western Europe the position was very different. There too men were often recruited by compulsion, but by compulsion for the most part unlike the direct and state-organized sort seen in the east of the continent. In France and even in Great Britain there can be seen at times elements of compulsory service. In France the drafting of militiamen into the regular army during the War of the Spanish Succession was in effect a sort of ad hoc and haphazard form of conscription. In Britain also the situation in these years of unprecedented effort was very difficult. Each year about 12,000 fresh men were needed to keep the army up to strength; and these proved very hard to raise. By 1704 there were no longer even enough guardsmen available to do ceremonial duty at Kensington Palace and the Tower of London. Press Acts for the forcible recruitment of debtors, vagrants and other marginal members of society were therefore in force in 1704–12 (and also at critical moments later in the century, in 1745–6, 1755–7 and 1778–9). In the last years of the Spanish Succession struggle Marlborough himself pressed for a more rigorous system of compulsory service. But in both Britain and France, and especially in Britain, the army was still essentially one of volunteers. Both countries used the carrot as well as the stick by offering recruits a lump sum, a version of the German *Handgeld*, when they enlisted: to men often unaccustomed to a money economy and to handling significant sums in cash this could be a real inducement. But as in the past, poverty and hunger produced most recruits. Some striking illustrations of this fact can be found in France. In a small town in the Beauvaisis in March 1694, for example, in conditions of virtual famine, recruits could be obtained for an enlistment premium of only a little over 6 livres; yet only two years later, when food prices were once more normal, it was necessary to pay 41 livres. A decade later, in 1706, the premium paid to attract men to the crack *Gardes Françaises* regiment was 50 livres; yet in 1710, after the terrible winter and famine of the previous year, a mere 20 were enough. In 1707 even the musicians of the opera-house in Marseilles joined up because, according to a contemporary, 'they were dying of hunger'.[33]

However it would be a mistake to think of the men who enlisted as being driven entirely by the need to find in the army a refuge from an even more intolerable situation in civilian life. As in the first half of the seventeenth century, more positive motives were sometimes of real importance. A desire for change and adventure, a wish to escape from a stultifying routine at the plough or the loom, counted for something

121

and motives for enlisting could be very varied. 'If we take the trouble to investigate the most important impulses which bring the lads to the free recruiting table,' wrote a commentator on the Habsburg army in the mid-eighteenth century, 'we shall find they are things like drunkenness, a frenzy of passions, love of idleness, a horror of any useful trade, a wish to escape from parental discipline, inclination towards debauchery, an imaginary hope of untrammelled freedom, sheer desperation, the fear of punishment after some sordid crime, or however else you care to define the motives of worthless people like these.'[34] There was also, at least in rural areas, quite often a surviving element of quasi-feudal trust and obligation involved. An officer member of one of the leading families of a district might well persuade, through his name and inherited position, young men to join his company or regiment when they would never have contemplated enlisting under someone unknown to them. This was still an age in which relationships were between individuals and families. The modern willingness to trust impersonal institutions and mechanisms was quite foreign to the ordinary man. A recruit might therefore feel some security when he enlisted if he knew he would be serving under a member of a family which he had all his life accepted without question as superiors and leaders. Readers of Scott will remember that when the young Edward Waverley joins his regiment for the first time just before the 1745 rebellion he takes with him twenty 'young fellows' from his uncle's estate who have enlisted in his troop of cavalry 'to attend his honour, as in duty bound'.[35] In this situation the soldier could feel that he had some moral claim on his officer for support in case of difficulty. Captains, on whom much of the work of recruiting for their companies still often fell, used to the full, as in the past, any family connections likely to be useful in this way: this was reflected in a continuing tendency for a high proportion of many companies to be drawn from their captain's home area. Indeed the ability of a local notable to attract recruits in his own district was one of the most searching tests of his real influence there, his 'interest' in English terms, and often seen as such. 'My Lord Mulgrave cannot brag of much interest in Yorkshire,' wrote an observer in the 1670s, 'where half his complement [of recruits] are not yet raised.'[36] In the French army, where quasi-feudal ties and loyalties of this kind were still unusually strong, it was not unknown in the early eighteenth century for recruits to claim that their agreement to serve was a purely personal one made with their captain, not with the king or the army in general, and that it was therefore nullified if he left the regiment. Personal ties of this kind sometimes did much to raise the morale of the man in the ranks and made him more willing to put up with the poor living conditions, disease and danger, all for a very meagre reward, which were his lot. While such ties existed he was spared what, at least for the peasant recruit, was the harshest and most traumatic experience of all, that of being suddenly thrust into a strange and frightening environment where he had no one to whom he could look for protection and who took any personal interest in his welfare.

Seigneurial recruiting of this kind was therefore still a factor of importance in western Europe. But it was inevitably one whose significance was declining. As armies became bigger and traditional ties and feelings weaker, it was less and less adequate as a means of recruitment. Increasingly it was replaced by the more impersonal and professional methods which had always been used to a considerable extent. More and more, at least in towns, the chief recruiting mechanism was now the officer or NCO who set up his table in or outside some tavern and tried by beat of drum (a cheerful, good-looking and richly dressed soldier was chosen as drummer whenever possible) and also increasingly by the distribution of printed leaflets,[37] to persuade young men to enlist. In the cities, where a more shifting and footloose population often made it easier to attract young men than in the countryside, professional recruiters, often former NCOs, were now becoming more important than in the past, while in France a variety of agents – old soldiers, minor judicial officials, members of the police force (*maréchaussée*), even sometimes the wives or sisters of NCOs – also helped to produce recruits. Inevitably this bred many abuses. On the one hand were often unscrupulous men who stood to profit by obtaining all the recruits they could by fair means or foul. On the other were their potential prey, often thoughtless, shiftless, drunken or downright criminal.[38] In such a situation deception, false promises, trickery of many kinds, and even occasionally something close to outright kidnapping, could flourish in spite of occasional official efforts to prevent them. Sometimes recruiters pretended that they were seeking men for the more popular and better paid cavalry and not for the infantry. Quite often a recruit would be released on the payment of a sum of money by his horrified relatives: this could mean that a family was in effect held to ransom by an unscrupulous officer or NCO. But no government could afford to be too tender-minded about the means by which its soldiers were obtained. As often, Louvois avowed openly what others tacitly accepted. 'It is a very poor excuse for a soldier, to justify his desertion,' he wrote in 1677, 'to say that he was recruited by force. If we admitted reasons of this sort, there would not be a single soldier left in the king's forces, for there is hardly one who does not believe that he has good reason to complain of his recruitment.'[39]

Naval recruiting posed different and in many ways more intractable problems. A foot-soldier needed no special knowledge or experience. Drill and the handling of his musket, learned in a mechanical fashion until the movements involved became automatic, could transform a ploughboy rapidly into an adequate infantryman. This training might well begin (as in Russia, for example) while a party of recruits was on the march to its regiment from the area in which it had been enlisted. The working of a ship, however, called for knowledge, experience, even perhaps a certain amount of individual initiative. Here ignorant and inexperienced landsmen were of little use. In Russia Peter I did indeed recruit peasants (mainly from the northern parts of the country) to serve in his new fleet: but he had no choice in the matter. All the navies of western Europe tried by various means, however, to draw on the manpower resources of their merchant and fishing fleets. The most systematic attempt to do this came in France. There, under the inspiration of Colbert, a series of ordinances issued in 1668-73 and codified in 1689 established the system of *inscription maritime*. This was based on the drawing up of lists of seamen in all the seagoing areas of the country. These men were to be divided into four (for the naval bases of Rochefort and Toulon, three) groups, the *classes*. In any given year one of these was to serve on the king's ships and another was to be held in reserve in the ports, drawing half-pay, while the others were free to serve in the merchant navy or the fishing fleet. A number of fringe benefits were promised to the men concerned – tax exemptions, free education for their children, payment of part of a seaman's wages to his dependants while he was serving, even pensions for widows of men lost at sea from a king's ship; but these promises were not kept, and apart from a wage increase in 1673 no effort was made to face the fundamental difficulty of the poor pay in the navy compared to what could be obtained elsewhere. A substantial new bureaucracy struggled to make the system work, and not altogether unsuccessfully. By 1690 about 60,000 seamen had been registered; and since the fleets which France put to sea in 1692, when her naval strength relative to that of England or the Dutch was at its peak, needed only 23,000 men, it seems that there was no absolute shortage of manpower.[40]

Yet the difficulties were great and often insuperable. The system was always deeply unpopular with the men subject to it, largely because of the low wages (often paid, as in England, only after long delays) and because it became increasingly difficult to provide the half-pay promised the *classe* held in reserve in the ports. To avoid naval service, French seamen posed as foreigners, served on foreign ships, took non-maritime jobs, went into hiding or simply left the area in which they were registered. Sailors more even than most other occupational groups, it must be remembered, lived from hand to mouth, so that interruptions of normal trade and the calling-up of men for the navy could inflict much hardship. In 1672–3 and 1689–90 the Atlantic ports were closed completely for a time to prevent their escape on board merchant ships, while in 1708 it was estimated that 30,000 had evaded call-up in the last two years. High officials on whom the working of the system partly depended, such as provincial governors and intendants, were often obstructive, particularly as many of them resented the claims of the new *commissaires* whom Colbert had established in the ports. There was often opposition to anything which restricted the supply of men to the merchant fleet; and municipal leaders (who were often elected and representative at least to some extent of popular feeling) were sometimes notably uncooperative in helping to man the navy. It was an implicit confession of the defects of the system when, in the 1690, eighty companies of soldiers meant to serve on French men-of-war, the *compagnies franches de la marine*, were created: they were to last until 1762. With all its shortcomings, however, Colbert's system remained in force in France with little essential change until the end of the old regime.

Moreover in spite of its difficulties it was widely admired and imitated elsewhere in western Europe. Denmark introduced a register of seamen available for naval service in 1679 and revived it in 1700, though this was on a voluntary and not a compulsory basis. In Spain something on roughly the same lines had been attempted as early as 1625; and in 1717 a register of seamen was established for the Basque maritime province of Guipúzcoa. This was extended to the whole country twenty years later, and by the end of the eighteenth century a huge structure of some three hundred edicts and orders had grown up to regulate its workings. As in France, seamen and fishermen, once registered, were to be liable to serve only in the navy; they were also to be freed from a number of other obligations, such as that of having soldiers billeted on them. As in France, however, the system was unpopular. Regulations meant to spread the burden of service equally between those liable to it were not observed in wartime, and although the number of men registered rose steadily in the second half of the eighteenth century there were complaints that because of the shortage of sailors the fleet could not be mobilized without crippling merchant shipping and foreign trade. As in France again, the system generated a good deal of corruption, favouritism and wire-pulling. In England also the idea of an official register of seamen had considerable appeal. There legislation of 1696 set one up, though only on a voluntary basis. This lasted for several years; but the inducements offered to those who entered their names (a payment of £2 a year, a double share of prize money and a guarantee of admission if necessary to Greenwich Hospital) proved far too little to attract the substantial numbers which had been hoped for. Bills for the setting-up of a compulsory register were later debated by the House of Commons in 1720, 1740 and 1744; but all of these foundered on the opposition of the seaports and a widespread feeling that anything of this kind smacked of despotism and was a threat to British liberty.

There were two other possible ways of manning Europe's navies. One was to make conditions of service good enough to attract an adequate number of volunteers. The other was to 'press' men, in effect by seizing seamen, and occasionally landsmen also, and forcing them on to men-of-war. No one doubted that the former was the preferable alternative; yet it was never seriously attempted anywhere. This was simply because it would have cost too much. The great disincentive to enlistment in every European navy was the fact that a sailor's wages compared so poorly in wartime with what he might expect in the merchant service (where wages usually rose with the outbreak of hostilities). Moreover in every navy he might have to face long delays before he received what he was owed; and in the British one at least he might expect to be paid not in cash but in tickets which could be cashed only at the office of the Navy Board in London. The badness of pay cut off the supply of volunteers as nothing else did. Compared to it, all other grievances were relatively unimportant. Discipline, though it inevitably depended heavily on the personalities and tempers of individual captains, was not in general as brutal as is often thought: there were relatively few complaints about it in the British navy at least, where it was more severe than in most others. Food, in an age of long sailing voyages when no means of preserving it other than salting and drying were known, was often of poor quality; but on British ships at least the quantities allowed were substantial, even generous. But without spending much more on wages than any government was willing, even if able, to afford, no great west-European navy could be manned on a voluntary basis.

Pressing, then, was unavoidable. Both the French and Spanish navies pressed men when necessary, in spite of their registers of seamen. Most strikingly of all, the great growth of British seapower in the later seventeenth and eighteenth centuries depended on pressing and would have been impossible without it. In Britain the press normally applied only to seaports and maritime counties, and in them only to able-bodied seamen, though in an emergency it could be applied to seamen anywhere. The seizing of men was done either by boat's-crews from naval vessels or by press-gangs, private business ventures paid by the navy and usually led by a retired naval officer or seaman. There were ample opportunities for abuse, notably by the pressing of foreigners or of men with no connection at all with the sea; and inevitably the system was deeply unpopular. It was universally admitted to be a bad and unfair method of manning the navy. Magistrates and municipal authorities, on whose cooperation it depended heavily, were often unwilling to help in its working. It intensified the ever-present problem of desertion. The men it produced were often of poor quality, as ship's captains repeatedly complained. Yet it continued to be used because there was no alternative, or none which the government or parliament was willing

127

to contemplate. The idea of easing the manning problem by raising wages was never seriously considered.

Sharp practice in recruiting was not confined to the recruiters. The practice of paying enlistment premiums made it possible for an enterprising man to enlist in a particular company, desert almost at once to enlist in another, and repeat this process until he was caught, collecting a premium at each enlistment. This was a frequent form of fraud. One unusually successful practitioner in England was said, when he was finally caught in the first years of the eighteenth century, to have made £60 (a substantial sum for the period) in a single year in this way. A generation later in France it was complained that some soldiers boasted of having enlisted with up to forty different captains in rapid succession.[41] The time-honoured fraud of padding the muster-rolls of a company or a regiment with the names of non-existent soldiers, whose pay could then be appropriated by the officers, was still far from unknown. It was still quite common, at least in the later seventeenth century, when the number of men actually present in a unit was being checked, for its commander to fill up the ranks with servants, cooks and other non-combatants, or to borrow men from fellow-officers to make up the numbers. Louvois waged war on these practices with predictable ferocity. In 1667 he ordered that substitutes of this kind (*passe-volants*) should be hanged, and in 1676 that they should have their noses cut off, while any soldier denouncing one was to have an immediate discharge (significantly regarded as a strong inducement) and a reward of 2–300 livres. As time went on, tighter accounting procedures and the slow weakening of the idea of the company or regiment as the property of its commander made this sort of deception less common; but in some armies at least it remained significant well into the eighteenth century.

All this, however, was relatively unimportant compared to the problem of desertion. Severe discipline, poor pay, oppressive or fraudulent recruiting, most of all the homesickness and disorientation felt by many young men when torn from an environment they had known all their lives and never before left; all these strengthened the incentive to flee from the army and its strange and unwelcome demands. Against desertion every government waged an unending struggle. Sometimes rewards were offered for the denunciation and arrest of a deserter. Five roubles, a considerable sum, could be obtained in this way in Russia under Peter I, and the amount was doubled in 1732. In France in 1701 anyone who arrested a deserter within the kingdom was promised 30 livres: the sum was to be doubled if he were arrested in a foreign country. In many German states peasants were paid a fixed reward for each deserter they caught, while if they helped or sheltered a runaway they might be fined or forced to pay the cost of recruiting and equipping a substitute. Almost everywhere there were frequent amnesties for deserters in the hope that some at least might be tempted to return to the colours. From at least as early as the 1680s there were formal agreements between states by which they promised to return deserters from each other's armies, and scores of these were signed in the eighteenth century; but they were often badly observed, at least in wartime, when many governments might be simultaneously on the lookout for men. The most widespread antidote, however, was simply severe punishment, sometimes backed by stringent precautions against flight. In France Louvois in 1684 replaced the death penalty for desertion by the mere cutting off of the nose and ears and a period of service in the galleys; but in 1716, when the coming of peace and the reduced size of the army had made recruitment easier, the death penalty returned. There were even proposals to make all Frenchmen of military age carry a passport as a means of fighting desertion, though these were never followed up. In Prussia Frederick I in 1711 ordered that deserters should have their nose and one ear cut off and be sent to hard labour for life. In Russia under Peter I they were for a time declared outlaws whom anyone could kill on sight with impunity, while in 1712 it was ordered that all recruits should be marked with a cross on the left hand to make escape more difficult.

There were well-identified situations in which desertion was particularly likely. One was when a body of recruits were being marched to their regiment from the point at which they had been assembled. It was then that the strain of adjusting to a new way of life was most intense and that those who had enlisted voluntarily were most likely to be regretting a rash decision; unusually strict precautions were therefore often needed. An English pamphleteer complained in 1718 that 'Officers conduct recruits as prisoners, sometimes marching them pinioned or handcuffed, or with the buttons of their breeches cut off'; and in London they were often placed for security in the Savoy prison, in notoriously bad living conditions, before being handed over to their regiments.[42] In Russia they were sometimes shackled to logs to prevent escape, as well as being imprisoned at the collecting-points.[43] Another moment of danger was when a body of troops was on the march, especially in wooded or broken country where it was easy to hide. The losses suffered in this way could be very severe. Of one party of 2277 men on the march in Russia in 1705, for example, 895 deserted, while of the French militia units sent in the same year to join the regular army in Italy a quarter had melted away by the time they reached Lyons. Forty years later in Spain, of 1068 who left Barcelona to march to Toulon only 500 reached their destination and all the rest disappeared en route.[44] It is not surprising therefore to find Prince Eugene in 1707 ordering that any soldier found more than a hundred paces away from the army on the march, or more than a thousand away from camp, should be hanged.

Yet none of this could halt or even much reduce the steady haemorrhage of men from every army and navy. The Prussian army lost over 30,000 in 1713–40 under that most militarist of rulers, Frederick William I. In Russia there were said to be 20,000 deserters from the army in 1732 – about a tenth of its total strength – while it has been calculated that during the War of the Spanish Succession at least one French soldier in four deserted. Desertion on this scale was often a real restraint on military and naval operations. It made it difficult to divide soldiers into small groups to forage for supplies and yet increased the need to see that they were regularly and adequately fed, since any shortage of food sharply increased the risk that discontented men might slip away into the countryside. It could substantially magnify the result of a battle, since prisoners, still often badly treated, were frequently tempted to desert to the victorious enemy. Marlborough estimated that 3000 of the French and Bavarian prisoners taken at Blenheim entered the British or Habsburg armies and half a century later, during the Seven Years War of 1756–63, 10,000 French prisoners and deserters joined the Prussian army, though they seem to have been half-hearted and rather useless recruits. At sea, where it was as big a problem as on land, desertion meant considerable restrictions on the movement and use of warships. British men-of-war often would not enter harbour until arrangements had been made for men in their crews regarded as untrustworthy to be moved to other ships which were to remain a certain distance from land. When they left dock after a refit they often did not take on most of their crews until the last moment before sailing: this meant a shortage of men to load stores and repair rigging, but these difficulties were less important than the need to prevent desertion.[45]

Status and ceremony

Bigger armies and navies, more effective central government control of them, growing standardization of weapons and uniforms, increasingly demanding systems of compulsory service – all this paints a picture of growing modernity. Nor is the picture false. Nevertheless the armed forces of the great European states were all to differing extents still influenced by assumptions and ideas inherited from the past, though these contributed little to making armies and navies more efficient and quite often made them significantly less so.

Nowhere were feudal military obligations by the end of the seventeenth century any longer a factor of importance. In France in 1674 there was a last effort to make some serious military use of the old feudal levies of the *ban* and *arrière-ban*. Royal letters-patent in August of that year summoned for service (which was to last only two months) half the nobility of those provinces within a hundred leagues of the frontiers thought to be threatened by enemy attack. These levies were given a month in which to prepare and equip themselves, and early in October some 5–6000 cavalrymen gathered in this way were assembled at Nancy. The experiment was a pathetic failure. The recruits proved completely useless. Marshal Turenne, the greatest French soldier of the century, to whose army in Alsace they were first attached, soon wished only to get rid of them; and when they were transferred to Lorraine and placed under the command of the Marshal de Créqui, one unit proved so lacking in fighting spirit that it allowed the enemy to seize Créqui's personal silver at the gates of Metz and refused to take part in an effort to recover it. Two or three hundred of the levies then left Metz to go home, against Créqui's direct orders. It is not surprising to find him writing, 'I ardently hope that the king may never need to call his nobles together, for it is a force incapable of

131

action and more suited to cause trouble than to cope with emergencies.' In the following year those nobles of the frontier provinces who had not been called on in 1674 were summoned for service. But this was a mere fiscal expedient. They were all excused personal appearance on payment of a tax graduated according to their income; and when the nobility of Normandy offered to serve in person rather than pay, this was refused.[46] This episode wrote the epitaph of feudalism as a military force. It was a clear indication that the mounted chivalry, which had for centuries ruled the battlefield and which had not been a negligible force even in the sixteenth century, was now completely useless even in France where more than anywhere else it had flourished. Henceforth the French nobility, traditionally one of the most warlike in Europe, could play no military role except in the organized and permanent regiments of the regular army.

On a less formal and organized level, however, the legacy of feudalism was still alive. Attitudes rooted in the past and difficult to reconcile with the needs of a modern fighting force still retained an obstinate vitality. It was only slowly and with difficulty that European nobilities were brought to admit that in a military context their inherited social status was less important than their place in a formal hierarchy of defined ranks. In France the decisive step in this process was taken in 1676, when it was decided that as between officers of the same rank the one with most seniority in the rank took precedence. The decision was needed to end a long series of personal quarrels, since a group of French marshals – Créqui, Bellefonds and d'Humières – had since the beginning of the war with the Dutch in 1672 refused to admit that they were in any way subordinate to Turenne, the commander-in-chief. A generation later, however, a diehard defender of noble privilege such as the Duc de Saint-Simon was still complaining bitterly of the subordination of inherited status to mere rank and seniority. To those who thought in this way status was an inalienable right given by birth which no official hierarchy could touch; military service to them was not a duty but a right. Occasionally this stress on the continuing importance of the high-ranking individual took much more bizarre forms. When Prince George of Hesse-Darmstadt was killed in the allied capture of Barcelona in 1705 his heart was enclosed in a casket to be sent to his mother in Germany. The English ship carrying it was forced ashore in Brittany by a French privateer and the heart taken prisoner. Though the Duchess of Orleans and the Electress of Hanover (both relatives of the prince) tried hard to have it released, the French government considered it of such importance, in view of the status of the body from which it had been taken, that they retained it until 1711, and then succeeded in obtaining twenty captured French naval officers in exchange for it.

The armies of the age of Louis XIV, then, though more modern than their predecessors, were still very far indeed from being meritocracies. The poor but able professional officer, to whom the poorly organized and loosely controlled armies of the first half of the seventeenth century had offered at least some limited opportunity for advancement (see pages 74–5 above) now found it more difficult to make his way in an age when military life, though much better organized, was also in some ways more self-consciously aristocratic in tone. In Prussia, for example, there had been one or two generals of commoner origins in the middle and later seventeenth century – Derfflinger, Hennigs von Treffenfeld, Lütcke – but by 1739 there was not one, and of fifty-seven colonels in the Prussian army only one was not noble. In France two outstanding commanders under Louis XIV, Catinat and Vauban himself, both of whom rose to the rank of marshal, were not of high aristocratic birth; but neither can be regarded as bourgeois. Catinat was the son of a high-ranking member of the *parlement* of Paris, and Vauban came from a minor family of the Burgundian nobility. In west-European armies, moreover, luxurious living and conspicuous display by aristocratic officers were taken for granted at least as much as in the past. The Duke of Marlborough, notorious for his love of money, earned much criticism for his resulting modest lifestyle. He was, however, exceptional. More typical was Saint-Simon who, when as an adolescent he made his first campaign as a volunteer private in the *mousquetaires du roi*, took with him a personal train of thirty-five horses and mules and numerous servants, including his tutor and his mother's steward who were to fight by his side in battle.[47] Later even in poverty-stricken Spain the Earl of Peterborough, who in 1705–6 commanded the allied forces in Catalonia and Valencia, had seventeen wagons, over fifty mules and several valuable horses to a total value of over £8000 to carry his own baggage. In 1698 Marshal Boufflers offered, at the French training camp of Compiègne, hospitality so enormously lavish that even the Duke of Burgundy, the grandson of the king, was ordered not to incur the impossible expense which would be entailed in competing with him.

This kind of conspicuous consumption is a good illustration of the aristocratic and still quasi-feudal tone which pervaded many armies during this period. Another is an emphasis on appearances and ceremony greater than had been possible in the badly paid and often ragtag forces which fought the Thirty Years War. This stress on ceremony and the performance of appropriate rituals was seen most clearly in the conduct of the sieges which played such a predominant role in west-European warfare. Every important step in the complex process of taking a fortress, from the opening of the approach-trenches by the besiegers to its final surrender, had an appropriate ceremonial associated with it, and few commanders were willing to neglect their performance.[48] The same values underlay the continuing passion, almost as strong as a century earlier (see page 58 above) for the firing of salutes on the slightest justification. Even the Dunkirk privateers wasted so much powder in this way that they had to be restrained by government order and threatened with being made to pay the cost of excessive firing. A victory on land was normally the occasion for an even more expensive *feu-de-joie*, a rolling salute which ran from one end to the other of the successful army, drawn up in battle array, and in which both cannon and small arms joined. It was most of all, however, on the level of personalities, in the ostentatious courtesies sometimes exchanged between opposing commanders, that the values of an officer-corps which was highly aristocratic, intensely conscious of individual status and honour (and also in its higher ranks markedly cosmopolitan in outlook) emerge most clearly. However ferocious war might sometimes be in its impact on the ordinary man, the highest ranks of society could use it to display their adherence to an aristocratic code of behaviour. Thus the severe treatment of high-ranking prisoners which had sometimes been seen during the Thirty Years War now became more and more rare, at least in western Europe, while there were some striking acts of generosity in this respect. When, to take an outstanding case, the French Marshal Villeroi was captured by the Habsburg forces in Italy in 1702 he was sent to live in complete freedom, first in a castle in Innsbruck and then in Graz. When, nine months later, he was allowed to return to France after Louis XIV had interceded personally on his behalf, he sent Prince Eugene 50,000 livres as a ransom, a sum which the prince at once returned. The ending of a war, again, often meant a ceremonial exchange of presents between the opposing generals. In 1697 the French commander in the Netherlands, to quote only one of a number of examples, received in this way valuable horses from the Elector of Brandenburg and a large quantity of lace from the governor of the Spanish Netherland provinces.

None of this did anything to soften the frequent brutality of old regime warfare. Yet side by side with much suffering, in western Europe at least, went ceremonials and traditional courtesies which emphasized a continuing and still significant aspect of war, that of an aristocratic game played according to gentlemanly rules. The contrast between the two aspects of conflict was too much taken for granted to arouse much contemporary comment, however striking it may appear to twentieth-century eyes.

The cost of war

What effect had war and preparations for war on Europe's economy and society during these decades? What were the gains and losses involved? Did the latter outweigh the former, and if so by how much? These are questions difficult to answer with any precision. The calculation is a complex one, for the losses and suffering inflicted by war were in part counterbalanced, and may occasionally have been outweighed, by beneficial stimuli which would not have existed, or would have been weaker, without the effects of large-scale conflict. The balance-sheet, therefore, is not simple. There are credit as well as debit items to be entered on it; and on both sides they are hard to measure accurately. Any satisfactory discussion of the impact of war, particularly as regards economic life, must be based largely on quantitative information; and though some fairly reliable figures exist for gains and losses over small geographical areas and short periods, it is impossible to extrapolate from these to large states and long time-spans. Morever the variations between different parts of

Europe, in wealth, in social structure, and not least in the violence and ruthlessness with which wars were fought, were very wide. Any discussion must therefore be to some extent vague, a matter of plausible conjectures and intelligent guesses as much as of established facts. All that is possible is to sketch a very impressionistic picture of gains and losses, much of which holds good for the whole period 1618–1789, and to supplement a number of points which have been touched on earlier (see pages 63–76 above).

On the debit side, war still often inflicted important demographic losses whose general nature is clear however difficult they may be to measure exactly. It tended to slow the growth of population, and under favourable conditions might reduce it quite sharply in absolute terms. Loss of life on the battlefield was a very minor element in this process. Some battles of the period were indeed remarkably bloody. At Blenheim in 1704 more than 30,000 men of the 108,000 engaged on the two sides became casualties, and at Malplaquet five years later the anti-French allies had a quarter of their forces killed or wounded. In a few limited areas the male population may have been seriously reduced by direct losses of this kind. Figures for Finland from the mid-eighteenth century (certainly more reliable than most such statistics for that age) show a remarkable predominance of women over men in the age-groups born in 1676–95; and this has been plausibly attributed in part at least to the battlefield sacrifices inflicted by the Swedish struggle of 1700–21 with Russia. But this was an exceptional case. Normally far more important, as in the first half of the seventeenth century, were the population losses caused by epidemics which, if they did not originate in army camps, were often spread by the movement of armies and made more lethal by the generally disruptive effects of war. The clearest and most destructive example is the great outbreak of plague which, beginning in Poland in 1708, was spread by the Swedish and Russian armies during the next five years to embrace the whole Baltic area and much of Scandinavia, with devastating results. Between a third and a half of the population of Danzig is said to have died in the outbreak there in 1709, while Copenhagen may have lost almost as high a proportion of its inhabitants in 1710–11. Even in more favoured parts of western Europe, where war was in general waged with more restraint than further east, it meant an increase in the constant danger of infections and contagious disease. In parts of the southern Netherlands, as a case in point, there were epidemics of dysentery in the mid-1670s and again in 1694 which were clearly the result of military operations. There were also, however, a number of more indirect ways in which wars impeded or even reversed population growth. The fact that a high percentage of soldiers were unmarried had in itself some effect of this kind. Also the presence of large armies in any area normally reduced, through the demands they made, the food supply of its inhabitants. Food shortage and high prices in peasant society meant postponed marriages, with a consequent reduction in their fertility when they did take place. There seems to be clear proof, for example, of marriage being delayed in the war-affected years 1692–4 and 1745–7 in the Basse-Meuse area of the southern Netherlands, one of the few parts of Europe for which reliable evidence of this phenomenon has been published.[49] It seems certain that this mechanism must have operated in many other areas, and perhaps often with more dramatic effect than in the Netherlands.

These demographic losses were frequently less obvious to contemporaries than the physical destruction which war still almost invariably involved. In western Europe the risk of considerable areas being devastated by unpaid, badly disciplined and even starving soldiers, as had happened so often during the Thirty Years War, was now much less. By the 1660s 'treaties of contribution' were becoming common in the Netherlands, for so long the greatest of all battlegrounds; and by the end of the century they had spread to western Germany. These meant that local authorities, municipal or provincial, negotiated with an invading army and agreed to pay it specified amounts in money or kind. In return the invaders promised not to pillage or destroy in the area covered by the agreement. A good example is the convention signed at Douai in July 1710 between representatives of the States-General and of the intendant of Amiens by which, in return for payment of 800,000 livres, the Dutch agreed that their army would not molest the inhabitants of the French territory covering Péronne, Doullens, Abbeville and St Quentin.[50] There are also some clear indications that European governments were becoming more willing to set reasonable limits to what their armies demanded from occupied territory. In 1677 Louis XIV ordered that the total contribution to be exacted from any area in French military occupation should not be more than it normally paid in taxes in a year to its legitimate sovereign. Moreover if the contribution were not paid it was not to be enforced by the time-honoured method of burning villages unless the inhabitants had first fled from their homes. If they remained they were to be coerced merely by the seizure of their livestock and the taking of hostages.[51] The ideas underlying this order were not given effective practical application until the War of the Spanish Succession; but it was the clearest official aspiration towards greater humanity in warfare hitherto seen in early modern Europe. The later seventeenth and early eighteenth centuries, then, saw a marked improvement in the general behaviour of armies in some parts of western Europe. The Duke of Marlborough, clearly a very important case, earned during his years of campaigning in the Netherlands (1705–11) a reputation for sparing civilians and smoothing over difficulties with them when they inevitably arose, and the Spanish Succession struggle seems to have had very little effect on civilian mortality in the Belgian provinces where so much of the largest-scale fighting took place.[52]

None of this meant that wars had ceased to be sometimes brutally destructive, even in the most developed parts of the continent. Entire provinces could still be devastated; but this was now usually the outcome of official policy and of political or strategic decisions taken in cold blood, of a deliberate policy of 'frightfulness'. It was much less likely than in the past to be, in this age of tighter discipline and somewhat more regular pay, the unplanned work of half-mutinous armies. The most famous example of this, one which shocked Europe and was to reverberate through generations to come, was the deliberate devastation of the Rhenish Palatinate by the French army in 1689 (it had also suffered very severely in the French invasion of 1674). Every significant town in the state – Mannheim, Worms, Speyer, Bingen, Oppenheim – was completely destroyed, together with many in neighbouring Baden. Louvois even ordered that any of the inhabitants of Mannheim, the capital, who attempted to return to their homes, were to be killed. To some extent this famous atrocity backfired. So much destruction and the drunkenness and looting (notably in the destruction of Worms) which accompanied it were very bad for discipline in the invading army, while they also provoked ferocious peasant resistance very similar to that sometimes seen in the Thirty Years War. Some of the sieges of the years which followed were also very destructive. The French bombardments of Koblenz in 1688 and Liège in 1691 were extremely severe, while that of Brussels in 1695 was compared by the Duke of Berwick, one of the French commanders, to the burning of Troy by the Greeks.[53] A few years later a parallel to the French action in the Palatinate was provided by the deliberate ravaging of much of Bavaria in 1704 by the English and Habsburg armies under Marlborough and Prince Eugene; perhaps 400 villages were burned in this calculated destruction. A little later again, in 1712, the Swedes were widely condemned when they burnt the town of Altona in north Germany (the fact that the inhabitants had offered to pay *Brandschatz* added weight to the condemnation). War then could still involve massive material losses, even in the parts of Europe where ideas of greater humanity in warfare were slowly making headway.

Obviously also war held back economic growth by diverting to unproductive purposes labour and capital which could have been more productively used. So far as the men who did the fighting were concerned, this point is perhaps not very important. Though armies were now generally larger than ever before they (and to a much less extent navies) were still recruited, at least in the west, mainly from the economically least valuable and least productive part of the population. The loss involved in having so many men employed in this way was therefore less than appears if only their numbers and not their quality are considered. Many of those who became soldiers would have made only a small contribution to society in civilian life; this can perhaps be seen in the difficulty which every state encountered in reintegrating them into society when a war ended and armies were sharply reduced. It must also be remembered that in peacetime soldiers in many armies were used on a large scale for civilian tasks of many kinds, particularly in the construction of public works such as canals and roads. In Russia, Prussia, France and later Spain (the Canal of Aragon completed in 1786 is a late example) they worked in great numbers on canal-building, while the road-building in the Highlands of Scotland after the Jacobite rebellion of 1715 is the best British example of this use of military manpower. In a poor country with a large army such as Prussia this sort of thing was very marked. There the frugal militarist Frederick William I ensured that off-duty soldiers were not idle: many were employed in particular in spinning wool and cotton. Under his successor a new recruit arriving in Berlin in 1756 was amazed to find on the river Spree 'hundreds of soldier-hands busy loading and unloading merchandise', while in the timber-yards 'everywhere was full of warriors hard at work' and 'everywhere I found soldiers similarly employed on hundreds of different jobs – from creating works of art down to plying the distaff'.[54] The value of this kind of labour is impossible to estimate with any accuracy; but it must have been an item of some significance to set against the growing financial and physical cost of armies.

War in these decades meant, nonetheless, a misuse of capital resources which were still scarce everywhere in Europe. The most striking example of unproductive investment of this kind remained, as in the first half of the seventeenth century, elaborate fortifications and great sieges. Even more than in the age of Richelieu and Olivares these were voracious consumers of materials and money as well as of labour. The building of the citadel of Lille in 1667–70 used 60 million bricks and 3½ million pieces of stone for its foundations: a canal had to be dug specially for the transport of the stone from a nearby quarry and entire forests were felled to provide the timber needed.[55] The capture of the city by the anti-French allies forty years later, in 1708, was by far the greatest single operation of the Spanish Succession war, involving immense and expensive siege-works and costing the besiegers some 15,000 casualties. The fortifications of Longwy, far from the biggest of Vauban's fortresses, involved moving 640,000 cubic metres of rock and earth and the construction of 120,000 cubic metres of masonry, while the lines of circumvallation built by the allies in 1711 to protect themselves from attack by any relieving French army during the siege of Bouchain (also hardly a first-rate fortress) were thirty miles long. Further east the new fortifications of Widdin in Bulgaria, built on marshy ground by the Habsburgs and finished in 1723, rested on almost 700,000 piles. Works of this kind were, by the standards of the age, enormous investments.

Moreover the efforts and sacrifices involved in a great siege were by no means confined to the soldiers engaged in it. They spread, in a kind of ripple effect, over wide surrounding areas. Peasants from miles around were conscripted to labour on the trenches and other works involved. Louis XIV, according to his own memoirs, demanded 20,000 for the siege of Maastricht in 1673, while Vauban in 1691 collected 21,000 when he attacked Mons and in the following year 18,000 were conscripted for the siege of Namur. Sometimes this was not too serious a sacrifice. If the siege took place at a time of year when there was not a great deal to be done on the land and if the labourers were given some small cash payment, as was now normal in western Europe, the peasant might regard work of this kind as a welcome chance to make a little money. The allied siege of Namur in 1695 was delayed by the refusal of labourers in the approach-trenches to go on working until they had been paid; and later, in 1748, the French army paid a florin a day to the men who built the siege-works for the attack on Maastricht. If, however, men were dragged from the fields at sowing or harvest time the results could be serious. More serious still, a large army engaged in a long siege made huge demands for food and forage on the countryside for many miles around. In 1674 the 6500 inhabitants of the little town of Verviers were compelled to provide 50,000 lbs of bread each day for the Dutch army then besieging Maastricht, as well as meat, 200 barrels of beer and 400 bottles of wine.[56] Sometimes these demands were impossibly heavy. In 1675 the village of Eysden, in the same area, was required to produce 1169 rations of forage for horses, each weighing 30 lbs, and found itself simply unable to do this. A generation later, when the French army after Malplaquet occupied the same camp for an unusually long period, this created such a shortage of forage all over the surrounding countryside that horses 'perished of hunger at their picket-ropes'.[57]

These decades also saw the emergence, on a much larger scale than ever before, of another type of heavy capital investment associated with war. This was the battle-fleet and the dockyards needed to build and maintain it. These were extremely expensive in several ways. A ship of the line was much larger, more heavily built and more expensive than any merchantman. It carried in proportion to its size a much larger crew. It was armed with a large number of guns (up to 100 for a first-rate man-of-war) and most of these were heavier than all but a few of the heaviest siege-guns used on land. A large fleet demanded enormous quantities of artillery. At the battle of La Hogue in 1692 the English and Dutch ships engaged carried 6756 guns, whereas the 'Great Convoy' of allied artillery for the siege of Lille in 1708 amounted to a mere 80 guns and 20 mortars – about as many as a really large man-of-war would carry. A great fleet also needed complex and expensive shore facilities. A dockyard meant not merely large stores of timber, cordage, sails and blocks, with storage space for them, but also sawpits, a mast pond where the valuable tall pine trees which made the best masts could be seasoned, a tar kettle, a pitch house and perhaps a rope walk, as well as dry-dock facilities. A great naval base was the biggest productive enterprise of the age, and significant towns grew up around some of them, depending almost completely on the work they provided – Deptford or Chatham in England and the entirely new dockyards at Rochefort in France (1666), Kronstadt in Russia (1703), and Ferrol in Spain (1726). A great navy, therefore, ate up resources faster than an army because it was so much more capital-intensive. Furthermore a navy could not, like an army, subsist in part at least on the resources it drew from occupied territory. Every army did this to some extent. But in the nature of things every navy had to be supplied and maintained almost exclusively from the resources of the country it served. Relatively poor countries such as Denmark, Sweden or even Russia, therefore, might for a time be important powers at sea. But it was difficult for them to become, and still more to remain for long, really first-class ones.

The relentless increase in the financial demands of war which had marked the age of Richelieu and Olivares continued in that of Louis XIV and Peter I. This applied both on the national level and on a more local one in areas such as the Netherlands, west Germany and parts of northern Italy where so much fighting took place. In every politically significant state, as in the past, expenditure on the armed forces accounted for much the greatest part of government spending. Where the state was poor and its ruler ambitious these costs could become overwhelming. In Russia already by 1679–80 the army seems to have taken over three-fifths of all government revenue; but by the first years of the eighteenth century its demands and those of the new navy had come to monopolize the budget. In some years perhaps as much as 95 per cent of all expenditure went to meet them. Even in 1725, when Peter I died, the army alone still absorbed 72 per cent of all the government's resources; and by then the yield of direct taxation had grown fivefold in real terms since 1680. Nor is it difficult to find in western Europe percentages which approach these. In Piedmont, one of the most heavily burdened western states in proportion to its wealth, over 68 per cent of all that the government spent went to the army in 1734–40, though in only three of these years was Piedmont at war. In England during the struggles of 1689–1713 about 40 per cent in round figures of government spending was taken by the army and about 35 per cent by the navy; and since total expenditure rose fast during this period, the absolute amounts going to the armed forces grew strikingly. Even in the peaceful decade of the 1730s they absorbed at least half of all British public spending. In France their share was comparable, though its distribution between army and navy was very different: in the war of 1689–97 the army took about 65 per cent of expenditure as against a mere 9 per cent for the navy. These figures are all subject to some margin of error and are an unreliable basis for exact comparisons: it is too difficult to be sure that like is really being compared with like. But the essential message is clear. The money governments raised by taxation or borrowing was still spent overwhelmingly on fighting wars or preparing to fight them.

Moreover these government demands might, in a town or village unlucky enough to find itself in a war zone, be supplemented by those of armies in the field; and whether these armies were officially friendly or hostile often made in practice little difference to the scale of their exactions. The imperial city of Nördlingen in Bavaria is a case in point. Though it had suffered a good deal in the Thirty Years War, recovery had begun even before 1648 and went ahead quite rapidly in the 1650s and 1660s. After this, however, there was a sharp retrogression so that by 1694 the wealth of the city (estimated from tax data) was only about 70 per cent of what it had been in 1579. This decline was the result of the demands placed on it by the wars of the Habsburgs with France in 1672–8 and 1689–97. In the 1670s it had to provide winter quarters for imperial regiments for five years running, and in the later decades of the century each citizen was normally paying more than twice as much in direct taxation as he had done in the 1650s. Only after the end of the French and Turkish wars of the Habsburgs in the second decade of the eighteenth century was there any recovery, and a petition of the magistrates to the Imperial Diet in 1721 gives, allowing for some inevitable exaggeration, a fair picture of what these struggles must have meant for a good many German cities. 'Because of the utterly ruinous Thirty Years War and the subsequent French wars,' they wrote, 'together with their consequent marches and counter-marches, camp-provisioning and winter-quartering, extortion from and plundering of the city's rural subjects, not to mention garrison costs, bombing, encampments and conquests, the city has gradually and unfortunately declined from its former position and has fallen into the uttermost ruin, so that not only has the citizenry – which formerly numbered 2000 men and included various nobles and other prosperous families – now been reduced to less than half its original size, and those who are left are in such a state that the many houses which burnt down in the bombardment [of 1647] have still not been rebuilt, but also such an unspeakable amount of money has been extorted from them over the years that one cannot read the financial records of these events without astonishment.'[58]

Often, however, the demands of armies in the field fell more heavily on the peasant than on the townsman. The towns had recognized authorities who could speak for them and with whom it was usually convenient for military commanders operating in the area to deal. The peasant in his village, and still more in an isolated homestead, often lacked even this limited protection. He was thus very vulnerable to demands for money, for food, for forage, for winter-quarters; and these were often still enforced, even in western Europe, by very brutal means. In one rather bizarre case in the village of Saive, in the Bishopric of Liège, for example, a party of French soldiers seeking supplies and money on Easter Sunday, 1677, found all the inhabitants in church in their best clothes, stripped them naked and besides taking their clothes, seized hostages to be held for ransom as well as all the animals they could find.[59] As well as food and money the peasant was often forced to provide transport-service on a large scale for both governments and armies in the field. Historians have seldom given this burden the prominence it deserves, and yet it could be one of the heaviest of all, especially in the eastern half of Europe where food and fodder had often to be moved over much longer distances than in the more densely populated west. In Brandenburg-Prussia this was a burdensome obligation even in peacetime. In Russia it weighed even more heavily, and became more onerous during the long struggle with Sweden. In 1702 4428 cartloads of bread and 8594 of other supplies were transported in this way from Moscow to the north-west of the country for army use; but only a year later the corresponding figures had grown to 5290 and 11,318.[60] Whereas in 1702 services of this kind had been demanded from only twenty districts (*uezds*), in 1703 fifty were forced to provide them. Carrying-services of this kind cost the peasant dear not merely because they took him away from his home and his fields, sometimes for long periods, but also because they exhausted and wore out his horses or oxen, an essential part of his working capital. Even in parts of western Europe this sort of burden could be far from negligible. In some parts of France, for instance, notably in the Pyrenees, the obligation to move newly felled timber to the nearest navigable river so that it could be floated down to the sea for the use of naval dockyards was a significant source of complaint. Though it was not in general an unbearable burden, it again could create serious difficulties if it fell at awkward times of the year, when carts and draught animals were urgently needed for other purposes.[61]

It is impossible to give even the vaguest estimate of the extent to which war, through its interference with rural life, reduced agricultural production in Europe during these decades. It has been calculated that in the Basse-Meuse district over the whole period 1620–1750, 'war's average effect was to reduce production at least fifteen per cent, and rarely more than forty per cent.'[62] However there were wide variations everywhere from year to year, depending on the nature and intensity of the fighting, the weather and other factors. In the Basse-Meuse there were years when production fell to less than a quarter of normal. Moreover in eastern Europe the effects of war on agriculture were sometimes far more destructive than almost anywhere in the west. The ravaging of the Swedish Baltic provinces by the Russian army from 1702 onwards and the devastation of Poland in the same years inflicted damage more extensive and lasting than anything to be seen in Germany, Italy or the Netherlands. The greater destructiveness of war in the east was seen perhaps most strikingly of all in the scorched-earth policy adopted in 1708 by Peter I for the defence of Russia against Swedish invasion. Throughout a wide belt of territory from Pskov in the north to Cherkassk in the south the peasants were forbidden on pain of death to keep grain or fodder in their houses or barns and ordered to bury or hide everything which might be of use to the enemy. The policy was effective. An English observer with the army of Charles XII in the following year reported: 'The country we stayed in was desolate; we found nothing but what was burnt and destroyed, and of large villages little left but the bare names.'[63]

The costs and losses described in the preceding paragraphs were all more or less direct and clearly recognizable ones. There were also indirect ones which are less easy to see and even more difficult to measure. The most important of these, and the one most extensively discussed by contemporaries, was the way in which war impeded the normal flow of seaborne trade. In this age, and for that matter until the second half of the nineteenth century, economic warfare was a commercial much more than an industrial struggle. Industry was as yet less developed than trade; and the difficulty and slowness of communications meant that markets for many industrial products on more than a local or at most a national scale were very fragmentary and imperfect. More particularly, the extreme difficulty of moving heavy and bulky goods by land meant that there was only limited international competition in the production of such things as many types of metal goods. By comparison, trade competition between the great maritime states of western Europe was now more active than ever before. These powers struggled not merely to increase their own exports, and increasingly also their re-exports of colonial products such as sugar and tobacco, but also to gain a greater share of the valuable carrying-trade of Europe generally, the trade which the Dutch had gone so far towards monopolizing during much of the seventeenth century. The intellectual climate was highly favourable to this kind of trade war. It was almost universally agreed that the total of Europe's wealth, and of the commerce which was an essential element in it, could not be increased, at least in the short term. What one state gained another must lose: international economic life was a zero-sum game. This idea had already been very frankly stated in justifications of the Anglo-Dutch conflicts of 1652–4 and 1665–7. 'What matters this or that reason?' wrote General Monck, soon to command an English fleet, advocating such a war in the early 1660s. 'What we want is more of what the Dutch now have.'[64] The same assumption permeates much of the correspondence of Colbert; and the French attack on the Dutch Republic in 1672 was inspired in part by trade rivalry and preceded by years of efforts to reduce Dutch trade with France. These attitudes were voiced, at least in England and the Netherlands, by a growing pamphlet literature: merchant interests and ambitions were in this period given considerably fuller expression than industrial ones. Thus when in the mid-eighteenth century a great

English merchant said of the French that 'our trade will improve by the extinction of theirs'[65] he was merely expressing succinctly what had for generations been the conventional wisdom.

A complete cutting-off of the enemy's seaborne commerce was never achieved by any belligerent during the great struggles of 1689–97 and 1702–13, in spite of the growing predominance of the English navy from 1692 onwards. On both sides in these conflicts there was an increasing use of neutral ships and of forged or illegitimately acquired papers to protect cargoes against enemy attacks, though the extent of this is difficult to measure. More important, on both sides there was reluctance to accept that trade with the enemy must be completely abandoned once war had been declared. The Dutch in particular were very unwilling to take such a radical attitude. Their traditional policy was to make war 'a purely military collision in an undisturbed context of industry and trade',[66] and the French invasion of their territory in 1672 was made possible partly by supplies of gunpowder and shot bought in Holland itself. English pressure forced them to agree at the outbreak of war in 1689 to end all trade with France; but in fact much Dutch trade continued until the peace of 1697. In 1703, again, the English government was able to force the republic to forbid all commerce and postal communication with the French; but this agreement was to last only for a year, was very unpopular in the Netherlands, and was not renewed when it expired. After 1705 there was relatively little effort even in London to end trade with France completely. Moreover although both the anti-French allies were very willing to cut off completely neutral (largely Danish and Swedish) commerce with French ports, this would have demanded a blockade for which they had neither the resources nor the organization.

This did not mean that the effects of war on seaborne trade were unimportant. In the War of the Spanish Succession, when Dunkirk enjoyed even more success than in the 1690s, over four thousand prizes were taken by French privateers; and this does not take into account the more than two thousand ransoms paid (as had also been done extensively in the war of 1689–97) by ships which were then allowed to go on their way. The very heavy English losses in the first half of the war (allegedly 3600 ships) led in 1708 to the passage of the Convoys and Cruisers Act by which Parliament, in an unprecedented interference in naval strategy, ordered that forty-three warships should be allocated to commerce-protection. At certain moments French privateers threatened completely to disrupt important branches of trade: in 1703 their activities meant that London had only a week's supply of coal in stock. Unquantifiable but important losses also stemmed from the need for ships, especially those with valuable cargoes, often to sail in convoy, and from the long delays while convoys were forming and awaiting their naval escorts. The Smyrna convoy, whose dispersal and partial capture in 1693 was the greatest success ever won by France against English trade, had been assembled and waiting for almost a year before it could sail. Half a century later, in 1742, a convoy for Portugal, a very important market for British goods, was held up for the same length of time. That to Jamaica in 1744, though it was ready in April, could not set sail until November. Hold-ups of this kind were a serious interference with normal commercial life. Big convoys might mean big losses when something went wrong, as in 1693; and the convoy system also meant that very large amounts of such things as West Indian sugar or Virginian tobacco might arrive suddenly in European ports. This could produce violent price fluctuations and increase the uncertainty which was always an important factor in much commodity dealing. It could also mean long delays in loading and unloading if ports became suddenly choked with ships when a convoy arrived. Moreover war almost invariably meant a rise in merchant seamen's wages and often a very steep rise in insurance charges, though these increased costs could be balanced by a rise in freight rates. Perhaps the best summing-up is to say that efforts at trade war increased the element of risk which was always present in seaborne commerce, especially over long distances. High freight-rates, temporarily high prices, lucky or skilful speculation, might bring windfall profits to merchants or shipowners. Bad luck or bad management might equally mean crippling losses.

War reduced the total amount of European seaborne trade. But this affected different maritime states to very different extents. France, for all her privateering successes, suffered relatively heavier losses than her rival across the Channel. Dutch trade was, in the early decades of the eighteenth century, in rapid decline absolutely as well as relatively. (Though this stemmed from the limitations of her own economy, her small population and restricted industrial potential, rather than from the effects of war.) England was the great gainer. Though her merchantmen were captured at a rate which sometimes seemed alarming, her trade grew nonetheless, sometimes rapidly. In 1688 nearly 286,000 tons of shipping cleared from her ports, of which nearly 191,000 were English. In 1699 337,000 tons cleared, and of this nearly 294,000 were English.[67] By the early eighteenth century England's seapower was allowing her to build a colonial empire in America and the Caribbean within which she had in theory and to a great extent in practice a trade monopoly. This empire gave her both markets for her goods, though as yet less important ones than in Europe, and sources of valuable tropical commodities much of which would be re-exported. The opportunities it was beginning to provide were to do more indirectly for British trade than the protection given by the navy in wartime did directly. Its importance, and the possible advantages of a successful maritime and colonial war, were by the 1720s at latest very widely recognized in Britain. One pamphlet of 1727 neatly epitomizes this recognition in its title: *Britain's Speediest Sinking Fund is a Powerful Maritime War, Rightly Manag'd, and Especially in the West Indies*.

Were there any ways in which war stimulated constructive change? There were: but here again the element of speculation and conjecture is large. War increased demand for certain sorts of manufactured goods – uniforms, small arms and cannon. This could mean sharp increases in their production and notably in the output of the metal-producing and metal-working industries. Russia is the most striking example of this. As she leapt, within a decade, from being a neglected and often despised state on the fringes of Europe to the position of a great military power, she was compelled to equip herself with a modern arms industry. The limited production of the later seventeenth century could not meet the demands it now faced. A new network of factories, most of them large, was therefore rapidly created to supplement it. In 1700 a commission, staffed by foreign experts as well as Russians, was set up to seek out new deposits of metal ores. In the years which followed, existing arms output in the Tula and Olonetz areas was rapidly increased and a great new source of metal production developed in the southern Urals. There rich deposits of iron and copper ores, cheap fuel and conscripted peasant labour made possible a spectacular growth in output. By 1723 one factory alone in the area was producing 350 field-guns each year. In the Olonetz district in north-west Russia, a traditional centre of arms production, government factories working for the new navy cast nearly 300 guns in 1704, while a few years later others in the south serving the fleet on the Sea of Azov were producing almost 250 a year. Growth in the production of small arms was equally rapid and needed to be: the establishment for the Russian army laid down in 1711 called for almost 123,000 muskets for the infantry and 50,000 for the cavalry regiments. Until at least 1712 Peter had still to buy substantial quantities of small arms abroad, mainly in the Netherlands; but by then Russia's output was beginning to meet her needs. In 1715 one new factory in Tula alone produced 11,000 muskets for the infantry and 7000 for the dragoon regiments, as well as 4000 pairs of pistols and other weapons: when it was rebuilt in 1720 its output grew further. This was as close to mass production as the early eighteenth century was to get. At Peter's death in 1725 there were about forty arms factories of differing sizes of Russia; and whereas at the beginning of the Great Northern War the whole empire had produced only 120–150,000 poods of iron (a pood = 36 lbs), this had grown to 1,165,000 at the end of the reign.[68] The same years saw a similar increase in Russia's production of gunpowder and a growth, though a less spectacular one, in the manufacture of woollen cloth for army uniforms. Hitherto this had been for the most part imported from England and the Dutch Republic, but here again new factories (for example near Voronezh in 1704 and in Moscow in 1705) sharply increased domestic production. There would have been some growth in output of metals and cloth even without the war; but it would certainly not have had this almost explosive quality.

In western Europe effects of this kind were less marked. France, England, the Dutch Republic, even the Habsburg hereditary provinces, were starting from a higher level of industrial development; and none of them made the sudden leap to great-power status which Russia did. Even in the west, however, war accelerated some aspects of industrial growth. In the Basse-Meuse region, which included the great metallurgical centre of Liège, 'it may have pushed the iron-working and weapons-producing parts of the economy from quiet prosperity to booming growth'.[69] In Spain, which at the beginning of the Succession war had been very heavily dependent on arms from abroad, the fighting of 1704–14 seems to have had a significant effect in stimulating their production. By the end of the war she could produce most of the artillery she needed; and by 1738 the government was able to insist that the army should use only domestically produced weapons – a very different situation from that at the beginning of the century.

War could stimulate sharply demand not merely for arms but also for food. The peasant and the farmer in battle areas might well still find themselves pillaged and subjected to harsh requisitioning. Increasingly, however, at least in one or two parts of western Europe, they might also hope to gain from higher food prices and from the growth in demand which war generated. So long as discipline in the contending armies remained reasonably good, the agricultural producer in or close to an area of military operations might sometimes make good profits. This appears to have happened in the Basse-Meuse area from the 1690s onwards, where after heavy losses in the 1670s and some recovery in the 1680s better behaviour by soldiers and rising prices meant that 'war turned from a burden to a benefit'.[70] The process was now in motion which was to allow Adam Smith to claim, seventy years or so later, that 'War is so far from being a disadvantage in a well-cultivated country that many get rich by it. When the Netherlands is the seat of war, all the peasants grow rich, for they pay no rent when the enemy is in the country, and provisions sell at a high rate.'[71] Even in 1763, when he uttered these words, they were an exaggeration. High wartime prices tended to benefit chiefly the bigger farmer who produced for the market, rather than the small peasant producer (though the distinction between the two was less marked in the Netherlands than almost anywhere else). Even in western Europe it was still very much the exception rather than the rule for the cultivator to profit from war. Nevertheless by the end of the seventeenth century, at least in some favoured parts of the continent, the man who worked the land had more hope of gaining by war and less fear of losing catastrophically by it than ever before. And even in peacetime armies might give some stimulus to agricultural production. A large garrison often provided a substantial and concentrated demand for food from which the surrounding countryside might benefit. In Prussia, for example, many fortresses provided a market which, in a poor country with a largely subsistence agriculture, was of real economic importance. Occasionally war needs might even lead to government action which could indirectly benefit agriculture. This can be seen in the efforts made by more than one government to improve horse-breeding and thus secure a better and more reliable supply of cavalry mounts for its army. In 1712 Peter I, in the best-known case of this, set up stud farms for the purpose in several Russian provinces, while efforts were made to improve horse-breeding as far away as Siberia. Again, however, the effect of efforts of this kind should not be overemphasized: their impact on economic life was very small.

The stimulus to economic growth which war might provide had another and quite different dimension. Through the demands which it made it sometimes stimulated forms of production and organization larger in scale, more complex and more administratively demanding, than those normal in civilian life. The equipping of armies and navies which were not merely bigger than ever before but also more rationally organized called not merely for large quantities of arms but for arms which conformed to standard patterns and were therefore, in some sense, mass-produced. This often created problems of organization which industry in general hardly had to face. It was, however, in the naval dockyards that the effect of war demands in fostering the growth of big and complex units of production was most clearly seen. These dockyards were large employers. By 1697 the English ones had over 4200 workmen, and this figure was considerably exceeded in the Spanish Succession conflict. A little later the Admiralty dockyard in St Petersburg, which was certainly the largest industrial complex in eighteenth-century Russia, employed over 7500 men in 1716, about two-thirds of them skilled: in 1721 it gave work to 3600 carpenters and 500 blacksmiths. But naval dockyards were also places in which a number of different processes had to be combined to produce the most complex artefact of the age, the large sailing warship. Not merely shipwrights and carpenters but smiths, caulkers, ropemakers, sailmakers and others had to contribute to this process. By the 1740s the more than fifteen hundred employed in the dockyard at Deptford were classified in thirty-one different trades. Moreover there was a marked seasonal rhythm to this work. In wartime there was a peak of demand in winter, because large ships did not normally keep the sea after September or October but instead returned to port for repairs and maintenance in preparation for the next summer's campaign. In peacetime the position was reversed and more work was done during the summer months. This combination of size, complexity and seasonal variations posed problems of a kind which no other industrial enterprise of the age had to face. It demanded a skill in planning and controlling the flow of work and in handling sometimes difficult labour relations which was called for nowhere else. It stretched the administrative capacities of the age to their limits.

Many aspects of the day-to-day supply of armed forces, indeed, now called for and often evoked administrative ability greater than that needed in the days of Richelieu and Gustavus Adolphus. This again was more marked where navies were in question. Armies, as well as being able to live to some extent on the country in which they operated, normally moved only slowly and often moved very little at all for quite long periods. A fleet, however, was completely dependent on the supplies provided for it and was in constant and usually unpredictable movement. To ensure that it never ran short, whatever the vicissitudes of its operations or the changes in the weather, demanded administrative skills of a high order. By the 1740s the British navy needed each year 12,000 cattle and 40,000 hogs to supply it with meat alone; and the Victualling Commissioners owned breweries, bakehouses, slaughterhouses and a wide range of storage facilities. They were, in fact, running the biggest business in Britain, probably the biggest effectively integrated one in all Europe; and the need for careful planning was intensified by the fact that as time went on, a bigger and bigger proportion of the fleet was likely to be thousands of miles from its home bases – about 40 per cent of it in the West Indies in 1740–1 and about the same proportion in the Mediterranean in 1743–4.[72] To varying degrees all over Europe, therefore, the needs of the armed forces stimulated administrative development and heightened administrative efficiency. They provided a school for administrators for which there was usually no parallel in civilian life. In Russia or Prussia this situation, pushed to extremes, meant that virtually all administrative processes were influenced by army needs and that most of them became completely subservient to army demands. In western Europe, however, it can be argued that war sometimes stimulated efficiency and fostered constructive innovation without distorting the entire administrative machine, and therefore had some beneficial effects which were slow-acting and unquantifiable but nonetheless real.

This was particularly so in one or two cases in the field of public finance. During this period money had to be raised on an unheard-of scale for wars which were unprecedentedly expensive. Sometimes it had to be transferred in large quantities from one part of Europe to another to pay soldiers or to subsidize allies. The improvement in financial and banking mechanisms which this stimulated is again seen most clearly in England. There the 1690s produced a revolution in public finance. Henceforth government loans were based on parliamentary guarantees, a broader and sounder foundation than they had ever had before. Simultaneously the Bank of England became the essential vehicle for raising loans and sustaining the government's credit. From 1709 onwards it was associated by statute with the issue of Exchequer bills, and in a variety of important ways helped mobilize the financial resources of the nation as a whole far more effectively than in the past. These fundamental changes took place against a background of war demands and would not have been introduced without them. In their turn they helped to make possible a trebling of government spending, essentially war-induced spending, from less than £2 million a year before 1688 to £5–6 million by the turn of the century. No other European state reacted so effectively to the financial demands of war. Throughout the eighteenth century Britain's international position was to benefit enormously from her ability in wartime to borrow more cheaply and spend more freely than any other power. Occasionally elsewhere there are signs that the financial pressures generated by war had some constructive effects. The efforts of both the French and English governments to pay and supply their armies in Spain during the Succession struggle probably helped to stimulate the growth there of an embryonic national money-market and of the sort of large-scale financial dealings needed to make it work, while international dealings by a small circle of Spanish financiers did something to bring a very introverted and xenophobic country into the mainstream of European economic life.[73] But in most states the response to war's financial demands took no more original form than heavier taxation; and where new financial mechanisms were introduced they were not necessarily more advanced ones. In Vienna, where the need was greatest, the army's demands for more money meant simply the appearance of the first 'Court Jew' to be seen there, the banker Samuel Oppenheimer whose death in 1703 meant that for a time the Habsburg government found itself completely penniless.

The balance-sheet then is not completely one-sided. War had constructive as well as destructive effects, and this continued to be true throughout the decades before the French Revolution. Yet although a final balance cannot be struck, it is impossible not to feel that it was a negative one. War inhibited population growth and physically destroyed real resources – houses, crops and animals. Probably more serious in western Europe, it diverted both labour and capital from relatively productive to relatively unproductive uses such as the building of fortifications and the conduct of sieges. It increased the risks and uncertainties of many forms of economic enterprise, notably seaborne trade. Against this, by helping to expand some existing industries and even occasionally to create new ones, it may have stimulated the use of resources which would otherwise have lain idle or been underemployed. It sometimes helped, by its demands, to set new standards of administrative efficiency (though how much this contributed to the happiness of the individual subject is another matter). It may also have been that the greater size and better organization of armed forces, the increase in the relative importance of naval warfare, the growing centralization of supply-systems and standardization of weapons, created a relatively steady demand for equipment and stores and thus helped somewhat to even out the marked peaks and troughs in prices which in that age were so readily produced by changing harvest-yields or trade conditions. Occasionally an entire society may have been revitalized, shifted on to new paths of development, by the impact of war. It has been suggested that the War of the Spanish Succession may have had this effect in Spain, shaking her out of the inertia and pessimism which had so marked the second half of the seventeenth century, and that 'to this extent . . . the war was beneficial, and the eventual benefits far exceeded in volume the damage caused to Spanish population, agriculture and commerce by a decade or more of civil conflict.'[74] In Russia an even greater jolt was felt as a result of the struggle with

Sweden, and with much more spectacular results. But here the balance of benefit is more doubtful. Important processes of change, some accelerated 'westernization' and a growth in the country's international stature, were well under way before the Great Northern War; and the changes of Peter's reign were carried out at the cost of mortgaging the country's future through the consolidation of serfdom and the creation of a military autocracy. The balance-sheet therefore varied widely from one state to another. Spain was to some extent revived by conflict. England was enabled to expand an overseas empire which was to contribute fundamentally to her commercial strength, and forced to modernize her system of public finance. But against this France was drawn into expenditures and sacrifices which were largely wasted and which clouded the last days of Louis XIV, while both the Dutch Republic and Sweden exhausted themselves in struggling to maintain international positions which were now beyond their powers. The average European, insofar as that phrase has meaning, would probably have lived better, and would certainly have been less heavily taxed and enjoyed greater physical security, if none of the great international struggles of this period had been fought.

PART THREE

Towards a New World: Nationalism and People's Armies, 1740–89

The struggles for power

The most spectacular change in the military balance of Europe in the half-century before the French Revolution was the sharp rise in the importance and prestige of Brandenburg-Prussia. During these decades the Prussian army became for much of the continent a model to be admired, even slavishly copied, in a way that none had ever been in the past. Its foundations had been laid long before 1740: more than anyone else King Frederick William I of Prussia, who died in that year, must be regarded as its creator. But he was too genuine a militarist to risk in battle the highly trained and rigidly disciplined force on which he lavished so much attention. It was his successor, Frederick II, who by his invasion of the Habsburg province of Silesia in December 1740 displayed to the world for the first time its potentialities. By 1745, when the German phase of the complex War of the Austrian Succession (1740–8) which this attack had triggered off came to an end, no one could doubt that a new and very powerful element had been added to the military balance of the continent. The supreme test for Frederick, his army and his subjects, was still to come. From the summer of 1756 onwards the Habsburgs, supported by France, Russia, Sweden and a number of small German states, struggled to defeat Prussia and destroy it as a significant power. In this Seven Years War Frederick more than once suffered defeats which seemed disastrous. That by the Russians at Kunersdorf in 1759 temporarily reduced him to despair; and by 1762, his resources almost at an end, it seemed that he could hardly hold out longer. From this desperate situation he was rescued by the death of the Empress Elizabeth of Russia, the most unyielding of his enemies; and when the war ended in the following year Silesia remained a Prussian province. In military if not in any other terms Prussia was now clearly one of the great powers, and such she remained in the eyes of all contemporaries to the end of this period.

There were other armies which maintained and sometimes increased their importance. British regiments fought doggedly though with no great success in west Germany and the Netherlands in the 1740s, and more successfully in Westphalia during the Seven Years War. Moreover during these mid-century struggles the military leverage given Britain by her financial strength, her ability to influence profoundly the progress of continental struggles by subsidizing a combatant with a large army but little money to pay and maintain it, was seen on a larger scale than ever before. From 1741 the Habsburg Empress Maria Theresa and from 1758 Frederick II benefited in this way; while the 'British' army which performed well in Westphalia from 1758 onwards consisted largely of hired German regiments and was commanded by a German prince. In the struggle of 1775–83 with her rebellious American colonies Britain suffered, it is true, the most serious defeat in her history; but this was the result of the appalling logistical problems of a war fought more than three thousand miles away and in a huge and relatively undeveloped country, more than of any strictly military shortcomings. The Russian army during this half-century confirmed that it was one of the most formidable in Europe. During the Seven Years War its soldiers showed themselves at least the equals of the Prussian ones in discipline and endurance, and in two difficult wars against the Ottoman Empire in 1768–74 and 1787–92 it won striking successes. The Austrian Habsburgs also, once they had been able to strengthen and reorganize their forces in response to the Prussian attack of 1740, had no reason to be ashamed of their army: after 1756 it showed that it could hold its own, or very nearly so, with that of Frederick II. France alone of the major European powers saw her military prestige decline. During the War of the Austrian Succession she suffered some considerable setbacks; but she also won important victories, and when the war ended in 1748 she had overrun the southern Netherlands (something Louis XIV had never achieved) and was threatening to invade the Dutch Republic. But the years 1757–62 were disastrous. The rout of a French army by the Prussians at Rossbach in 1757 was the most humiliating defeat suffered by any power during the century, and the Westphalian campaigns of the following years did nothing to retrieve France's military reputation. The same years, in spite of her having the support of Spain from 1761 onwards, saw her suffer great defeats at sea at the hands of the British and lose her colonies of settlement in Canada and Louisiana and her hopes of empire in India. By 1763 her opportunity of becoming a true world power had disappeared, as events were to prove for ever, though this was hardly clear to contemporary observers. The rebellion in America allowed her, by joining the colonists against Britain from 1778 onwards, to revenge herself for the failures of twenty years earlier; but her successes in this war she owed to her navy at least as much as to her army. This lack of military achievement, allied with other factors, meant that France, far more than any other European state, saw in the generation before the Revolution pressures for drastic military reform, for the creation in effect of a new type of army. The shaking of old assumptions and the explosive release of new energies which began in the later 1780s gave these pressures a scope and importance they would not have otherwise achieved. The new army of which some reformers in France had dreamed could thus become a reality and lead Europe into a new era of intensified military effort and still heavier war demands.

The heritage of the past

The great struggles of the generation 1690–1720 gave old-regime warfare a scale and intensity which were not to be surpassed before the transformation brought about by the French Revolution. During the eighteenth century, as has just been seen, the balance of military strength between the great states altered considerably. But many of the essential characteristics of armies and navies, in their armament and tactics, in the ways in which they were recruited and controlled, did not change fundamentally from what they had been in the days of Marlborough and Prince Eugene.

The armies which fought the wars of 1740–8 and 1756–63 were no larger than those which had faced each other in the War of the Spanish Succession; sometimes they were smaller. A notable example was that of France, which in the critical year 1710 had numbered about 380,000 but was only about 280,000 strong (even including about

100,000 militia) fifty years later, in the last stages of the Seven Years War. In peacetime military burdens were sometimes, by the standards of the past, relatively light. The Swedish army which in 1709, when the country was making the greatest military effort in its history, had numbered about 110,000 men, had only about 45,000 at the end of the century, although the population from which it drew recruits had grown by perhaps 40 per cent. The Spanish army in 1759, before the country entered the Seven Years War, was much smaller, at perhaps 59,000 men, than the crushingly large forces which Olivares had struggled to maintain. Further east the story was rather different. In the first years of the eighteenth century the Habsburgs had had great difficulty in keeping on foot a force of about 100,000: without English subsidies they would at times have been unable to achieve even this. In the 1780s, strengthened by the territorial gains made in the southern Netherlands and Italy and still more by the administrative and fiscal reforms of the 1740s and 1750s in the hereditary provinces, they were able to support an army which approached a quarter of a million. More striking still was the case of Prussia. The standing army of 80,000 which Frederick William I left to his son in 1740 had grown to 194,000 when Frederick II died in 1786. In the crisis years of the Seven Years War it had reached 260,000 or more, the equivalent of about 7 per cent of the total population of the state and an achievement unequalled in any other. The Russian army grew less rapidly, and the existence of Cossack and other irregular forces makes it difficult to estimate its strength accurately; but by the end of the century it was around the 300,000 mark.[1] The military centre of gravity of the continent had therefore moved markedly to the east. Compared to the western states, those of eastern and central Europe were now much stronger than they had been in the seventeenth century or even the first half of the eighteenth, a change of immense political importance. It was now impossible for France, Spain and Great Britain to settle their disagreements and fight out their conflicts, as they had done in the sixteenth and seventeenth centuries, with little or no attention to Europe east of the Elbe.

The navies of the western powers during this period grew much more than their armies, a reflection of the fact that the struggles between them were now more than ever before conflicts for colonial empires and the markets and trade which these brought. The British navy, now unquestionably the largest, had 247 ships of all types by 1714; but in 1760, at the peak of its success in the Seven Years War, it had 412 and by 1783, the last year of the very difficult American war, it numbered 468, of which a remarkable 174 were ships of the line.[2] That of France had a much more chequered history; as in the past, strength at sea seemed to many French statesmen clearly secondary to strength on land and therefore to be sacrificed when the two services competed for resources. The years after the Spanish Succession struggle saw France's naval power reduced so sharply that in 1719 she had only 49 warships of all classes. Yet by the end of the 1730s she had nearly 50 ships of the line and was once more clearly the second-greatest naval power in the world; and by 1754, in spite of losses in the naval struggle of 1744–8 with Britain, she had still 57. The Seven Years War saw her suffer the most severe setbacks in her entire maritime history; in its later years she virtually gave up all naval building. Yet by 1773 she had once more 66 ships of the line; and the War of American Independence, a unique opportunity to take revenge on Britain for past defeats, saw her make the greatest naval effort in her history. From 35 million livres in 1776 the French naval budget jumped to 200 million in 1782. The 81 ships of the line she possessed in that year marked her out once more as the only possible threat to British naval leadership. The two other states whose seapower grew during this period, Spain and Russia, underwent vicissitudes as sharp as those of France. The Spanish navy, which by the end of the seventeenth century had almost ceased to exist, was rapidly revived during the two decades or more after the Succession war, and again during the 1750s; by 1774 it had 58 ships of the line, a force comparable to that of France. In Russia, once the passionate support of Peter I had been removed, the navy declined rapidly under his successors, none of whom shared his obsessive interest in it. Not until the 1760s, under Catherine II, did it begin to revive; but it then grew fairly rapidly. By 1788 the Russian Baltic fleet numbered 37 ships of the line, and its quality was shown in its generally successful showing in the war of 1788–91 against the very respectable Swedish navy. Moreover by then Russia had built a second powerful squadron in the Black Sea (22 ships of the line in 1791) although she was still unable to pass it through the Straits into the Mediterranean.

In terms of their demands for men, the armed forces of Europe as a whole were almost certainly less of a burden during this period than they had been in 1690–1720. As a proportion of the population from which they were drawn, European armies in aggregate were no larger and probably smaller than in the past. Europe west of the Urals, which had perhaps 118 million inhabitants in 1700, supported 140 million by 1750 and 187 million in 1800; a growing population and armies which grew less rapidly if at all meant that for the continent in general the load had been lightened. Navies, though the major ones were growing, were less demanding than armies in terms of man-power. This certainly did not mean that the weight of war demands was lessening everywhere. The greater cost of navies as opposed to armies meant that a state whose naval power was increasing found itself inevitably faced by growing financial pressures. The outstand-ing example of this was Great Britain. From just over £62 million for the war with Spain and France of 1739–48, her total military and naval expenditure rose to close on £105 million for that of 1756–63 and then to nearly £140 million during that of 1775–83.[3] Even on land and in western Europe the burdens were not necessarily much less than in the past. It has been estimated that in the Seven Years War perhaps one in every seven adult males in France made some sort of direct contribution to the national war effort (100,000 militiamen, 42,000 members of the *milices garde-côtes* and possibly 200,000 others who served briefly in some auxiliary capacity, as well as those in the regular army). In the Spanish Succession struggle the proportion had been about one in six; there had been some alleviation but not a very striking one.[4] This easing of the weight of war demands was unequally distributed geographically. The southern Netherlands, for gener-ations the great cockpit of western Europe, saw no serious fighting after 1713 except for a short period in 1745–8. Italy, another traditional area of great-power conflict, was untouched by war after 1748. But in Prussia, parts of which suffered as badly in the struggle of 1756–63 as in the Thirty Years War, the situation was very different. Even in England, whose position was so much more favoured, the raising after 1757 of a new and more effective militia, deeply and almost universally unpopular, rubbed in the fact that war was expensive in human terms and that its cost was not entirely financial.

The armies of 1740–89 were recruited essentially as their predecess-ors had been. In Russia and to a large extent in Prussia they were raised by conscription. In western Europe men were found by a mixture of voluntary enlistment and a variety of forms of forcible recruitment applied in time of need to the more expendable and less economically valuable members of society. Sometimes as in the past economic pressures meant that voluntary enlistment was hardly voluntary at all; but, again as in the past, there were positive as well as negative forces which attracted men to the colours. These might be strong enough to offset the discouraging effects of a military discipline which was tending almost everywhere to become more strict. Personal loyalties still played some role, though with declining effect as the years went by. The landsmen who entered the British navy, for example, were still often recruited on or near the estates of their officers; the flagship of at least one admiral in the mid-century was manned partly by men whom he had himself raised in this way. A captain changing ships still tried and expected, with the support of the Admiralty, to take as many as possible of his followers with him.[5] To the ordinary man the most frightening and repugnant aspect of service continued to be not poor living conditions (still often no worse than those he encountered in civilian life and sometimes better) or harsh discipline, but the trauma of being thrust into a strange environment in which he felt alone and unprotected. The long-standing belief that armies should be recruited as far as possible from men valueless for anything else or, even better, from foreigners, was now more widespread and explicit than ever before. 'It would undoubtedly be desirable,' wrote in the 1780s the Comte de Saint-Germain, the greatest French war minister since Louvois, 'if we could create an army of dependable and specially selected men of the best type. But in order to make up an army we must not destroy the nation; it would be destruction to a nation if it were deprived of its best elements. As things are, the army must inevitably consist of the scum of the people and of all those for whom society has no use.'[6] A few years earlier Frederick II had argued that 'useful hard-working people should be guarded as the apple of one's eye, and in wartime recruits should be levied in one's own country only when the bitterest necessity compels.'[7] The assumption that the role of the productive and the educated was to work, not to fight, to pay for wars but not to play any direct role in them, was now beginning to be challenged as never before (see pages 199–201 below). But it had perhaps never been stronger in ruling circles than in the decades just before the French Revolution.

This desire to protect the more economically valuable parts of society meant that, as in the past, the towns, because of the privileges and exemptions they enjoyed, often bore much less than their share of the burden of conscription where it existed. This was notably the case in Prussia; while in Spain in 1745 the city of Seville, one of the largest in the country, claimed that only 201 of its male inhabitants were liable for military service, since all the rest were in one way or another exempt. Where voluntary enlistment was concerned, on the other hand, the townsman, because he was more accustomed to change and movement and less wedded to an unchanging environment and a traditional routine, was often an easier target than the peasant. This was the case in the Austrian Netherlands, where the towns contributed, in proportion to their population, many more recruits than the countryside,[8] while in France the army was drawn increasingly from the cities, notably from Paris itself. The armies of the second half of the eighteenth century resembled those of its earlier decades in two other ways; in the high proportion of foreigners which many of them still contained and in the fact that all of them (and still more navies) were plagued to varying degrees by the problem of desertion. Both points have already been made at some length: neither needs elaboration here. On the first it may be enough to quote as illustrations the admittedly extreme cases of Prussia and the Swiss cantons. In the former, even at the death of Frederick II, less than half the army consisted of native-born Prussian subjects, while in 1789 there were still a dozen different armies which included Swiss regiments, and probably one Swiss in every twelve of military age was serving in a foreign army in time of peace. In wartime the proportion may have risen to one in eight. Moreover the hiring by one ruler to another in wartime of substantial auxiliary forces was now better established than in the first years of the century and easier to take for granted than ever before. More than ever, it was a practice particularly useful to Britain with her great financial resources and rather unmilitary population. She obtained substantial forces in Germany in this way during both the great mid-century struggles with France, was able to hire Russian auxiliaries in 1747–8, and confidently – though in the event mistakenly – expected to have them again in 1775 for use against the rebellion in America. Other powers could also benefit in this way, however. During the Seven Years War the Habsburg government hired regiments from several of the smaller German rulers – the Archbishop of Mainz, the Duke of Württemberg and the Bishop of Würzburg – who often found this a convenient way of meeting the cost of armies larger than their own territories could support.

Desertion remained, at least until late in the century, as much of a problem as in the past. Frederick II was as preoccupied by it as his father had been; under him Prussian infantry units, when marching through wooded country in which desertion would be relatively easy, were often surrounded by cavalry patrols, while men detached from camp to fetch wood or water were when practicable accompanied by an officer. When the Sound was frozen over in a severe winter both the Danish and Swedish armies took special precautions to prevent men escaping across it, though the pickets stationed for this purpose sometimes themselves deserted, taking their NCOs with them. Such precautions were by no means excessive; in the Seven Years War Frederick II is said to have lost about 80,000 men by desertion and his Habsburg opponents about 62,000. In the 1780s of the men raised in Ireland for the British army about a sixth deserted each year. Navies could suffer even more severely. In Britain the Navy Board estimated that in 1755–63 185,000 seamen and marines were employed in the war which more than any other created the British Empire. Of these possibly 110,000 were pressed men; and the inevitable result was a continual risk of large-scale desertion. In the three years 1755–7 only 147 men in all were killed in battle or died of wounds, yet in the same period well over 12,000 deserted from the navy.[9] A generation later, in the American war, little more than 1200 were killed in the years 1776–80, but over 42,000 deserted. It is true that these figures, because of the way in which the navy kept its records, somewhat exaggerate the number of true desertions;[10] but they are nonetheless impressive ones. In France the problem was much less acute, especially in the Atlantic squadrons where desertion had always been less marked than on the Mediterranean coast. (A naval war with Britain in the eighteenth century severely damaged France's transatlantic trade, reduced the demand for merchant seamen and therefore made service in the navy a rather more attractive alternative than it would otherwise have been for men in such ports as St Malo or

Bordeaux.) Nevertheless the *inscription maritime* was still as unpopular and as open to evasion as ever, as can be seen in, for example, the fierce resistance from 1748 onwards to efforts to bring the bargemen of the River Garonne within its ambit.

Almost as much as in the past, moreover, armies continued to be essential for the maintenance of public order, for the repression of large-scale crime, rioting or outright rebellion, for the preservation of the existing structure of society. Every state still lacked an adequate police force. Even in France, the best-equipped in this respect, the *maréchaussée*, the most effective of a number of different police forces (it was recruited mainly from old soldiers), numbered only about 3900 in the last decades of the century. In an immense and thinly populated country such as Russia policing in the modern sense was practically non-existent. The result was that soldiers still performed, as they had for generations, a very wide range of policing duties. Sometimes these bulked so large that they had considerable implications for military efficiency. It has been calculated that during the eighteenth century infantry regiments stationed in the British Isles may have spent an eighth of their time on police work, and cavalry ones (more useful for some sorts of policing because of their greater mobility) up to a fifth. The fact that much of the British army was usually widely dispersed in small detachments and acting as a police force seriously hampered its training and probably reduced its military effectiveness. Soldiers everywhere were used to fight organized large-scale crime, as when in the early 1750s French troops broke up the gang led by Louis Mandrin, the most famous criminal of the age (and himself a deserter from the army), which had for some years terrorized a large area of south-eastern France. They were used to repress the smuggling which was rampant over much of Europe: in 1778 a detachment of English militia even fought at Southwold something like a pitched battle with smugglers, when an armed ship tried to land contraband goods under cover of a bombardment of the shore. They were used to repress the riots in capital cities which were one of the most serious of all forms of challenge to existing authority since they attacked it at its centre – in Madrid in 1766, when there were dangerous demonstrations against an unpopular minister; in Moscow in 1771, when a serious outbreak of plague led to hysteria and widespread disorder; in London in 1780, when in the Gordon Riots of that year 12,000 soldiers and militia had to be used to control the situation and almost 300 people were killed in the process. They were used to repress the grain riots which were a normal accompaniment of bad harvests and high prices: in 1775, in the *guerre des farines*, a considerable military effort was needed to combat outbreaks of this kind in the area around Paris. On the largest scale, they were used to crush serious and sustained rebellion. In Brittany in 1675 perhaps 20,000 soldiers had been employed to repress a peasant rising, while in Russia in 1707–9 54,000 were needed to put down rebellions of the Don Cossacks and the Bashkir people of the Volga basin. The extreme case also came in Russia during the great outbreak led by the Cossack Emelyan Pugachev which in 1773–5 affected a huge area in the south-east of the country. This involved pitched battles with large regular forces before it was finally crushed. To the end of the period covered by this book the protection of the political and social status quo within states remained an essential function of armies, arguably the most essential of all. The great upheaval in France which has made 1789 one of the best-known dividing-lines in European history was made possible partly by an unprecedented reluctance of the army to act effectively in this traditional role.

In many ways, then, the armies and navies of Europe and the purposes for which they were used were not radically different in the age of Frederick II and Catherine II from what they had been in that of Louis XIV and Peter I. Nevertheless there were new factors in the situation, and some of them were important.

The Prussian model and the growth of militarism

The emergence of Brandenburg-Prussia as a great military power in the middle of the eighteenth century was the most striking event of its kind that Europe had ever seen. In the seventeenth century and even in the first decades of the eighteenth Prussia could still be written off as, in the words of one historian, 'a thinly populated, poverty-stricken sandbox'.[11] Its army was known to be large and well organized, and it had performed respectably in the Spanish Succession struggle; but it had won no spectacular victories and in the 1720s and 1730s it had

167

seen very little active service. The successes achieved against the Habsburgs in the early 1740s changed this situation at a blow. Before the end of the decade some of Frederick's contemporaries were already beginning to refer to him as 'the Great'. Prussia's victorious survival against apparently overwhelming odds in the Seven Years War was even more impressive. Europe was now faced almost for the first time in its history (the only earlier example is the Sweden of Gustavus Adolphus) by a state which had leapt suddenly to at least a kind of great-power status through military efficiency and nothing else. The France of Louis XIV had been the greatest military power of its day; but it had also been the wealthiest and most populous of all and the cultural leader of the continent. It had stood for far more than naked military strength, and in organization and discipline its army had not been notably superior to some of those which opposed it. Moreover its rise to military leadership had been a process which extended over generations and involved failures as well as successes. Russia under Peter I had deeply impressed Europe by her sudden and new-found military importance. But it was well understood that, however remote and barbaric, she was a gigantic country with enormous material potentialities. Unlike these, Prussia had built a spectacular structure of military strength on very slight material foundations. Her successes owed nothing to natural resources, population or wealth and everything to organization and leadership. Her new status, more than that of Russia, was a work of art, the handiwork of her rulers. Frederick II who, to his own age, appeared as a great commander as much as an 'enlightened despot', was in fact building on foundations laid by his father, as he himself admitted. But this was far from clear to contemporaries. Rather like Peter I but with far smaller material resources to draw on, he seemed to have raised the state he ruled, by his own vision and leadership, to an entirely new level of significance; and in his case much more than that of Peter this achievement rested upon purely military foundations.

Contemporaries lavished admiration not merely upon Frederick himself but almost as much upon the army he commanded. For the first time in its history Europe was presented with a model of military organization which commanded almost universal admiration and inspired widespread efforts to imitate it. In the later decades of the century the great army manoeuvres held each year in Prussia became a kind of graduate school for high-ranking officers from all over the continent, a showcase of the best contemporary military practice. Sometimes this imitation was mechanical, a copying of externals which, by its very slavishness, is the most telling proof of the impression which Prussia's achievements had made. Such was the adoption in the Habsburg army from the middle of the century of Prussian styles of uniform. Sometimes it went rather deeper, as in the widespread copying of the systems of drill and tactics which seemed an essential ingredient in Frederick's victories. Marshal Daun, one of the most able Habsburg commanders of the century, was given the task in its middle years of working out a new drill and tactical code which was based completely on the Prussian model. The first English translation of the Prussian regulations was published in 1754, and four decades later the drill-book which became standard in the British army after 1792 was modelled on the Prussian one; its author, General Dundas, had himself attended the manoeuvres of 1785 and 1788 and learned much by the experience. Thousands of miles away across the Atlantic a Prussian staff-officer, Friedrich von Steuben, became in 1778 inspector-general of the Continental Army under George Washington and did much to improve its training and discipline. Even in the last years of the century a well-informed commentator could still speak of 'this discipline which all the world has rushed to imitate'.[12] Occasionally imitation extended further, to such basics as recruitment, as with the introduction in Hesse-Kassel in 1762 and many of the Habsburg territories in 1781 of a cantonal system based on the Prussian one (it did not extend to the Austrian Netherlands, the Italian possessions or, until 1784, Hungary and the Tyrol).

This admiration for the Prussian army was not total or universal. It was well realized that its achievements rested in large part on a foundation of ferocious mechanical discipline – 'no end of cursing and whipping by sadists, jumped-up junkers, and the yelling of the flogged in return', as one unwilling recruit, himself inveigled into the army by fraud, described it.[13] This many observers in western Europe found repugnant. James Boswell, visiting Berlin in 1764, was unpleasantly impressed when he went 'to the Park, where I saw a Prussian regiment exercised. The soldiers seemed in terror. For the least fault they were beat like dogs.' But he went on to admit, in terms which most contemporaries would have accepted, that he was 'doubtful if such fellows don't make the best soldiers. Machines are surer instruments than men.'[14] Six years earlier a British general had been if not condescending at least ambiguous. 'The service is certainly done with exactness,' he wrote in 1758, 'but with less life and gaiety than anywhere I have yet seen. A pensive attention to their duty is the prevailing turn, and I never saw an army where the officers were so little communicative, or where it was so difficult to get any information.'[15] A closer student, at the end of Frederick's reign, pointed to the badness of army medical services in Prussia and the poorness of its military engineers, and even criticized the king himself for his lack of skill in siege warfare as opposed to field operations.[16] But the contemporary verdict on both Frederick and his army was a strongly favourable one, often quite excessively so.

This admiration of Prussia was an important aspect of the growth of militarism in eighteenth-century Europe. This was a new development, one of the most significant of the period. Over most of the continent there can now be seen a growing tendency to regard armies not merely as essential tools for the defence and possible expansion of the state, and for the equally necessary maintenance of internal order, but as something to be valued in and for themselves. They could even be seen as setting standards and exhibiting virtues to which all society should aspire. The clearest and most extreme examples of armies as institutions whose demands shaped society, and which themselves more or less openly controlled it, were of course to be seen in Russia and Prussia. But even in much of western Europe a revaluation of them and a willingness to import military standards and behaviour into society in general can be seen. At the highest social level this showed itself in a tendency for many monarchs now to regard military uniform as their normal dress. Even in the first years of the century this had been true of Charles XII, of Frederick William I and to a rather less extent of Peter I. As it went on, Frederick II, Joseph II in the Habsburg dominions and Peter III in Russia showed very clearly the same preference, and this attachment to uniform and the externals of military life culminated in its last years in the 'paradeomania' of the Tsar Paul. Seventeenth-century rulers had given little sign of this. Louis XIV, whose reign was so shaped by warfare, was not a soldier by taste, outlook or training. He never himself wore uniform and would have regarded it as a breach of etiquette for a French nobleman to present himself at court in it. He was deeply interested in his army, even down to the quality of the bricks used in fortress-building, as his letters to Louvois show, but interested as a supreme bureaucrat, not as a soldier. Nor did this change in attitudes affect every eighteenth-century monarch. Louis XV and Louis XVI were also civilian kings, if anything more so than Louis XIV. Even in the 1780s the only men who normally wore uniform at the French court were officers of the guards and colonels coming to take leave of the king before joining their regiments. The Spanish Bourbons were no more military in their tastes: a traveller in 1797 was struck by the fact that in a fairly long stay in Madrid he had never seen any member of the royal family appear in public wearing uniform.[17] In the Habsburg empire it was only after 1780, under Joseph II, that military uniform became a permissible form of dress at court; earlier in the century Prince Eugene himself had to appear there as a civilian. Nonetheless, over much of the continent it was now more normal than ever before for the ruler to be seen and wish to be seen as a soldier, and to take a detailed and professional interest in his army. Even in England, where the environment was less favourable to the growth of militarism than in any other major state, this is visible in the attention paid by George I and George II to army organization.

Growing militarism also sometimes meant a tendency to remove armies from civilian control and make them more autonomous. In Britain the Secretary at War was, as in the past, always a politician and not a soldier. In the Dutch Republic, almost as unmilitary as Britain, ultimate control remained firmly in civilian hands. In the Habsburg territories the *Kriegskommissariat*, even after its reshaping by the great reforming minister Count Haugwitz in the 1740s, was a largely civilian body. In France, however, there was a significant change. Le Tellier, Louvois and their successors had been civilians, administrators without military rank or experience. Though the Marquis de Chamlay, the most important military adviser of Louvois and of Louis XIV in his later years, held high army rank, he had little experience of active service and was often employed on non-military tasks. In 1758, however, the post of Secretary of State for War was for the first time given to a soldier (the Marshal de Belleisle, who had a distinguished record of command in the field), and many of his successors were also military men. The pressure for army reform in

France during the later decades of the century (see pages 197–201 below) came entirely from soldiers, a situation quite unlike that a century earlier; and the *Conseil de la Guerre*, established in 1788 as part of this striving for efficiency, was made up entirely of generals. Moreover in the second half of the century there was a slow but steady tendency for an increasing proportion of the *intendants d'armées* and *contrôleurs des guerres* to be army officers, something Louvois would have bitterly opposed. The greatest army in western Europe was now much more of an autonomous and self-regulating entity than ever before.

Not merely at the highest administrative levels but also at much more humble ones the distinction between soldiers and civilians was now becoming sharper. More and more it was a distinction between different outlooks and psychologies as well as between different modes of life. It was given material and visible form by the barracks in which, increasingly, soldiers lived. Their building was slow to develop on a large scale; it proceeded in many states only by fits and starts, and even in the last years of the century and in western Europe it was not complete. To the end of this period many soldiers were quartered on the civilian population in the way traditional for generations. In France there had been some barrack-building as early as 1692 for élite units – the *Maison du Roi*, the *Gardes Françaises* and the Swiss regiments; and in 1719 an ordinance envisaged housing soldiers in this way over most of the country. Such an ambitious plan, however, was abandoned within a few years as too costly. Though there was a certain amount of building over the following decades it was not until fairly late in the century that most French soldiers began to live in barracks; it was calculated that by 1775 200,000 were doing so. Elsewhere a similar process can be seen. In the Habsburg territories, for example, one of the main motives behind the military reforms embarked on after 1748 was to make the army more professional and efficient by separating it more completely from the civilian population; this meant that in the second half of the century an increasing proportion of soldiers were housed in barracks.

Costs alone, however, meant that everywhere in Europe a separation of this kind was achieved only rather slowly. Purpose-built barracks were expensive, too expensive for poor countries to provide easily on a large scale. In Russia, although Peter I had hoped at the end of his reign to house much of the army in this way, the idea was abandoned immediately he died. To the end of the century there were barracks only in Moscow, St Petersburg and one or two provincial towns. Outside these the soldiers still shared the huts of peasants in the countryside. Even in Prussia it was only in the later years of Frederick II that barracks began to be provided in all the major towns. Frequently, disused buildings, often old ones intended for some other purpose, and even former monasteries in some cases, were pressed into service; and very often barracks, whether newly built or taken over from some other use, were gloomy and unhealthy places, damp, badly ventilated and insanitary. Those in the Habsburg provinces at the end of the century, for example, consisted mainly of huge rooms in which up to 160 men had to sleep and cook their meals, evil-smelling chambers in which the windows were never opened.

But barracks separated the soldier from the civilian more effectively than ever before. This, and in particular the tighter discipline and more effective control by officers and NCOs which went with it, were the main objectives of building them, in spite of their cost. The French ordinance of 1719 specified that the new barracks should be completely enclosed by a wall ten feet high which should be at least thirty feet from the building on all sides. This was to enforce on the soldiers 'order and discipline, so that an officer will be in a position to answer for them'.[18] Some decades later an English observer made the same point, writing approvingly of barracks that 'those garrisons which have them are much more quiet, on account of the convenience which noncommissioned officers have to visit the quarters every evening, and to see that the soldiers are shut up in their quarters, which cannot be done when they are lodged among the inhabitants, where they have the liberty of going out and in whenever they please'.[19] In Russia and Prussia the army now controlled and directed society; but in western Europe armies were becoming more than ever before separate and distinct societies enclosed within larger civilian ones. Another index of this separation is the slowly declining numbers in the later seventeenth and eighteenth centuries of the women, children and miscellaneous hangers-on who had encumbered so many armies during the Thirty Years War and later, making their camps resemble gipsy encampments and slowing their movements. In the Habsburg army it was decided in 1756 that in future the wives and children of recruits must be left at home, and in 1775 this was reinforced by an order forbidding wives to follow their husbands in the field. But long before this the trains of civilian dependants who had in a rough-and-ready way acted as a link between the soldier in the field and the civilian world had been markedly reduced, though far from eliminated, in all major armies.

This increasingly sharp distinction between professional soldier and civilian tended to mean a decline in the significance of militias as the eighteenth century went on. As military technology very slowly advanced, as armies became more disciplined and professional in their outlook, it became more difficult for any militia force to retain what military value it might have had in the past. This decline was not universal. In England a substantial and reasonably effective militia came into existence when it was re-established in 1757 after decades of insignificance. This force was a replica of rural society almost to the same extent as the Prussian army, for the Militia Act specified property qualifications for its officers – a colonel must possess an income from real estate of at least £400 a year, a lieutenant-colonel or major one of £300, a captain one of £200, and so on – and the rank-and-file was made up mainly of those too poor to pay for substitutes. It was more efficient than its predecessors; but it played no direct role either in the war of 1756–63 or in that of 1778–83. In Russia the land-militia in the Ukraine which Peter I had created as a defence against the Turks was of more military significance. Its numbers increased during the 1730s, and it was mobilized en masse during the Russo-Turkish war of 1736–9; but in 1769 it was formally abolished (though in fact its regiments simply became regular infantry and dragoon ones). Elsewhere, however, the importance and effectiveness of formations of this kind tended to decline. In France militiamen were still drafted into the regular army in time of war during the 1740s and 1750s, though on a much smaller scale than during the critical years of the Spanish Succession struggle. But the weakness of the French militia when faced with any sort of serious challenge is perhaps seen in the way in which Mandrin and his gang were able to seize quite large towns such as Autun without the local militia units offering any real resistance. In Spain the militia was even less militarily effective, and everywhere militia service continued to be unpopular and avoided whenever possible. In many countries militias still performed minor but useful police functions. They escorted groups of army recruits or prisoners of war. They helped to keep order at the executions which were one of the most popular and sometimes disorderly of all public spectacles. In some towns, in France at least, they still patrolled at night to guard against thieves and fires. But as a link between the soldier and the civilian, insofar as they had ever been one, they were in general becoming less effective.

There were a number of ways in which regular soldiers could be infused with a new psychology and given a stronger sense of belonging to a distinctive institution in which they could take pride. One was by the award of decorations for acts of courage, for good conduct or merely for completing a long period of service. Most of these were reserved for officers, and gallantry on the battle-field by a common soldier was usually still rewarded, if at all, as it had been for centuries, by a gift of money from his commander. However among officers the creation of these new awards – the Order of St Louis in France in 1693, the Order of the Sword in Sweden in 1748, the Order of Maria Theresa in the Habsburg empire in 1757, the Order of St George in Russia in 1769, the *Pour le Mérite* in Prussia (though until 1810 this was also awarded to civilians) had some real importance; and the Order of St Louis at least was open to NCOs and privates who performed deeds of outstanding gallantry. Moreover in France an ordinance of 1771 created a long-service medal for veterans, awarded after twenty-four years in the army, which was the first of its kind. An old soldier wearing it (a handful of hardy souls served for forty-eight years and obtained two) felt himself marked out from the population at large by bearing a tangible symbol of achievement which entitled him to respect. This sense of distinctiveness was no doubt enhanced by the fact that in France from the 1760s onwards veterans became entitled as of right to a pension after very long service and were also periodically given a new uniform to wear in retirement. The same growth of a corporate consciousness can be seen in a psychologically very significant form in the evolution in most armies of an elaborate code of ceremonies governing military funerals. That finally systematized in France in 1761 prescribed the number of volleys to be fired by a guard of honour at the graveside for different ranks and also the number (varying with the rank of the dead man) of those who must attend the burial of a comrade. Even a simple private was entitled to a guard of ten men under a corporal.[20] To an age still deeply attached to ceremony, and particularly to the ceremonial of death, the importance of this development was considerable.

The striving for increased efficiency which was one aspect of the new military spirit showing itself by the mid-eighteenth century was far from completely victorious. Everywhere tradition and vested interests placed obstacles in its way. Even in the Prussian army every field regiment continued to have a colonel-proprietor, as in the past, by whose name it was normally referred to. In the Habsburg army it was only in 1769 that regiments began to be designated by numbers. Old habits died hard. In the French army, one of the most easy-going, it was claimed in the early 1780s that only a third of the infantry officers and a quarter of the cavalry ones stayed with their men in winter quarters, while the richer officers bought up the leave entitlements of the poorer ones and disappeared to Paris or their estates for long periods each year. Yet in at least one important respect the new attitudes did begin to take effect. This was in the creation in several armies of embryonic general staffs. All of these were small and some of them had only short or intermittent lives. Nevertheless they were anticipations of the much greater developments of the following century. By the 1750s a number of European states were beginning to feel the need for some central organization which would supervise the administration and movement of large bodies of soldiers, make ready in peace plans for possible future campaigns, and in particular prepare the more detailed and accurate maps which were now increasingly seen to be needed for successful operations. As communications slowly improved and armies became more mobile, as written orders slowly supplemented and replaced verbal ones, the advantages to be gained from better staff-work gradually became more apparent. Some movement towards this can be seen in the Habsburg army after the War of the Austrian Succession, in efforts to provide every general in command of an army with a *General-Adjutant*, in effect his chief of staff, and also a *Generalquartiermeister* to regulate the movements of the army and the building of camps and field fortifications. A few years later, in 1763, an embryonic general staff appeared in Russia, intended in wartime to control, under the commander-in-chief, the movement of the army in the field, and in peacetime to carry out cartographic work and train officers for service as quartermasters. In

France some provision began to be made in 1765 for the training of staff-officers, and though it ceased in 1771 it was re-established in 1783. The elaborate planning undertaken in Paris in the later 1760s for a possible invasion of England is perhaps the first example of this aspect of staff-work, a foreshadowing of the far better known achievements of Moltke a century later. Even the Piedmontese army acquired a small general staff in 1793, though there were still significant powers which lacked anything of the kind: little effort was made to create such a body in Britain, and Spain had no approach to one until the outbreak of war with Portugal in 1801. The most important material result of these developments, and of the effort to make war more planned, controlled and scientific which underlay them, was the production of a number of great large-scale military maps more complete and reliable than anything seen before – that of France begun by Cassini de Thury in 1750, that of the Habsburg territories, in 5400 sheets, made under Joseph II, and that of Prussia completed in 1796 (though Frederick II always discouraged activity of this kind as likely to be more useful to an enemy than to his own army). The growth of general staffs, therefore, was not without constructive aspects. Its central importance, however, was as part of the process which was making armies more conscious of themselves as autonomous professional entities.

Nothing did more to create a modern professional military class than systematic training for officers; and this grew considerably during these decades. In this respect there was a marked difference between armies and navies. A naval officer needed technical knowledge in a way that most army officers did not; and even before the end of the seventeenth century some states had begun to provide organized professional training for at least a proportion of those who were to serve at sea. Denmark established such a school in 1663 and gave it its final form in 1701. France set one up in 1669; and by 1718 the naval academy established in St Petersburg by Peter I, the most important of a number of such institutions in Russia, had 500 pupils. Its successor, the *Morskoi Shlakhetskii Kadetskii Korpus* (Noble Naval Cadet Corps), came into existence in 1752. Although in England and the Dutch Republic there continued to be deep suspicion of formal training of this kind and a marked preference for practical experience, a naval academy was set up in Portsmouth in

1729. Though it attracted few students (by 1773 there were only fifteen) this was the first English school of any kind financed entirely by the state and with state-appointed teachers. In Spain a professionalization of the officers of the newly resurrected navy stemmed from the creation in 1717 at Cadiz of a training company of *Guardias Marinas*, which was later to be supplemented by others at Ferrol and Cartagena in 1776. The products of these, drawn from the middle and lesser nobility, largely replaced the old-style Spanish officer of the seventeenth century, who had very often come from a merchant ship (especially one trading to South America) or a privateer.[21]

So far as armies were concerned, the need for effectively trained officers was obviously greatest in the technical branches, the artillery and engineers. Here real progress was made. The academy set up at Woolwich in 1741, the engineering school established at Mézières in 1748 (the finest of its kind in Europe), the combined artillery and engineering school created in Russia in 1756, the artillery school set up in Segovia in 1764, were outstanding examples. From establishments of this kind, notably from that at Mézières, came a high proportion of the flow of expert and often technical writing on military problems which was another characteristic of the period. So far as the ordinary infantry or cavalry officer was concerned, however, the position was rather different. In an age when military technology changed only very slowly, he needed little or nothing in the way of specialized knowledge. Moreover there was often a feeling that book-learning might dilute the physical courage and qualities of leadership which were really essential to young officers, and that it was hard to reconcile with the noble status which most of them enjoyed. Every army to the end of this period therefore still included many officers who had learned their trade simply by practical experience, and many included an element of promoted long-service NCOs with little formal education of any kind. Considerable efforts to develop systematic training were made, however. As early as 1682 Louvois had set up nine cadet companies to produce officers for the French army, and two years later there were well over four thousand young men being trained in this way at an annual cost of almost a million livres. But from the start this French initiative left a good deal to be desired. There was no test of any kind for entry to the companies and even completely illiterate applicants were accepted. Duelling and disorderly behaviour were very common,[22] and in 1694 the companies were broken up and the cadets dispersed to different regiments to learn by experience as in the past. Few eighteenth-century efforts at officer-training were as ambitious as this. For young nobles from important families there were a number of select schools with high social prestige which would prepare them for a military career – the Noble Cadet Corps which was established in St Petersburg in 1731, the École Royale Militaire set up in Paris in 1751, the Austrian military academy at Wiener-Neustadt (1754), the Spanish one at Zamora (1790). In Germany the cadet schools established in Prussia in 1717 were paralleled by others in Saxony in 1725 and Bavaria in 1756. But these could cater only for a fortunate minority. They were supplemented in some countries, notably in France, by privately owned schools which offered some preparation for a military career; but these were expensive and often concentrated on riding and fencing rather than on any intellectual accomplishments.

For the poor noble, the petty *dvoryanin* in Russia, the *hobereau* in France, the *hidalgo* in Spain, the possibilities were less enticing. Peter I used his guards regiments as schools for training officers, and this continued all through the eighteenth century. In 1776, after a number of not very successful experiments, twelve military schools were set up in provincial cities to cater for the poor nobles who were the backbone of the French officer-corps. These were relatively effective: one of them, at Brienne, was soon to have the young Napoleon Bonaparte among its pupils. In Spain there were at different times a number of military schools which were meant to provide two-thirds of the officers needed (the remainder being made up of promoted NCOs); but these were often short-lived and rather unsuccessful. In Prussia more was achieved. The cadet schools set up by Frederick William I produced during the reign of his son 3000 officers of whom 41 rose to the rank of general; but even this was only a part of what was needed. No army in this period was able to solve the problem of giving all its officers a really effective training; and nowhere was any amount of formal training, intellectual ability or long and faithful service able to compete with high noble birth when it came to promotion. In every army, as in the seventeenth century, there were still a good many young noblemen whose status and family assured them of high military rank while they were still little more than boys. Everywhere there were plenty of poor, hard-working, long-serving officers with no hope of rapid promotion and hardly any of rising above the new ranks of major or lieutenant-colonel, however great their merits. Yet more systematic training than in the past, with all its limitations, was another of the factors helping to produce armies more professional, more a distinct and distinctive element in society, than ever before.

The effects of war: law, humanitarianism and their limitations

The social and economic impact of war in the half-century which followed the Prussian invasion of Silesia was not essentially different from what it had been in the age of Louis XIV and Peter I. Its negative and destructive effects for the continent as a whole were less. The complicated struggles of 1740–8 imposed in general less strain on the combatants than those of 1701–13; and though the Seven Years War inflicted great loss and damage, its worst direct effects were confined to a few areas of Germany – Silesia, Saxony, Brandenburg and Pomerania. After 1763 there was for a generation no sustained large-scale land warfare in western Europe. The Russo-Turkish struggle of 1768–74 was a long and exacting one; but it was fought in poor, remote and undeveloped areas whose very lack of highly developed economic life tended to limit its disruptive effects.

This does not mean that these wars could be taken lightly by those who lived through them. Large numbers of men still died on the battlefield. In the Seven Years War the Prussian army lost about 180,000 men in all. Devastation could still be great. Prussia lost about a ninth of her small population of 4.5 million during the same struggle; and in some provinces the proportion was considerably worse – about a fifth in Pomerania and even a quarter in the Neumark of Brandenburg. Frederick himself when the war ended had to admit that most of his subjects 'had nothing left except the miserable rags which covered their nakedness'. Large-scale conflict and the movements of armies could still spread disease, as in the past. The plague which in 1771 terrified Moscow and may have killed up to 60,000 people there, as well as 14,000 in Kiev and 10,000 in other towns of the Ukraine, was brought from the south Russian steppe by soldiers fighting the Turks. War still disrupted trade and increased the uncertainties which impeded its growth. Privateering never regained the importance it had enjoyed in the generation after 1690. In France it generally declined from the 1740s onwards, though Bayonne remained an active centre until the end of the Seven Years War and Dunkirk was still prominent in this way during the struggle for American independence. Nevertheless even in decline it could inflict great losses on seaborne trade. One contemporary estimate is that in the naval struggles of 1739–48 Britain lost 3238 merchant ships and her French and Spanish opponents 3434. On both sides a high proportion of these captures was the work of privateers (one Spanish privateer took 120 British ships before being itself taken), and in the last years of the Seven Years War French warships were handed over to private entrepreneurs for use in privateering very much as had been done from the 1690s onwards. In 1776–83 probably over 3000 British merchantmen were again lost, for the most part to French, Spanish and American privateers. However these losses have to be seen in the context of a volume of British seaborne trade which grew steadily throughout the century, apart from the years 1778–83. They were a serious nuisance; but they never inflicted unbearable losses on economic life. The financial demands of war, however, could still be crippling. Prussia survived them in 1756–63 only by a ruthless exploitation of the Saxon territory which she occupied for much of the war (this was forced to contribute 48 million thalers against only 45 million drawn from all the Prussian provinces combined) and by judicious use of the British subsidies she received in 1758–62. France by her expenditure on the struggle with Britain in 1778–83 reduced her finances to a plight from which they never recovered and which paved the way for the collapse of the old regime there from 1787 onwards. Even in Britain during the last years of the American war, years which saw the one sustained fall in her foreign trade during the century, the government could borrow only at well over 5 per cent interest, historically a very high rate. Yet in western Europe at least the attitude to war had changed by the 1760s and become more confident and optimistic than ever before. Observers above the battle in London or Paris could now see it as a nuisance, an irrationality, expensive and destructive no doubt but hardly the devastating and almost uncontrollable scourge which it had hitherto so often seemed.

Moreover as in the past, losses continued to be offset, however incompletely, by the opportunities and stimuli which war provided. There was a tendency during these decades for artillery to become a more prominent element in the makeup of armies than ever before and for the proportion of guns to men to increase, so that in 1759 Frederick II, who disapproved of this as restricting rapid movement, complained that 'If this war goes on a few years more I believe that we shall eventually have detachments of 2000 men marching with 6000 cannon.'[23] This growing importance of the gun, as in previous decades, did something to stimulate the demand for iron. Similarly the copper-sheathing of warships as a protection against the growth of weeds on their hulls and the ravages of the teredo worm, which was general in the British navy by the 1770s and then spread fairly rapidly to other fleets, clearly raised the demand for copper. A 74-gun ship of the line, it was calculated, needed 1455 large copper plates to protect it, and by the 1780s there were about 470 ships of the line in all the European navies combined. The result was a significant boost to copper production in Wales, in Sweden and even in Spain, where in 1784 the Cadiz dockyard began to use metal from the Rio Tinto mines.[24] There were some technological benefits. Cannon bored out to give the inside of the barrel a smoother and more regular surface were more accurate than those merely cast around a clay core, while better-quality iron meant that fewer of them proved defective when put to the proof. Stimuli of this kind were not, however, evenly spread over the continent. The more developed states of the west, technological leaders with relatively sophisticated industries, and most of all Britain, benefited from them more than central or eastern Europe. Thus in England Henry Cort began his experiments on wrought iron, which culminated in the 'puddling' process of 1784, largely to achieve a higher quality of metal for the production of guns and anchors for the navy; later the Admiralty would accept only iron produced by his methods. The development in 1774 by the industrialist and inventor John Wilkinson of the cannon-lathe, the result of a decade of work in the production of artillery, made it possible to bore reasonably accurate cylinders and thus did more than anything else to make Watt's steam-engine a practical proposition.[25] However qualitative benefits of this kind were small. The technology of weapons production was advancing only slowly, probably more slowly than industrial technology in general, so that the contribution it could make to the growth of industry was necessarily limited.

War needs were of greater importance in quantitative than in qualitative terms. The British iron industry benefited from the impetus they gave to increasing the production of metals, and therefore making them cheaper through such things as the use of coal and coke in smelting in place of increasingly scarce and expensive charcoal, while this in turn may have given some impetus to coal-mining.[26] The growth of iron production in south Wales, for example, owed much to the demand for munitions during the American war, which stimulated an influx of capital into the industry from such trading centres as Bristol and London.[27] It would be very hard to argue that war did anything significant to accelerate the coming of the Industrial Revolution in Britain. One leading authority at least has asserted the contrary.[28] But its overall effect on British industry in these decades seems to have been a mildly stimulating one; and to a lesser extent this may well have been true of Europe in general. Even in medicine there was arguably some desirable spin-off. There was a strong incentive, purely on grounds of increased fighting efficiency, to find some cure for the scurvy which had for generations weakened and decimated the crews of ships which were long at sea; and in fact systematic testing of various possible antidotes went on, with considerable success, in the British navy during the War of American Independence. It is noteworthy that there was never any corresponding effort to counteract the disease in the merchant fleet, where it certainly existed in the more distant trades, or in the civilian population where it had been widespread during the seventeenth century. This, then, appears to be a clear case of the desire to wage war more effectively stimulating an important advance in preventive medicine.[29]

More important than these rather peripheral benefits for Britain, however, was the fact that the wars of 1739–63 made her the most successful and dynamic imperial power in the world and allowed her markedly to expand her foreign trade. This meant that except in quite unusual circumstances (notably in September 1745 to February 1746, because of the Jacobite rebellion) she was able in wartime to borrow each year very large sums (rising to a peak of £12 million in 1761) without great difficulty and on relatively easy terms. The American war years of the later 1770s and early 1780s were more difficult; but even then the British government was able to borrow more easily than its French rival, now rapidly approaching bankruptcy. This financial strength was crucial to Britain's military and naval success. In the 1730s the philosopher George Berkeley described it as 'the chief advantage England has over France', and three decades later a leading continental expert on commercial questions spoke of it as 'the permanent miracle of her policy, which has inspired both astonishment and fear in the states of Europe'.[30] In an age when armed forces had ceased to be feudal and had not become national in any complete sense, but were becoming increasingly professional, wars were won by those best able to pay for them. This is well illustrated by the incessant harping by Frederick II in his voluminous writings, particularly in his *Political Testaments* of 1752 and 1768, on the urgent need for every Prussian ruler to accumulate the largest possible reserve of hard cash for use in wartime, so that in a war of attrition Prussia could hold out longer than her enemies.[31] Britain defeated France in the eighteenth-century struggle for empire largely because of her ability to spend money more lavishly and over a longer period than her opponent. This she owed partly to her much superior system of public finance. It was also, however, the result of the trading opportunities opened by her growing colonial empire; the expectations which had been aroused earlier in the century (see page 149 above) were now being realized. Above all, her West Indian islands and their valuable tropical products, of which sugar was much the most important, were a cornerstone of her commercial and financial system without which, many contemporaries believed, it was likely to collapse. In September 1779, with French and Spanish squadrons temporarily in control of the Channel, George III himself argued that 'our Islands must be defended even at the risk of an invasion of this Island. If we lose our Sugar Islands it will be impossible to raise money to continue the war.'[32] By waging war successfully and on a large scale against her European rivals, Britain expanded her empire and her trade and thus gained some of the resources needed to wage war equally successfully on an even larger scale in the future. For her success bred success.

In the decades before the French Revolution the naturalness and inevitability of war were still taken almost as much for granted as they

184

had been in the first decades of the seventeenth century. The churches and the theologians continued to proclaim that peace was inherently a higher state of human affairs than war, and one more pleasing to God, and to distinguish between just and unjust wars; but this had no more influence on the decisions of statesmen than in the past. Nevertheless in educated and opinion-forming circles in western Europe, as the century progressed, a growing hostility to war, a desire to limit and weaken its role and even to eliminate it altogether, can be seen. The Enlightenment, that great movement of generally liberating ideas which was at the height of its influence from the 1740s to the 1770s, was by implication, and often explicitly, hostile to international conflict on two counts. In the first place it was profoundly humanitarian. It sprang from a deeply held belief that a vast amount of human suffering was self-inflicted, the result of ignorance, of the selfishness of ruling groups and of the dead weight of obscurantist prejudice and tradition from which all societies suffered. This suffering, of which war was the most obvious aspect, was therefore easily avoidable if the peoples of Europe were provided with enlightened leadership and made aware of their own potentialities. They must refuse to be sacrificed in trivial state and dynastic quarrels. They must learn to distrust spurious ideals of self-sacrifice and heroism. 'The combined vices of all ages and all places,' wrote Voltaire in the article on 'War' in his *Dictionnaire Philosophique* (1764), the book which of all his enormous output best summarizes his essential ideas, 'will never equal the evils produced by a single campaign. . . . Philosophers, moralists, burn all your books. So long as the caprices of a few men make us loyally cut the throats of thousands of our brothers, that part of human life devoted to heroism will be the most frightful thing in the whole of nature.' Secondly, as well as being humanitarian the Enlightenment was markedly cosmopolitan. It was the product of a tiny minority of intellectuals who thought of themselves, on the whole rightly, as above selfish national prejudices; for the most part they believed deeply in the essential similarity, in needs and capacities, of all men and certainly of all civilized Europeans. It was easy for them to think of Europe as a genuine unity, bound together politically by diplomatic ties and the workings of the balance of power, intellectually by the ideas of the Enlightenment, morally by a simple 'natural religion' of goodwill and benevolence which ought to transcend all confessional and doctrinal differences, and culturally by the predominance of the French language. Such a Europe must therefore be one in which differences and rivalries would become progressively less important. 'Europe', wrote the most influential international lawyer of the age, Emmerich de Vattel, 'is a political system, a body in which all are bound together by the interrelations and the various interests of the nations inhabiting this part of the world. . . . The continual attention of rulers to all that goes on, permanently resident diplomats, continual negotiations, make modern Europe a kind of republic the independent members of which, bound together by common interests, unite to maintain there order and liberty.'[33]

This intellectual and emotional rejection of war, now stronger, better argued and more self-conscious than ever before, found expression in a number of ways. One was in a proliferation of schemes for the creation of some sort of international organization which would bind together the states of Europe and make impossible war between them. Early schemes of this kind, such as those of the Quakers William Penn (1693) and John Bellers (1710), were usually religious in inspiration and owed nothing to the ideas of the Enlightenment. The most famous and frequently reproduced of all, that of the Abbé de Saint-Pierre first published in 1712, was largely a response to the sufferings of France in the War of the Spanish Succession. But all those of the later eighteenth century – the adaptation of Saint-Pierre's project by Rousseau in the early 1760s, the schemes produced by the English radicals Richard Price in 1776 and Jeremy Bentham a decade later, and the *Zum Ewigen Frieden* of the great German philosopher Immanuel Kant in 1795 – were all to varying degrees products of the Enlightenment. Most of these projects aimed at achieving peace and security by the creation of some effective international authority which could override the aggressive ambitions of any individual ruler and compel him, if necessary even by force, to respect the rights of his neighbours. In other words there was to be created between states a binding 'social contract' analogous to that between individuals from which civil society was usually thought to have originated. From the 1770s onwards this approach began to be supplemented or replaced by another, more clearly derived from the mainstream of Enlightenment thinking and particularly from the Physiocrats, the school of economic theorists who were very influential in France, and later in the intellectual world of Europe generally, from the later 1750s onwards. This was the belief that an essential harmony and cooperation between peoples, expressing itself in trade and cultural contacts, was natural and would come about if only artificial barriers and destructive traditions of rivalry could be broken down. From this it was easy to go on to argue that peoples were naturally peace-loving and that it was only the selfishness and shortsightedness, if not the positive wickedness, of kings, statesmen, commanders and diplomats, which kept them apart. In other words a state's international behaviour was determined by the sort of society and government it had: the more effectively power within it could be removed from traditional élites and given back to the people, the more peace-loving it was likely to be. Though these were ideas still only taking shape in the last years of this period, and doing so more insistently in the new American republic than anywhere in Europe,[34] they had an important future before them.

But the practical effect of all this was negligible. No statesman paid much serious attention to these peace-plans. Most probably knew very little about them. Twentieth-century historians, forced to contemplate two world wars and two grandiose attempts at international organization, have sometimes given them a significance which they hardly deserve. Yet they meant that the problem of war was now being discussed more extensively than ever before; and for the first time in completely secular and practical terms. Discussion hitherto had been the work of theologians and lawyers. It had been largely concerned with distinguishing between just and unjust wars and deciding what methods were or were not legitimate in waging war. Now for the first time there had appeared a substantial body of political and social comment which sought practical means of ending war and was not content merely to tame it somewhat.

That war was being slowly tamed, however, gradually limited and made less deadly, many writers of these decades had no doubt. To some it seemed that it was becoming outdated through its mere irrationality and inability to achieve very much. The most celebrated of the German cameralist writers of the century, for example, claimed that the real strength of a state depended on the quality of its government rather than mere accumulation of territory, and that any war, however successful, was an economic disaster.[35] A decade later one of the most intelligent of British economists, Sir James Steuart, asserted that 'nothing is so evident, from the consideration of the total revolution in the spirit of the people of Europe, as that war is inconsistent with the prosperity of a modern state.'[36] The disappearance of war as an instrument of state policy, he went on, might therefore not be far off. Europe, it was also argued, was now so developed, the major states so strong and so evenly balanced in their strength, that it was hardly possible for any of them to make great gains at the expense of the others. 'Conquests,' proclaimed the Scottish historian William Robertson, 'are never very extensive or rapid, but among nations, whose progress in improvement is very unequal.' Alexander the Great or Genghis Khan had been able to build up huge empires of conquest because they were fighting peoples at a very different level of civilization from their own. But now the states of Europe were all at the same stage of development, had all great and varied internal resources and were well protected by the workings of the balance of power. As a result, 'After the fiercest and most lengthened contest, all the rival nations are exhausted, none is conquered. At length a peace is concluded, which reinstates each in possession of almost the same power and the same territories.'[37] (A good summary of the results of the Seven Years War which had ended only a few years before Robertson's book was published.) It was easy to feel that war, if it could achieve so little, must be of declining importance.

Moreover there was a persistent and largely justified feeling that it was not merely losing much of its effect as an instrument of policy but also becoming milder and more controlled. The religious hatreds which had envenomed the conflicts of the Counter-Reformation had largely died away. True national hatreds had hardly yet appeared. Even dynastic rivalries had, by the middle of the century, become perceptibly less important than in the age of Louis XIV. War was, it could therefore be argued, less emotionally charged than it had been for generations past. Now, wrote one of the Scottish founders of sociology, Adam Ferguson, 'war is made with little national animosity, and battles are fought without any personal exasperation of those who are engaged; so that parties are, almost in the very heat of a contest, ready to listen to the dictates of humanity or reason.'[38] A leading figure in the first stages of the French Revolution put it even more forcibly. 'We find that wars are less bloody among us,' he wrote, 'than with nations which are savage and ignorant: our legions thunder upon one another politely; the heroes salute before they proceed to kill; the soldiers of the hostile armies pay mutual visits before the battle, as a party sits down to supper before the dice-box is called for. They are no longer nations that fight, nor even kings, but armies and men payed [sic] for fighting: it is a game, where they play for what is staked, and not for all they have in the world; in fine, wars which in old times were a madness, are at present only a folly.'[39]

There is a tragic irony in the fact that these words were written not much more than a year before the French *levée en masse* of August 1793 opened the era of the 'armed horde', of the nation in arms. Yet it was reasonable throughout most of the eighteenth century to feel that war was becoming milder, less destructive and less demanding. Armies were still commanded by aristocrats, and the officers of opposing forces could therefore easily feel themselves still united by a fellowship in which community of class and outlook made differences of nationality almost irrelevant. All over western and central Europe the officer-corps continued to be permeated by aristocratic values, those of personal status and personal honour, and in its upper ranks, at least, often highly cosmopolitan and little influenced by national prejudices. The continuing stress on appearances even at the expense of efficiency is clearly visible in the excessive and irrational emphasis which many armies still placed on obtaining, even at considerable extra cost, tall and handsome recruits. In France this emphasis was so heavy that men who had served satisfactorily for long periods were sometimes dismissed from the army when it was belatedly decided that they were not tall enough. In the German states, where the fad for tall soldiers was more pervasive than anywhere else, the *Handgeld* paid to recruits often varied with their height. As late as 1760 the Bavarian government laid down a scale of recruitment premiums based simply on height, while that of Prussia (where Frederick William I's passion for tall soldiers had been carried almost to the pitch of mania) continued to discriminate in this way until very near the end of the century. Such an attitude shows a genuine kind of militarism, a feeling that armies are valuable in and for themselves, not merely as tools for the achievement of political ends. But militarism of this kind is not at all the same thing as aggressiveness or ruthlessness in the waging of war. A feeling that armies were almost works of art, entities whose formal perfection must be safeguarded, was likely to limit rather than extend the scope of warfare.

The belief that war was becoming more regulated and restricted had, however, other foundations. There were now available a considerable number of general and theoretical discussions by lawyers of how it was permissible to wage it and the limits which must be set to it, of which in the eighteenth century *Le Droit des gens ou les principes de la loi naturelle* (London, 1758) of the Swiss Emmerich de Vattel was the most popular and influential. But, probably more important in practice, these were now supplemented by detailed printed instructions issued to many armies and intended to govern their behaviour in time of war. These regulated such things as requisitioning and the raising of contributions, courts-martial and relations between soldiers and civilians in general. In 1665 a German, Von Tratzberg, published in his *Corpus Juris Militaris* a collection of twelve such codes, and this was reissued several times with additions to keep it up to date. In 1680 the French government began the systematic publication of the instructions of this kind which it issued, so that by 1706 fifteen volumes of them had appeared; and in 1709 a Swedish officer published in Paris his *Code militaire, ou compilation des règlements et ordonnances de Louis XIV faites pour les gens de guerre*, which was meant to provide a handy portable guide to the subject. Detailed regulation such as this, however imperfectly observed in practice, was a far cry from the conditions of the Thirty Years War. Side by side with these codes, moreover, there was growing up a network of agreements between states and rulers which attempted to outlaw in war specific practices agreed to be illegitimate and uncivilized; these can be seen as an effort to apply in practice some of what the international lawyers were enunciating in theory. In 1696 Louis XIV suggested to his opponents that both sides in the war then raging should agree not to bombard any city unless they were actually besieging it (though this was in large part simply an effort to stop English naval bombardments of the French Channel ports, against which France had no defence, and achieved nothing). The 1690s, however, saw a series of proposals to prohibit the use of particularly destructive weapons such as bombs and red-hot cannonballs; and in 1692, in one of the earliest such agreements, Louis XIV, the Emperor Leopold I and a number of lesser German rulers undertook not to use poisoned projectiles or any made of materials other than lead.[40] Though the subject does not seem to have been explored by historians, there were almost certainly a good many similar agreements in the eighteenth century: the French and Habsburg governments, for example, signed conventions of this kind in 1735 and 1742.

More and more, then, soldiers were now hemmed in by clearly defined official criteria and requirements against which their actions could be judged. The effectiveness of formal restrictions of this kind can be easily overestimated. They were far from being universally observed and were perfectly compatible with some of the most bloody battlefield confrontations in European history – for example between Russians and Prussians at Zorndorf (1758) and Kunersdorf (1759). But in western Europe warfare was, in general, becoming milder and less destructive. This growing mildness was at bottom a matter of spirit, of atmosphere, of unspoken assumptions. Increasingly there was widespread agreement that it was not merely foolish and counterproductive but also morally wrong for war to be waged in a spirit of all-out struggle, that damage and loss should be inflicted on civilians only when this was clearly justified in terms of military necessity, that resistance to obviously superior forces was to be condemned as perverse rather than admired as heroic. Already in the seventeenth century the propensity of the Turks to resist to the last gasp rather than surrender to superior Christian strength seemed to many observers one of the things which marked the Ottoman Empire as a non-European state. The Turkish commander of the fortress of Neuhausel in Hungary, wrote one pamphleteer in the 1680s, deserved no mercy when it was taken, 'because he had stood it out beyond all Reason and the Rules of War. Which allow not Men to do all the Mischief they can, when there is no hope left, nor possibility of defence.'[41] It was most clearly in the defence of besieged fortresses that this unwillingness to push conflict to extremes could be seen. The accepted convention, that once a 'practicable breach' had been made in the walls the garrison could surrender with honour, and that it was not entitled to expect good treatment if it held out longer, did not necessarily preclude a stubborn defence. A long series of great sieges in the Netherlands showed this very clearly. Sometimes, however, the spirit of limited risk which underlay the convention meant that a siege might become mere show, almost a farce. When, for example, the Austrian garrison of the Castel Nuovo in Naples was attacked by the Spaniards in 1734 a Florentine observer noted that 'the besieged, no less considerate of the city than the besiegers, make signs with a handkerchief when they decide to fire and give warning in a loud voice so that the populace can withdraw, and when these are out of danger they proceed. Before destroying a small house, they allowed time for the furniture to be removed. As soon as a cannon is fired the lowest people run up to search for the ball, and the garrison waits before firing again.' During this siege there were precisely three casualties on each side.[42] Behaviour such as this was exceptional and was seen by contemporaries as being so; but it is clear that in western Europe at least the conduct of war was by the middle of the century more restrained and more governed by a spirit of moderation than ever before.

This is well illustrated by the way in which the treatment of prisoners had improved. In the seventeenth century it had usually been assumed that it was the duty of a captain to ransom members of his company who fell into the hands of the enemy. Since he had very often recruited them himself, and since they sometimes thought of themselves as serving him rather than any higher or more impersonal authority, it could be argued that if he failed to obtain their liberty his contract with them was nullified and they could be ransomed by any other captain who wished to have their services. The distinction between prisoners and deserters was still not always clear, and there was a likelihood that a prisoner left unransomed would soon take service with his captors; in 1673 Louis XIV ordered his captains to ransom men as quickly as possible to minimize this risk. By the eighteenth century, however, ransoming by captains in this way was being supplemented and largely replaced by the signature in wartime of agreements (cartels) for the exchange of prisoners, under which the side receiving more men than it gave up paid a cash ransom for the surplus. A Franco-Dutch agreement of this kind was made in 1673; and the French and English governments signed one in 1691 for the exchange of naval prisoners. In the first half of the following century formal cartels of this kind were still only coming into use; a French attempt in 1711 to negotiate with Britain a general agreement for the exchange of prisoners was a failure. However from the end of 1744 France and the Habsburg monarchy exchanged prisoners on a large scale, while the Seven Years War saw the signature of a number of exchange cartels. Prussia made such agreements with the Habsburgs and France in 1757 and with Russia and again with France in 1759, while in the latter year an Anglo-French convention for the exchange of prisoners taken on land came into force. Men captured at sea benefited from cartels between Britain and Spain in 1742, 1781 and 1782, and from another Anglo-French agreement in 1780.

Difficult questions sometimes arose in these negotiations. How was the ransom to compensate for an excess of prisoners on one side or the other to be calculated? How many ordinary soldiers or seamen should be considered the equivalent of an officer of a given rank for exchange purposes? Could a sick or wounded man be exchanged against a healthy one? Each side, inevitably, tried to use or misuse such an agreement for its own purposes. The English in the later 1690s, as their superiority to France at sea became more marked, tried to disregard the cartel of 1691; while the French made such an agreement in 1780 only because of the failure in the previous year of their hopes of invading England. Nevertheless when a cartel was in operation it often meant that prisoners were returned with remarkable speed. The Anglo-French agreement of 1759, which was not unusual in this respect, laid down that all existing prisoners on the two sides should be exchanged or ransomed within a month and any taken in the future within fifteen days at most. Moreover quite apart from these formal agreements there were a great many local and informal arrangements for the exchange of prisoners, in batches or even as individuals, while by the middle of the century it was not uncommon for men to be freed in return for nothing more than a promise not to serve in the future against their captors. The Habsburg army released considerable numbers of French soldiers on this basis in 1745–6, and the same thing happened on quite a large scale during the Seven Years War. Men who were not active combatants – surgeons, chaplains, almoners, secretaries, etc. – were often not treated as prisoners at all, while from the middle of the century one or two states began to pay small allowances to their servicemen while they were in enemy hands: the French did this for their naval prisoners during both the Seven Years War and the American war, and the Spanish government adopted the same policy in 1780. None of this meant that a prisoner could be sure of good treatment. A British soldier after the battle of Malplaquet in 1709 found two French captains 'almost naked and prodigiously wounded' after they had been stripped and robbed by men of Marlborough's army; but the same soldier, when as a prisoner two years earlier he had been beaten by his French captors, had had the satisfaction of seeing them immediately arrested by their own officers.[43]

Of course there was another side to the picture. Though military and naval technology developed only very slowly, new and more destructive weapons were sought and sometimes found. The British from 1778 onwards produced in large numbers the carronade or 'smasher', a large-bore naval gun with a low muzzle velocity which was murderous at short ranges, and a year or two later they adopted shrapnel for use against enemy troop-formations. Both British and French experimented unsuccessfully with explosive shells, while Frederick II's army might even have used a flame-thrower proposed to him but for the fact that it turned out to project its jet over too short a distance. There were still examples even in the most civilized parts of the continent of extreme brutality, especially when a fortified city was taken by storm. When the French captured Bergen-op-Zoom in the Netherlands in September 1747 the killing, raping and pillaging was so savage that one of the officers in the victorious army wrote of the scene that 'far from depicting it, I want to forget it for ever'.[44] As in the past, the chance of behaving in this way could act on an army rather as the hope of prize money did on the crews of men-of-war, spurring them on to extra efforts. The commander of the French army besieging Eger in Bohemia in the early 1740s found that 'the thing which keeps all the soldiers so cheerful and makes them work with superhuman energy is the promise I made to them that they could plunder the town, if they took it by storm.'[45] Sometimes the threat of destruction and massacre was used with effect to force the surrender of a fortress. In 1713 the French commander Marshal Villars, a tough professional, after he had captured the city of Freiburg refused to allow wounded men and non-combatants to be evacuated and threatened to destroy the town and slaughter the wounded if the citadel, which was still holding out, did not surrender at once. Half a century later across the Atlantic the Earl of Albemarle, the British commander at the capture of Havana from the Spaniards in 1762, threatened to massacre the garrison, apart from a few senior officers, if it were taken by storm; and the Duc de Crillon, the commander of the Franco-Spanish forces during the great siege of Gibraltar in 1779–82, used the same threat, though this time without success. Though civilians were generally treated with far more consideration than a century earlier there were still exceptions to this, sometimes important ones; the behaviour of the French army in Westphalia in 1759 made contemporaries draw comparisons with the devastation of the Palatinate seventy years before. In spite of the improvement in the position of prisoners there were still striking cases, at least in the earlier decades of the century, of their maltreatment. Some of the Swedish prisoners taken by the Danes during the Great Northern War were sold to Venice for use as galley-slaves, while in 1758, after the terrible battle of Zorndorf, the most fiercely contested of the century, Russian wounded left on the field were buried alive by local peasants with the help of Prussian soldiers.[46]

Finally there must be remembered the contrast, which has been stressed so often in earlier pages, between western and eastern Europe. In the west war could still mean much suffering and loss, and even serious atrocities; but these were usually the result of poor organization and breakdowns in discipline rather than of deliberate cruelty or violent hostility between the opposing armies. Further east the struggles of the Habsburgs and even more of Russia with the Ottoman Empire had a different character. These were still in some real sense wars of religion and clashes between different and mutually antagonistic civilizations. A feeling that the Muslim was outside the scope of the laws of war, deeply felt religious prejudices, a long tradition of violent mutual hostility, even a difficult physical environment, all combined to produce acts of cruelty which would have been difficult to perpetrate in western Europe. The great Turkish siege of Vienna in 1683 saw both a massacre of Christian prisoners by the Turks after their defeat and the burning alive by the garrison of three thousand sick and wounded left by the besieging army (though the ringleaders in this, who had acted without orders, were afterwards punished). The Habsburg capture of Buda three years later led to the slaughter of most of the inhabitants. On the Russian side the Turkish wars of 1711, 1736–9 and 1768–74 produced no such spectacular incidents, though the Tatars of the Crimea, a vassal-state of the Ottoman Empire, suffered severely in the second and third of them. However the struggle of 1787–92 saw the worst military massacres of the century at the storming of Ochakov in 1788, when ten thousand Turks were killed, and of Izmail two years later when as many as thirty thousand may have perished. The harshness of conflict in Hungary or the Balkans, moreover, rubbed off to some extent on other parts of the continent. It was noted in the 1690s that the Habsburg regiments most likely to behave brutally to their French opponents were those with recent experience of the Turkish wars, while the Russian ravaging of East Prussia in 1757, which aroused widespread condemnation in western Europe, was largely the work of Cossack and Kalmyk irregulars accustomed to a very different environment and institutions.

Towards the future: the nation in arms

In many ways, then, the armies of the eighteenth century, even in its last decades, were backward-looking and tradition-bound. Everywhere their rank-and-file was still drawn predominantly from the lowest strata of the social pyramid. Everywhere they were still officered by men who were, in some sense of that overworked word, nobles. Everywhere military technology advanced with painful slowness. Everywhere, moreover, strategy and military thinking generally were still based mainly on ideas of limited war, of caution and avoidance of the uncertainties of great pitched battles. The Marshal de Saxe, the most successful French general of the mid-century and in many ways a radical, believed that a commander might enjoy sustained success without ever fighting a battle, while the Saxon *Dienstreglament* of 1752 wrote that 'A battle is at once the most important and the most dangerous operation of war. A great general shows his mastery by attaining the object of his campaign by sagacious and sure manoeuvres, without incurring any risk.' To outwit and outmanoeuvre the enemy rather than destroy him by a decisive stroke, most of all to be able to take up winter quarters in his territory and lay it under contribution, depleting his resources while economizing one's own, were the great objectives of every commander. Even Frederick II, though he fought so many battles, never seriously hoped to destroy any of his adversaries by a single overwhelming blow, in Napoleonic style. (He claimed in his *Political Testament* of 1768 that he had aimed at something of the kind when he invaded Saxony in 1756, hoping to advance quickly to Vienna and dictate peace terms there, but it is doubtful whether the claim was justified: a campaign of this kind was beyond Prussia's strength.[47])

Yet by the middle of the century or soon after, at least in one of the greatest European states, demands for very far-reaching change were being voiced. There the vision of a new sort of army, more austere, more national, imbued with a passionate fighting spirit, was now being put forward. This ferment of new ideas was in France and largely confined to her. It is not difficult to see why this should have been so. For the French army the eighteenth century was in general a sad anti-climax after the victories of Condé, Turenne and Luxemburg in previous generations. By the early 1760s the humiliation at Rossbach and the depressing performance of the French forces in west Germany, under third-rate commanders such as the Duc de Richelieu, had produced a widespread feeling of outraged national and professional pride. This helped to strengthen and focus ideas which were already taking shape and to generate a new spirit, active and aggressive, intolerant of weaknesses and inefficiencies, a kind of military puritanism. No other power experienced in this way the crumbling of a great military tradition. In no other, therefore, was there the same reaction.

Nor was discontent merely a matter of poor performance on the battlefield. By the later eighteenth century the French officer-corps was grossly inflated. In 1775 (when there was an officer for every fifteen soldiers) it included 1200 generals, whereas Prussia, with a standing army almost as large, had only 80 and even the Habsburg empire, with a comparable force, managed with a fraction of the French figure. Though every European army was officered overwhelmingly by nobles, the French one was unique in the extent to which its higher ranks were stuffed with holders of high-sounding titles. In 1789 of the 109 commanders of infantry regiments 9 were princes, 5 dukes, 25 marquises, 40 counts, 12 viscounts, 7 barons and 9 chevaliers, leaving only 2 untitled, both of whom had noble status.[48]

Far too many officers, and far too many who had achieved high rank through birth rather than achievement, made for an army which was lax, self-indulgent and unprofessional, one in which officers did not take their duties seriously, went on campaign with excessive amounts of baggage and numbers of servants, and often neglected their men. Moreover there was a widespread feeling that wealthy bourgeois were now invading the officer-corps to a dangerous extent, using their money not only to buy government offices which conferred noble status on the holder but also to acquire companies and even regiments. They lacked, it was claimed, the military tradition of true nobles and helped to spread laxity and indiscipline in the army as a whole.

The years before the revolution saw distrust and dislike of civilian influences, of the allegedly corrupting effects of mere wealth unsupported by military tradition and spirit, rise to a climax. In 1780-4 a committee of lieutenant-generals under the Marshal de Contades met regularly to discuss army reform; and in 1781 the Secretary of State for War, the Comte de Ségur, made a determined effort to root out these unwelcome influences. This was done by a regulation which demanded that in future officers entering the French army must show that their families had been noble for at least four generations, or failing this that their fathers had performed substantial military service and had been awarded the Order of St Louis. This was not intended to make the officer-corps more aristocratic as an end in itself. It aimed rather to exclude those who sought to make wealth alone a stepping-stone to military rank, and who might therefore weaken the fibre of the army and dilute its fighting spirit. Such an attitude had clear moralistic overtones. It was an expression of the distrust of luxury and self-indulgence, the admiration of Spartan virtues, which had been one element in the Enlightenment and had been spread by a galaxy of writers from Rousseau downwards.[49] There was much in it, therefore, which appealed to the poor provincial nobles who still provided the great majority of French officers. These had always suffered from the preemption of the highest ranks by members of great and powerful families or nobles with court connections. Now they felt themselves threatened from another direction, by the invasion of the officer ranks by the power of money; and the fact that they were poor and often heavily dependent on their salaries as officers added edge to their feelings. In the decades before the revolution their resentment was more acute and vocal than ever before.

Ségur and those who thought like him were genuine reformers. But they aimed at reforms of a strictly limited kind. What they wished to create was a military caste, one with high standards and a high sense of duty, but still essentially an hereditary closed group. They had no aspiration towards equality of opportunity or a 'career open to talents' of the sort which the revolutionaries were soon to attempt, with considerable success, to introduce. Nor had they any idea of changing the essential nature of the army. They assumed that it would be recruited as in the past and did not envisage any fundamental change in the way it fought. Already, however, very far-reaching and radical proposals for change in these respects had begun to be made. For the first time the ideal of a nation in arms, with all its potential appeal and all its dangers, was being put forward. A true mass army produced by truly universal conscription was now being seriously proposed.

Already in the 1750s the Marshal de Saxe, in his *Rêveries sur l'art de la guerre* (published in 1757 but written considerably earlier) had demanded universal military service for a five-year period for all men between the ages of twenty and thirty, insisting that 'it is essential to make no distinctions, to be immovable on this point, and to enforce the law particularly on the nobles and rich'. This demand implied a total break with the past. It meant a complete rejection of the traditional view of military service as both a career for the nobly born, entitled as of right to command, and a burden to be imposed on the lowest strata of society and on elements otherwise of little value. Saxe indeed anticipated many of the attitudes which were being put forward more and more insistently in France by the 1770s and 1780s. He was an outstanding apostle of duty, effort, professionalism and plain living in military life, of that stress on the Spartan virtues which was to reach its full flowering only a generation after his book appeared. He too distrusted wealthy officers and thought the only ones worth having were 'the poor gentlemen who have nothing but their sword and their cape'. To him the good officer was fulfilling an almost sacred obligation. 'The man who devotes himself to war should regard it as a religious order into which he enters. He should have nothing, know no other home than his troops, and should hold himself honoured in his profession.' He disliked intensely in a soldier any sort of self-indulgence. Cavalry horses must be given violent exercise to keep them fit and prevent their putting on weight. Baggage should be regularly inspected and anything not immediately useful thrown away as an impediment to speed of movement. Men must be worked hard. 'It is absolutely necessary to accustom soldiers to labour. . . . Continual exercise makes good soldiers because it qualifies them for military duties; by being habituated to pain they insensibly learn to despise danger.'[50] All this was again a long way from many of the norms of old-regime warfare in western Europe – the officers who left their regiments for months on end to enjoy themselves in society or look after their estates, and who left the training of their men entirely to NCOs or at best to a few despised colleagues who had been promoted from the ranks; the exchange of elaborate courtesies between opposing commanders; the long baggage-trains, many servants, richly decorated tents and fine dinner-services of the wealthier officers.

Saxe's ideas were in his own lifetime, as he realized, merely dreams. But the generation which followed the appearance of his book saw at least in France growing demands for armies which were leaner, tougher, more professional and, most important of all, directly representative of the society of which they must be an integral part. In the early 1770s an anonymous French author repeated Saxe's call for a physically fit army capable of forced marches, and for a new sort of tactics which placed more emphasis on mass attack and was less preoccupied with siege warfare and the use of artillery.[51] In Germany the political writer Justus Moser, in the many volumes of his *Patriotische Phantasien* which he began to publish in 1775, envisaged some kind of German national militia. The Frenchman Servan de Gerbey in his *Le Soldat citoyen* (written in 1768–71 though published only in 1780 in Switzerland) proposed something similar for France, stressing in particular the educative effect of such service and the way in which it might help towards greater national unity: this was a new idea with a long and important future before it. It was no accident that the words *patriote* and *citoyen* occurred in the titles of these books. Already the feeling that national unity was an ultimate value and the belief that all Frenchmen were, or ought to be, bound together in some common citizenship, ideas to which the Revolution was to give an immense impetus, were rapidly gaining ground. France was becoming a *nation* or a *patrie* and ceasing to be a mere *royaume*.[52] This great emotional transformation was reflected in these proposals for radical military change.

More important than any of these books, however, was the *Essai général de tactique* published in 1772 by the Comte de Guibert. This, almost alone of such writings, faced squarely the fact that a radically new army meant a new society. Guibert demanded complete unity both within society and between society and government. Internal reform of this kind was essential. It alone could give a country real strength. Compared to it the normal preoccupations of foreign policy and diplomacy were trivial. 'How easy it is', he wrote, 'to have invincible armies in a state where the subjects are citizens, where they cherish the government, where they love glory, where they do not fear labour.'[53] This ideal society, strong in its unbreakable unity, would be able, when attacked, to wage war to the death. 'Terrible in its anger, it will carry fire and sword to its enemy'; and once embarked upon a struggle it would never give up until it had obtained full reparation for the injury done it. In all this the anticipations of the Jacobin attitudes of 1793–4 are very clear. In more specifically military terms, Guibert demanded that armies become smaller, more mobile, more aggressive, less encumbered by artillery and supply-wagons, less preoccupied by the attack and defence of fortresses and strong positions. Soldiers must be able to carry heavy burdens, make forced marches, dig trenches and swim rivers. This book is the most forcible of all statements of the impatience, even the contempt, with which many French theorists now regarded old-regime warfare. More clearly than any other work of the period it looks forward to the cataclysm which shook France and Europe from the end of the 1780s onwards. The first stages of the Revolution, indeed, saw the putting forward of a great many proposals for army reform along the lines which the radicals of the 1770s and the 1780s had advocated – universal military service and the opening of officer rank to all men of ability, justified by the need to have soldiers who were also citizens and the immense defensive strength which this would give.[54]

In the last decades of the old regime this sort of radicalism was ineffective even in France and very rare outside it. There were some signs that a new attitude was beginning to filter downwards to the rank-and-file of the French army. Desertion became less of a problem. Just before the Revolution, in the year from July 1786 to July 1787, only a little over 2300 men deserted, and of these almost 500 returned to their units of their own accord.[55] Moreover in the last decades of the century ideas of the heroic death appropriate to a soldier who lost his life on the battlefield underwent a significant change in France: whereas hitherto it had been seen as a mark of the personal glory and achievement of the individual, it now became an exemplary sacrifice, the fulfilment of a supreme duty to the motherland.[56] There were also signs that popular mass nationalism of an active, self-conscious, modern kind was beginning to show itself. When in 1763 a public subscription was opened to pay for the rebuilding of the French fleet after its disastrous losses in the Seven Years War it produced a remarkable response: the 13 million livres it raised paid for fifteen new ships of the line. But the nation in arms remained the dream of a few highly untypical theorists. In the wars of the mid-century, as often before, armed peasants on occasion played a role, sometimes a significant one. They put up considerable resistance to the Prussians in Moravia in 1741, for example, and helped defend Genoa and her territory against the Habsburg army in 1746–8. But between this semi-instinctive impulse of men to defend their own homes and immediate surroundings and any sort of universal military service was an immense gulf, one which no government could envisage crossing. To some even a limited and spontaneous local mobilization seemed suspect and dangerous: Frederick II, the exemplar of military achievement for the age, notably took this view. Even in the darkest days of the Seven Years War he recoiled from any idea of arming the mass of his subjects, which seemed to him a perilous invasion of his own rights and those of the regular army. In 1757 he forbade the inhabitants of the island of Borkum in East Friesland to resist French attack; and two years later he turned down the suggestion of his brother, Prince Henry, that those of the eastern provinces should be armed to resist Russian invasion. To every ruler of the decades before the French Revolution the nation in arms was not merely an unacceptable idea but an almost inconceivable one.

The demand that armies should be more mobile, flexible and aggressive in their tactics was met in part by the development of light infantry units which were used for scouting, attacking the enemy's communications and supply-lines, and irregular warfare of all kinds. The earliest example of these, the Croat regiments from the Habsburg military borders, achieved a formidable reputation for their fighting abilities and even more for their capacity to loot and ill-treat civilians: Frederick II thought them the most dangerous of all the opponents he had to cope with. By 1763 as much as a quarter of the Habsburg army could be described as 'light troops'. Other armies soon realized the potentialities of this sort of warfare. The British created a light infantry regiment in 1757 for use against the French in North America. The Spanish army, after earlier experiments, had two in 1762, and almost at the same time Russia began to equip herself with units of this kind. France had *chasseur* regiments of light infantry and several German armies had *Jaeger* ones in which foresters and gamekeepers, good shots accustomed to moving in difficult country, often figured prominently. The first book on irregular warfare (*la petite guerre*) appeared in 1752 and by 1800 something like fifty had been published. But none of this altered fundamentally the character and outlook of armies; and the Prussian army, the most widely admired and copied, adhered more closely than any to the tactics of the past. More than any other it was held together by rigid discipline and nothing else. This forced it to rely, in an essentially traditional way, on fire-power, the badly aimed volleys of soldiers in rigid line formation, since its soldiers were too unreliable to be allowed to charge with the bayonet or to be used extensively in mobile irregular warfare.[57]

By 1789, then, the grip of the past on most European armies was still strong. Most of them were still no bigger than in the days of Marlborough and Prince Eugene. Weapons developed only slowly: such changes as the introduction of lighter and more mobile field artillery from the middle of the century, notably in the Habsburg empire by Prince Joseph von Liechtenstein and in France by J. B. de Gribeauval, do little to undermine this generalization. The social composition of armies had not altered in any important way. Nowhere was it easy to find enough volunteers of acceptable quality to serve in the ranks, while officers in general were probably more self-consciously aristocratic and more hostile to bourgeois interlopers, however able, than in the seventeenth century. A few limited efforts had been made to narrow the gap between the noble majority of officers and the non-noble minority; but these took the form of a limited concession of noble status to some of the latter, not of any attempt to ease access to officer-rank for the plebeian. Thus in France a decree of 1750 granted nobility to families in which for three generations male members had served as officers, while in 1757 the Empress Maria Theresa was persuaded to confer noble status on all officers who had served without blemish for thirty years. But such measures did nothing to modify in any serious way the predominantly noble and privileged character of the European officer class: if anything they strengthened it. Yet it is easy enough, from the perspective of two centuries later, to see that things were changing, or at least beginning to change. The demand for a new style of war, one more exacting, in many ways harsher, in a sense more idealistic, was beginning to be audible. Side by side with this went the new vision, so alluring to some idealists and so pregnant with dangerous possibilities, of the nation in arms. As yet these demands and that vision were being put forward in only one country; but it was that country which, in the decade which followed, was to transform warfare and impose on it a quantum jump in scale and scope. For eastern Europe a war of entire peoples was not unprecedented. The struggle of 1700–21 between Russia and Sweden, and perhaps earlier that of 1654–67 between Russia and Poland, had been such. For the western part of the continent, however, struggles of this scale and intensity had hitherto been very exceptional; that of France in the critical years of the Spanish Succession conflict had been perhaps the only really striking example. In 1789 their day was about to begin.

Notes

(Authors of books and articles listed in the Bibliography are in small capitals)

INTRODUCTION

1. J. R. Hale, *War and Society in Renaissance Europe, 1450–1620* (London, 1985).
2. See the examples quoted in BOYNTON, pp.281–4.
3. Quoted in SCHWOERER, p.13; see also Sir John Smythe, *Certain Discourses Military*, ed. J. R. Hale (Ithaca, 1964), Introduction, p.1xxiv.
4. THOMPSON, pp.149, 151.
5. M. D. Feld, *The Structure of Violence: Armed Forces as Social Systems* (Beverly Hills and London, 1977), p.191.
6. J. A. Lynn, 'Tactical evolution in the French army, 1560–1660', *French Historical Studies*, xiv (1985), 179.
7. D. Buisseret, *Sully and the Growth of Centralized Government in France, 1598–1610* (London, 1968), pp.163–4.
8. BABEAU (1884), ii, 12.
9. CRUIKSHANK, p.13.
10. Buisseret, *Sully*, pp.152–3.

PART ONE

1. R. A. Stradling, 'Olivares and the origins of the Franco-Spanish war, 1627–1635', *English Historical Review*, ci (1986), 90.
2. PARKER (1984), p.100.
3. ROBERTS (1953–8), ii, 676.
4. ROY, p.28.
5. BURNE and YOUNG, p.14.
6. ROBERTS (1953–8), ii, 494, fn.1.
7. H. H. Rowen, *John de Witt, Grand Pensionary of Holland, 1625–1672* (Princeton, 1978), p.600.
8. DUFFY (1979), p.169.
9. WIJN, p.223.
10. ELLIOTT, pp.384–5.
11. PETERSEN (1975), pp.143–4.
12. The process is well illustrated in the account by a long-serving professional soldier of his raising a regiment for Dutch service in 1657, in TURNER, p.127.
13. MALLETT and HALE, p.324.
14. REDLICH (1964–5), i, 170.
15. MALLETT and HALE, p.282.
16. The most accessible account of the Swedish recruiting system is that in ROBERTS (1958), ii, 208ff.
17. REDLICH (1964–5), i, 265.
18. I. Gentles, 'Arrears of pay and ideology in the army revolt of

1647', *War and Society: a Yearbook of Military History* (London, 1975), pp.44, 52.
19. TURNER, pp.5–6.
20. TURNER, p.7.
21. POYNTZ, p.58.
22. D'AVENEL, iii, 103; ANDRÉ, p.30; CORVISIER (1983), p.80.
23. D'AVENEL, iii, 97fn.
24. OPPENHEIM, pp.213, 300.
25. OPPENHEIM, pp.212–13; LA BRUYÈRE, p.120.
26. BAMFORD, p.72.
27. D'AVENEL, iii, 84.
28. TURNER, pp.128–9.
29. PARKER (1972), p.164.
30. OPPENHEIM, p.355.
31. URLANIS, p.47.
32. LA BRUYÈRE, pp.29–30.
33. HUTTON, p.134; BURNE and YOUNG, p.220.
34. D'AVENEL, iii, 182.
35. PARKER (1984), p.193.
36. HUTTON, p.28.
37. BRUNEEL, p.465.
38. D'AVENEL, iii, 106.
39. PARKER (1984), p.124.
40. ROUPNEL, pp.30–2.
41. FRANZ, p.47.
42. KAMEN (1968), p.45.
43. ISRAEL (1985), pp.89–109.
44. CABOURDIN, i, 64, fn.42.
45. C. Tilly, *The Contentious French* (Cambridge, Mass., 1986), pp.134–5.
46. FRANZ, p.98.
47. ROUPNEL, p.235.
48. R. Crummey, *Aristocrats and Servitors: the Boyar Élite in Russia, 1613–1689* (Princeton, 1983), pp.48–9.
49. PARKER (1975), p.65.

PART TWO

1. CORVISIER (1983), pp.325, 344–5, 330.
2. CORVISIER (1964), i, 153–4.
3. ROBERTS (1979), p.45.
4. LENMAN, p.153.
5. *Oeuvres de Louis XIV* (Paris, 1806), iv, 15.
6. There is an interesting discussion of the difficulties of movement and their implications in MILOT, 269–90.
7. SCOULLER, p.185.
8. KEEP, pp.56ff.
9. ROTHENBERG, p.105.
10. DOMINGUEZ ORTIZ (1955), pp.368, 372–3.
11. MALO (1912–14), ii, 329–30.
12. COLONIE, p.253.
13. SALUCES, i, 292.
14. J. W. Fortescue, *History of the British Army*, 2nd ed. (London, 1910), ii, 27–8.
15. On this episode see EHRMAN, pp.526–7.
16. ROUSSET, i, 223.
17. SCOULLER, p.149.
18. SCOULLER, p.193.
19. BUTLER, i, 278.
20. JONES (1980b), 204–5.
21. KEEP, pp.39, 192–4.
22. *The Spirit of France and the Politick Maxims of Lewis XIV laid open to the World* (London, 1689), pp.33–4.
23. KAMEN (1969), p.59.
24. KEEP, pp.110–11, 175.
25. REDLICH (1964–5), ii, 228, 192.
26. BROMLEY and RYAN, p.831.
27. BUSCH, p.80.
28. KEEP, pp.131–4.
29. V. O. Klyuchevsky, quoted in KEEP, p.131.
30. KEEP, pp.146–55, is the only good discussion in any western language of the complexities of this system and their results.
31. (GUIBERT), pp.104–5.
32. Quoted in M. Raeff, *Origins of*

the Russian Intelligentsia: the Eighteenth-century Nobility (New York and London, 1966), p.183.

33. CORVISIER (1964), p.317.
34. Quoted in DUFFY (1977), pp.48–9.
35. Sir W. Scott, *Waverley* (Oxford, 1981), pp.25, 30.
36. CHILDS, p.41.
37. For French examples see BABEAU (1889–90), i, pp.46–9.
38. The heavy drinking which recruiting often involved is well brought out in an English soldier's account of how he joined up in 1706, in BISHOP, pp.124–35.
39. ROUSSET, ii, 479.
40. ASHER, p.91.
41. SCOULLER, p.122fn.; CORVISIER (1964), p.334.
42. SCOULLER, p.105.
43. BESKROVNYI (1958), p.30.
44. BESKROVNYI (1958), p.29; CORVISIER (1964), p.738; DESDEVIZES DU DEZERT, ii, 315.
45. BAUGH, p.209.
46. ROUSSET, ii, 96–101, 128.
47. BABEAU (1889–90), ii, 14–15.
48. WRIGHT, pp.634–44.
49. GUTMANN, p.189.
50. CORVISIER (1964), p.75.
51. GUTMANN, p.63.
52. BRUNEEL, p.470.
53. BERWICK, i, 126.
54. BOWMAN, p.123.
55. DUFFY (1975), p.36.
56. GUTMANN, p.39.
57. COLONIE, p.346.
58. FRIEDRICHS, pp.116, 168–9.
59. GUTMANN, p.42.
60. G. D. Kapustin, 'Guzhevoi transport v severnoi voine', in *Voprosy voennoi istorii Rossii XVIII i pervaya polovina XIX vekov* (Moscow, 1969), p.162.

61. P.W. Bamford, *Forests and French Sea Power, 1660–1789* (Toronto, 1956), pp.51–4.
62. GUTMANN, p.89.
63. HATTON, pp.252–3, 259.
64. WILSON, p.107.
65. Quoted in *Cambridge Economic History of Europe*, iv (Cambridge, 1967), 561.
66. CLARK (1923), p.139.
67. EHRMAN, p.172.
68. The figures in this paragraph are taken from BESKROVNYI (1958), pp.75–93.
69. GUTMANN, p.80.
70. GUTMANN, p.110.
71. *Lectures on Justice, Police, Revenue and Arms* (London, 1896), p.273.
72. BAUGH, pp.407, 432–40, 488.
73. KAMEN (1969), pp.229, 224, 74.
74. KAMEN (1969), p.381.

PART THREE

1. The figures in this paragraph are taken from CORVISIER (1976), p.126.
2. Sir W. Laird Clowes, *The Royal Navy: a History* (London, 1897–1903), iii, 7, 328.
3. J. R. T. Hughes, *Fluctuations in Trade, Industry and Finance* (Oxford, 1960), p.26.
4. CORVISIER (1964), p.65.
5. RODGER (1984), p.68.
6. Quoted in J. U. Nef, *War and Human Progress* (London, 1950), p.306.
7. Quoted in EARLE, p.54.
8. RUWET, pp.41–2.
9. L. Neal, 'The cost of impressment during the Seven

Years War', *Mariner's Mirror*, vol. 64 (1978), 48–9; GRADISH, p.70.

10. On this see the very interesting article of RODGER (1984), *passim*.

11. S. E. Finer, 'Military forces and state-making', in C. Tilly, ed., *The Formation of National States in Western Europe* (Princeton, 1975), p.110.

12. (GUIBERT), p.2.

13. BOWMAN, p.127.

14. *Boswell on the Grand Tour: Germany and Switzerland, 1764*, ed. F. A. Pottle (London, 1953), p.80.

15. P.Yorke, *The Life of Lord Chancellor Hardwicke*, iii (Cambridge, 1913), 227.

16. (GUIBERT), pp.57–8, 85–90, 6.

17. DESDEVIZES DU DEZERT, ii, 215.

18. Quoted in M. Foucault, *Discipline and Punish: the Birth of the Prison* (London, 1977), p.142.

19. J. Muller, *A Treatise Containing the Practical Part of Fortification* (London, 1755), p.222.

20. CORVISIER (1975), p.21.

21. MERINO NAVARRO, p.34.

22. COLONIE, Chap.i, *passim*, gives a good picture of cadet life in one of these companies.

23. DUFFY (1985a), p.315.

24. MERINO NAVARRO, pp.292–5.

25. TREBILCOCK, p.477.

26. JOHN, 330–4.

27. A. H. John, *The Industrial Development of South Wales, 1750–1850* (Cardiff, 1950), pp.24–5, 99–100.

28. 'If England had enjoyed unbroken peace the Industrial Revolution might have come sooner,' ASHTON, p.83.

29. F. Mathias, 'Swords into ploughshares: the armed forces, medicine and public health in the late eighteenth century', in J. M. Winter, ed., *War and Economic Development: Essays in Memory of David Joslin* (Cambridge, 1975), p.76.

30. Quoted in F. Braudel, *Civilization and Capitalism* (London, 1981–4), iii, 378.

31. See, among many other examples, his 'Exposé du gouvernement Prussien' (written c.1775–6) in FREDERICK II, ix, 183–4.

32. *Correspondence of George III*, ed. Sir J. Fortescue (London, 1927), iv, no. 2773.

33. VATTEL, pp.39–40.

34. F. Gilbert, *To the Farewell Address: Ideas of Early American Foreign Policy* (Princeton, 1961), *passim*.

35. J. H. G. von Justi, *Der Grundriss einer guten Regierung* (Frankfurt, 1759), pp.426–7.

36. Sir James Steuart, *An Inquiry into the Principles of Political Economy* (London, 1767), i, 448.

37. W. Robertson, *The History of the Reign of the Emperor Charles V* (London, 1769), iii, 431.

38. Adam Ferguson, *Principles of Moral and Political Science* (Hildersheim, 1975), p.295.

39. J. P. Rabaut de Saint-Étienne, *The History of the Revolution of France* (London, 1792), p.256.

40. CLARK (1953–5), 175.

41. *Observations upon the Warre of Hungary* (London, 1689), p.26.

42. Quoted in H. Acton, *The Bourbons of Naples (1734–1825)* (London, 1956), pp.20–1.
43. BISHOP, pp.152, 216.
44. BUTLER, i, 707.
45. DUFFY (1979), p.253.
46. HATTON, p.517; DUFFY (1974), p.183.
47. K. Lehmann, 'Ermattungsstrategie – oder nicht?', *Historische Zeitschrift*, cli (1935), 55–8.
48. DURUY, p.84.
49. The pressures for this type of reform are well discussed in BIEN (1979), *passim*. See also SCOTT, Chap.i.
50. PHILLIPS, pp.102–3, 106–7, 120, 123, 140. This collection provides perhaps the most conveniently accessible printing of Saxe's book.
51. *Reflexions d'un soldat patriote* (London, 1773), especially Pt I, pp.102ff., Pt. II, pp.12–15, 44–5.
52. J. Godechot, 'Nation, patrie, nationalisme et patriotisme en France au XVIIIe siècle', *Annales historiques de la révolution française*, xliii (1971), 481–501.
53. MENARD, p.63.
54. Many of these schemes can be found in the British Library in a volume of proposals submitted in 1790 to the *Comité militaire* of the National Assembly (pressmark F.R.276). A typical example is (General Joseph Servan), *Projet de constitution pour l'armée des François* (Paris, 1790).
55. BABEAU (1889–90), i, 329.
56. CORVISIER (1975), p.23.
57. See the comments of (GUIBERT), p.136.

Select Bibliography

This list of suggestions for further reading does not pretend to be exhaustive: a complete bibliography of the subject would constitute a sizeable volume in itself. Works which deal wholly or mainly with the details of military and naval operations have not been included; and preference has been given to those in English which are likely to be accessible to the student who can make use of a good university library.

Aberg, A., 'The Swedish army, from Lutzen to Narva', in M. Roberts, ed., *Sweden's Age of Greatness, 1632–1718* (London, 1973)

Acerra, M., J.P. Merino Navarro, J. Meyer, eds., *Les Marines de guerre européennes, XVIIe–XVIIIe siècles* (Paris, 1985)

Anderson, Olive, 'The treatment of prisoners of war in Britain during the American War of Independence', *Bulletin of the Institute of Historical Research*, xxviii (1955)

——, 'The establishment of British supremacy at sea and the exchange of naval prisoners of war, 1689–1783', *English Historical Review*, lxxv (1960)

André, L., *Michel le Tellier et l'organisation de l'armée monarchique* (Paris, 1906)

Andrews, K.R., *Elizabethan Privateering: English Privateering during the Spanish War, 1585–1603* (Cambridge, 1964)

Asher, E.L. *The Resistance to the Maritime Classes: The Survival of Feudalism in the France of Colbert* (Berkeley/Los Angeles, 1960)

Ashlund, Lt.-Col., 'L'Armee suèdoise de 'soldats-cultivateurs' à la fin du XVIIIe siècle et au début du XVIIIe siècle', *Revue internationale d'histoire militaire*, xxx (1971)

Ashton, T.S., *Economic Fluctuations in England, 1700–1800* (Oxford, 1959)

Atkinson, C.T., 'The cost of Queen Anne's War', *Journal of the Society for Army Historical Research*, 33 (1955)

Babeau, A., *La Vie militaire sous l'ancien régime*, 2 vols. (Paris, 1889–90)

Baetens, R., 'The organization and effects of Flemish privateering in the seventeenth century', *Acta Historiae Neerlandicae*, ix (1976)

Bamford, P.M., *Fighting Ships and Prisons: the Mediterranean Galleys of France in the Age of Louis XIV* (Minneapolis, Minn., 1973)

Barker, T.M., 'Military entrepreneurship and absolutism: Habsburg models', *Journal of European Studies*, 4 (1974)

——, *Army, Aristocracy, Monarchy: Essays on War, Society and Government in Austria, 1618–1780* (Boulder, Colorado, 1982)

Barudio, G., *Das Teutsche Krieg* (Frankfurt, 1985)

Baugh, D.A., *British Naval Administration in the Age of Walpole* (Princeton, N.J., 1965)

Bayard, Françoise and Dessert, D., 'Les Finances dans l'état monarchique en guerre au XVIIIe siècle', in *Les Monarchies*, ed. E. Leroy-Ladurie (Paris, 1986)

Benecke, G., 'The problem of death and destruction in Germany during the Thirty Years War', *European Studies Review*, ii (1972)

Berwick, James Fitz-James, first Duke of, *Memoirs of the Duke of Berwick*, 2 vols. (London, 1779)

Beskrovnyi, K.G., *Ocherki po istochnikovedeniya voennoi istorii Rossii* (Moscow, 1957)

——, *Russkaya armiya i flot v XVIII veke* (Moscow, 1958)

Bien, D., 'La réaction aristocratique avant 1789: l'exemple de l'armée', *Annales*, xxxix (1974)

——, 'The army in the French Enlightenment: reform, reaction and revolution', *Past and Present*, 85 (Nov., 1979)

Bishop, M., *Life and Adventures of Matthew Bishop from 1701–1711* (London, 1744)

Black, J., *A Military Revolution: Military Change and European Society, 1550–1800* (Basingstoke, 1991)

——, *European Warfare, 1660–1815* (London, 1994)

Blackader, Col. John, *The Life and Diary of Colonel John Blackader* (Edinburgh, 1824)

Blanchard, Anne, *Vauban* (Paris, 1996)

Bois, J.P., 'Les anciens soldats de 1715 à 1815: problèmes et méthodes', *Revue Historique*, 265 (1981)

Bowman, D., ed., *The Life-Story and Real Adventures of the Poor Man of Toggenburg* (Edinburgh, 1970)

Boynton, L., *The Elizabethan Militia, 1558–1638* (London, 1967)

Brancaccio, N., *L'Esercito del vecchio Piemonte* (Rome, 1922)

Braun, R., 'Taxation, sociopolitical structure and state-building: Great Britain and Brandenburg-Prussia', in C. Tilly, ed., *The Formation of National States in Western Europe* (Princeton, N.J., 1975)

Brewer, D.C., *Servants of the Sword: French Intendants of the Army, 1630–1670* (Urbana, Ill., 1976)

Brewer, J., *The Sinews of Power: War, Money and the English State, 1688–1783* (London, 1989)

Bromley, J.S., 'The French privateering war, 1702–1713', in *Historical Essays, 1600–1750, presented to David Ogg*, ed. H.E. Bell and R.L. Ollard (London, 1963)

——, and Ryan, A.N., 'Navies', in *New Cambridge Modern History*, vi (Cambridge, 1970)

Bruijn, J.R., *The Dutch Navy of the Seventeenth and Eighteenth Centuries* (Columbia, South Carolina, 1990)

Bruneel, C., *La Mortalité dans les campagnes: le Duché de Brabant aux XVIIe et XVIIIe siècles*, 2 vols. (Louvain, 1977)

Burton, I.F., 'The supply of infantry for the war in the peninsula', *Bulletin of the Institute of Historical Research*, xxviii (1955)

Busch, O., *Militärsystem und Sozialleben im alten Preussen 1713 bis 1807* (Berlin, 1962)

Butler, R. d'O, *Choiseul*, i (all published) (Oxford, 1980)

Cabourdin, G., *Terre et hommes en Lorraine (1550–1635)*, 2 vols. (Nancy, 1977)

Carrias, E., *La Pensée militaire française* (Paris, 1960)

Casey, J., *The Kingdom of Valencia in the Seventeenth Century* (Cambridge, 1979)

Castex, R., *Les Idées militaires de la marine du XVIIIe siècle* (Paris, 1911)

Ceva, L., 'Il Commando degli eserciti in Europa fra 'l'età di mezzo e restaurazione', *Rivista Storica Italiana*, xcviii (1986)

Chandler, D.G., 'The art of war on land', in *New Cambridge Modern History*, vi (Cambridge, 1970)

——, *Marlborough as Military Commander* (London, 1973)

——, *The Art of War in the Age of Marlborough* (London, 1976)

——, ed., *The Marlborough Wars* (London, 1968). Contains extracts from the memoirs of Captain Robert Parker and the Comte de Merode-Westerloo.

Chernov, A.V., *Vooruzhennye sily russkogo gosudarstva v XVI–XVII vv.* (Moscow, 1954)

Childs, J., *The Army of Charles II* (London, 1976)

——, *Armies and Warfare in Europe, 1648–1789* (Manchester, 1982)

——, *The British Army of William III, 1689–1702* (Manchester, 1987)

Clark, G.N., *The Dutch Alliance and the War against French Trade, 1689–97* (Manchester, 1923)

——, 'War trade and trade war, 1701–1713', *Economic History Review*, i (1927–8)

——, 'The character of the Nine Years War, 1688–97', *Cambridge Historical Journal*, xi (1953–5)

——, *War and Society in the Seventeenth Century* (Cambridge, 1958)

Coleman, D.G., 'Naval dockyards under the later Stuarts', *Economic History Review*, 2nd ser., vi (1953–4)

Colonie, Colonel J.M. de la, *Chronicles of an Old Campaigner, 1682–1718*, trans. W.C. Horsley (London, 1904)

Cooper, J.C., 'Sea Power', in *New Cambridge Modern History*, iv (Cambridge, 1970)

Cornette, J., *Le Roi de guerre: essai sur la souveraineté dans la France du Grand Siècle* (Paris, 1993)

Corvisier, A., *L'Armée française de la fin du XVIIe siècle au ministère de Choiseul: le soldat* (Paris, 1964)

——, 'La Mort du soldat depuis la fin du moyen age', *Revue Historique*, ccliv (1975)

——, *Armies and Societies in Europe, 1494–1789* (Bloomington, Ill./London, 1979)

——, *Louvois* (Paris, 1983)

——, 'Les Armées et la guerre', in *L'Europe à la fin du XVIIIe siècle (vers 1780–1802)*, ed. J. Berenger and others (Paris, 1985)

——, ed., *Histoire militaire de la France*, i (ed. P. Contamine), ii (ed. J. Delmas) (Paris, 1992)

Cruickshank, C.G., *Elizabeth's Army* (Oxford, 1966)

D'Avenel, Vicomte G., *Richelieu et la monarchie absolue*, 2nd ed., iii (Paris, 1895)

Davis, R., *The Rise of the English Shipping Industry in the Seventeenth and Eighteenth Centuries* (London, 1962)

Deane, J.M., *A Journal of the Campaign in Flanders, A.D. MDCCVIII*, ed. J.B. Deane (London, 1846)

Dickson, P.G.M., and Sperling, J., 'War finance, 1689–1714', in *New Cambridge Modern History*, vi (Cambridge, 1970)

Dominguez Ortiz, A., *La Sociedad espanola en el siglo XVIII* (Madrid, 1955)

——, *La Sociedad espanola en el siglo XVII* (Madrid, 1963)

Downing, B.M., *The Military Revolution and Political Change: Origins of Democracy and Autocracy in Early Modern Europe* (Princeton, N.J., 1992)

Duffy, C., *The Army of Frederick the Great* (London/New York, 1974)

——, *Fire and Stone: The Science of Fortress Warfare, 1660–1860* (Newton Abbot, 1975)

——, *The Army of Maria Theresa: The Armed Forces of Imperial Austria, 1740–1780* (London, 1977)

——, *Siege Warfare: The Fortress in the Early Modern World, 1494–1660* (London, 1979)

——, *Frederick the Great; A Military Life* (London, 1985)

——, *The Military Experience in the Age of Reason* (London/New York, 1989)

Duffy, M., 'The foundations of British naval power', in *The Military Revolution and the State*, ed. M. Duffy (Exeter, 1980)

Duruy, A., *L'Armée royale en 1789* (Paris, 1888)

Ehrman, J., *The Navy in the War of William III, 1689–1697* (Cambridge, 1953)

Elliott, J.H., *The Revolt of the Catalans: A Study in the Decline of Spain (1598–1640)* (Cambridge, 1963)

Ergang, R.R., *The Myth of the All-Destructive Fury of the Thirty Years War* (Pocono Pines, Pa., 1956)

Esper, T., 'Military self-sufficiency and weapons technology in Muscovite Russia', *Slavic Review*, xviii (1969)

Fayle, C.E., 'Economic pressure in the war of 1739–48' *Journal of the Royal United Services Institute*, lxviii (1923)

——, 'The deflection of strategy by commerce in the eighteenth century', *Journal of the Royal United Services Institute*, lxviii (1923)

Fernandez Duro, C., *Armada espanola, desde la unión de las reinos de Castilla y de Aragon*, vi–vii (Madrid, 1900–01)

Francis, D., *The First Peninsular War, 1702–1713* (London, 1975)

Franz, G., *Die dreissigjährige Krieg und das deutsche Volk*, 3rd ed. (Stuttgart, 1961)

Frederick II, King of Prussia, *Oeuvres de Frederic le Grand*, ix, xxviii–xxx (Berlin, 1856)

Friedrichs, C.R., *Urban Society in an Age of War: Nordlingen, 1580–1720* (Princeton, N.J., 1979)

Gaya, L. de, *Gaya's Traité des Armes, 1678*, ed. C. Ffoulkes (Oxford, 1911)

Gilbert, A.N., 'Military recruitment in the eighteenth century', *Journal of the Society for Army Historical Research*, lvii (1979)

Girard, G., *Racolage et milice: le service militaire en France à la fin du règne de Louis XIV* (Paris, 1912)

Glete, J., *Navies and Nations: Warships, Navies and State Building in Europe and America, 1500–1860*, i (Stockholm, 1993)

Goodman, D., *Spanish Naval Power, 1589–1665: Reconstruction and Defeat* (Cambridge, 1997)

Gradish, S., *The Manning of the British Navy during the Seven Years War* (London, 1980)

Guibert, J.A.H. de, *Observations sur la constitution militaire et politique des armées de S.M. Prussienne* (Berlin, 1777)

——, *General Essay on Tactics* (London, 1781)

Gutmann, M.P., *War and Rural Life in the Early Modern Low Countries* (Princeton, N.J., 1980)

Guy, A.J., *Oeconomy and Discipline: Officership and Administration in the British Army, 1714–1763* (Manchester, 1985)

Hale, J.R., 'Incitement to Violence?: English divines on the theme of war, 1578 to 1631', in his *Renaissance War Studies* (London, 1983)

Hatton, R.M., *Charles XII of Sweden* (London, 1968)

Helleiner, K.F., 'The population of Europe from the Black Death to the eve of the vital revolution', *Cambridge Economic History of Europe*, iv (Cambridge, 1967)

Hellie, R., *Enserfment and Military Change in Muscovy* (Chicago, Ill., 1971)

——, 'The Petrine army: continuity, change and impact', *Canadian-American Slavic Studies*, viii (1974)

Houlding, J.A., *Fit for Service: The Training of the British Army, 1715–95* (Oxford, 1981)

Hutton, R., *The Royalist War Effort, 1642–1646* (London, 1981)

Ingrao, C.W., *The Hessian Mercenary State: Ideas, Institutions and Reform under Frederick II, 1760–1785* (Cambridge, 1987)

Irvine, D.D., 'The origins of capital staffs', *Journal of Modern History*, x (1938)

Israel, J.I., *The Dutch Republic and the Hispanic World, 1606–1661* (Oxford, 1982)

——, *European Jewry in the Age of Mercantilism* (Oxford, 1985)

John, A.H., 'War and the English economy, 1700–1763', *Economic History Review*, 2nd ser., vii (1954–5)

Johnston, J.A., 'Parliament and the protection of trade, 1689–1694', *Mariner's Mirror*, lvii (1971)

Jones, C., 'The military revolution and the professionalization of the French army under the ancien regime', in *The Military Revolution and the State, 1500–1800*, ed. M. Duffy (Exeter, 1980)

——, 'The welfare of the French foot-soldier from Richelieu to Napoleon', *History*, 65 (1980)

Jones, D.W., *War and Economy in the Age of William III and Marlborough* (Oxford, 1988)

Joslin, D.M., 'London bankers in wartime, 1739–84', in *Studies in the Industrial Revolution*, ed. L.S. Pressnell (London, 1960)

Kahan, A., *The Plow, the Hammer and the Knout: An Economic History of Eighteenth-Century Russia* (Chicago, Ill./London, 1985)

Kamen, H., 'The economic and social consequences of the Thirty Years War', *Past and Present*, 39 (1968)

——, *The War of Succession in Spain, 1700–1715* (London, 1969)

Keep, J.H.L., *Soldiers of the Tsar: Army and Society in Russia, 1462–1874* (Oxford, 1985)

——, 'Feeding the troops: Russian army supply policies during the Severn Years War', *Canadian Slavonic Papers*, 29 (1987)

Kennett, L., *The French Armies in the Seven Years War: A Study in Military Organization and Administration* (Durham, NC, 1967)

Kent, H.S.K., *War and Trade in the Northern Seas* (Cambridge, 1973)

Kiraly, B.K. and G.E. Rothenberg, ed., *War and Society in East Central Europe*, i, *Special Topics and Generalizations in the 18th and 19th Centuries* (New York, 1979)

Kitchen, M., *A Military History of Germany from the Eighteenth Century to the Present Day* (Bloomington, Ind./London, 1975)

Knyvett, Sir H., *The Defence of the Realme*, ed. C. Hughes (Oxford, 1906)

La Bruyère, R. *La Marine de Richelieu: Maillé-Brézé, Général des Galères, Grand Amiral (1619–1646)* (Paris, 1945)

Leclerc, M., 'Les réformes de Castries (14 Octobre 1780–23 Aout 1787)', *Revue des Questions Historiques*, cxxviii (1937)

Le Donne, J.P., 'Outlines of Russian military administration, 1762–1796', *Jahrbücher für Geschichte Osteuropas*, 31 (1983), 33 (1985), 34 (1986)

Lefèvre, J., *Spinola et la Belgique, 1601–1627* (Paris, 1947)

Le Goff, T.J.A., 'Problèmes de recrutement de la marine française pendant la Guerre de Sept Ans', *Revue Historique*, 283 (1990–91)

Lenman, B., *The Jacobite Clans of the Great Glen, 1650–1784* (London, 1984)

Leonard, E., *L'Armée et ses problèmes au XVIIIe siècle* (Paris, 1958)

——, 'La Question sociale dans l'armée française au XVIIIe siècle, *Annales*, iii (1948)

Lewis, M., *England's Sea-Officers: The Story of the Naval Profession* (London, 1939)

Linderen, J., 'The Swedish 'miliary' state, 1560–1720', *Scandinavian Journal of History*, 10 (1985)

Lloyd, C., 'Armed forces and the art of war: navies', *New Cambridge Modern History*, viii (Cambridge, 1965)

Loir, M., *La Marine royale en 1789* (Paris, 1892)

Longworth, P., *The Cossacks* (London, 1969)

Losch, P., *Soldatenhandel* (Kassel, 1933)

Lundkvist, S., 'The expansion of empire; Sweden as a great power', in *Sweden's Age of Greatness, 1632–1718*, ed. M. Roberts (London, 1973)

Luvaas, J., ed., *Frederick the Great on the Art of War* (New York, 1966)

Lynn, J.A., 'Food, funds and fortresses: resource mobilization and positional warfare in the campaigns of Louis XIV', in J.A. Lynn, ed., *Feeding Mars; Logistics in Western Warfare from the Middle Ages to the Present* (Boulder, Col., 1993)

——, 'How war fed war: the tax of violence and contributions during the *Grand Siècle*', *Journal of Modern History*, 65 (1993)

——, 'Recalculating French army growth during the *Grand Siècle*, 1610–1715', *French Historical Studies*, 8 (1994)

McKay, D., *Prince Eugene of Savoy*, (London, 1977)

Malo, H., *Les Corsaires dunkerquois et Jean Bart*, 2 vols. (Paris, 1912–14)

——, *La grande guerre des corsaires: Dunkerque, 1702–15* (Paris, 1925)

Mallett, M.E., and J.R. Hale, *The Military Organization of a Renaissance State: Venice, c. 1400 to 1617* (Cambridge, 1984)

Martin, R., 'The army of Louis XIV', in P. Sonnino, ed., *The Reign of Louis XIV: Essays in Celebration of Andrew Lossky* (Atlantic Highlands, N.J., 1990)

Memain, R., *Matelots et soldats des vaissaux du roi: levées d'hommes du département de Rochefort, 1661–1690* (Paris, 1937)

Menard, General, ed., *Ecrits militaires, 1772–1790, par le Comte de Guibert* (Paris, 1977)

Mention, L., *L'Armée de l'ancien régime* (Paris, 1909)

Merino Navarro, J.P., *La Armada espanola en el siglo XVIII* (Madrid, 1981)

Merode-Westerloo, Comte J.P.E. de, *Mémoires du Feld-Maréchal Comte de Merode-Westerloo*, 2 vols. (Brussels, 1840)

Michaud, Helen, 'Aux origines du secrétariat d'état de la guerre: les règlements de 1617–1619', *Revue d'Histoire Moderne et Contemporaine*, xix (1972)

Milot, J., 'Un problème operationnel du XVIIIe siècle illustré par un cas régional', *Revue du Nord*, 53 (1971)

Mols, R., *Introduction à la démographie historique des villes d'Europe du XVIe au XVIIIe siècle*, 3 vols. (Louvain, 1954–6)

Murray, Sir O., 'The Admiralty', *Mariner's Mirror*, xxiii (1937), xxiv (1938)

Nordmann, C., 'L'Armée suèdoise au XVIIe siècle', *Revue du Nord*, 54 (1972)

Oppenheim, M., *A History of the Administration of the Royal Navy, 1509–1660* (London, 1896; repr. 1961)

Owen, J.H., *The War at Sea under Queen Anne* (Cambridge, 1938)

Palmer, R.R., 'Frederick the Great, Guibert, Bulow: from dynastic to national war', in *Makers of Modern Strategy*, ed. P. Paret (Oxford, 1986)

Paret, P., 'Colonial experience and European military reform at the end of the eighteenth century', *Bulletin of the Institute of Historical Research*, xxxviii (1964)

Parker, G., *The Army of Flanders and the Spanish Road: The Logistics of Spanish Victory and Defeat, 1567–1659* (Cambridge, 1972)

——, 'Mutiny and discontent in the Spanish Army of Flanders, 1572–1607', *Past and Present*, 58 (1973)

——, 'War and economic change: the economic costs of the Dutch revolt', in J.M. Winter, ed., *War and Economic Development: Essays in memory of David Joslin* (Cambridge, 1975)

——, 'The "Military Revolution", 1560–1660 – a myth?', *Journal of Modern History*, 48 (1976)

——, *Spain and the Netherlands, 1559–1659: Ten Studies* (London, 1979)

——, *The Military Revolution: Military Innovation and the Rise of the West, 1500–1800* (Cambridge, 1988)

——, and others, *The Thirty Years War* (Cambridge, 1984)

Parker, Captain, R., *Memoirs of the Most Truly Remarkable Military Transactions . . . 1683–1718*, 2nd ed. (London, 1741)

Perré, J., *La Guerre et ses mutations des origines à 1792* (Paris, 1961)

Petersen, E.L., 'From domain state to tax state', *Scandinavian Economic History Review*, xxiii (1975)

——, 'Defence, war and finance: Christian IV and the Council of the Realm, 1596–1629', *Scandinavian Journal of History*, vii (1982)

Polisensky, J.V., 'The Thirty Years War and the crises and revolutions of seventeenth-century Europe', *Past and Present*, 39 (1968)

——, *The Thirty Years War* (London, 1971)

——, ed., *War and Society in Europe, 1618–1648* (Cambridge, 1978)

Poyntz, S., 'The relation of Sydnham Poyntz, 1624–36', ed. A.T.S. Goodrick, *Camden Society Publications*, 3rd ser., xiv (1908)

Prinzing, F., *Epidemics Resulting from War* (Washington, D.C., 1915)

Pritchard, J., *Louis XV's Navy, 1748–1762* (Montreal, 1987)

Rabb, T.K., 'The effects of the Thirty Years War on the German economy', *Journal of Modern History*, xxxiv (1962)

Rebelliau, A., *Vauban* (Paris, 1962)

Redlich, F., *De Praeda Militari: Looting and Booty, 1500–1815* (Wiesbaden, 1956)

——, 'Contributions in the Thirty Years War', *Economic History Review*, 2nd ser., xii (1959–60)

——, *The German Military Enterpriser and his Workforce*. 2 vols. (Wiesbaden, 1964–5)

Regele, O., *Der österreichische Hofkriegsrat, 1556–1848* (Vienna, 1949)

Roberts, M., *Gustavus Adolphus*, 2 vols. (London, 1953–8)

——, *The Military Revolution, 1560–1660* (Belfast, 1956)

——, *The Early Vasas* (Cambridge, 1968)

——, *The Swedish Imperial Experience, 1560–1718* (Cambridge, 1979)

Robson, E., 'The armed forces and the art of war', in *New Cambridge Modern History*, vii (Cambridge, 1957)

Rodger, N.A.M., 'Stragglers and deserters from the Royal Navy during the Seven Years War', *Bulletin of the Institute of Historical Research*, lvii (1984)

Rothenberg, G.E., *The Austrian Military Border in Croatia, 1522–1747* (Urbana, Ill., 1960)

Roupnel, G., *La Ville et la campagne au XVIIe siècle: étude sur les populations du pays dijonnais* (Paris, 1922)

Rousset, C., *Histoire de Louvois et de son administration politique et militaire*, 4 vols. (Paris, 1862–3)

Roy, I., 'The English civil war and English society', in *War and Society: A Yearbook of Military History* (London, 1975)

Russell, C.S.R., 'Monarchies, wars and estates in England, France and Spain, c. 1580–c. 1640', *Legislative Studies Quarterly* (May, 1982)

Saxe, Marshal Count M de, *Reveries or Memoirs upon the Art of War* (London, 1757)

Schwoerer, Lois G., *'No Standing Armies!' The Antimilitary Idealogy in Seventeenth-Century England* (Baltimore, Maryland/London, 1974)

Scott, S.F., *The Response of the Royal Army to the French Revolution* (Oxford, 1978)

Scouller, Major R.E., *The Armies of Queen Anne* (Oxford, 1966)

Silberner, E., *La Guerre et la paix dans l'histoire des doctrines économiques* (Paris, 1957)

Stearns, S., 'Conscription and English society in the 1620s', *Journal of British Studies*, 11 (1972)

Stoye, J.W., 'Soldiers and civilians', in *New Cambridge Modern History*, vi (1970)

Stradling, R.A., 'Catastrophe and recovery: the defeat of Spain, 1639–43', *History*, 64 (1979)

——, 'The Spanish Dunkirkers, 1621–48: a record of plunder and destruction', *Tijdschrift voor Geschiednis*, xciii (1980)

——, *Europe and the Decline of Spain: A Study of the Spanish System, 1580–1720* (London, 1981)

——, 'Spain's military failure and the supply of horses, 1600–1660', *History*, 69 (1984)

——, *The Spanish Monarchy and Irish Mercenaries: The Wild Geese in Spain, 1618–1668* (Dublin, 1994)

Symcox, G., 'The Navy of Louis XIV', in P. Sonnino, ed., *The Reign of Louis XIV: Essays in Celebration of Andrew Lossky* (Atlantic Highlands, N.J., 1990)

Tallett, F., *War and Society in Early Modern Europe, 1494–1715* (London, 1992)

Thompson, I.A.A., *War and Government in Habsburg Spain, 1560–1620* (London, 1976)

Trebilcock, C., 'Spin-off in British economic history: armaments and industry, 1760–1914', *Economic History Review*, 2nd ser., xxii (1969)

Tuetey, L. *Les Officiers sous l'ancien régime* (Paris, 1908)

Turner, Sir J., *Memoirs of His Own Life and Times, 1632–1670* (London, 1829)

Urlanis, B., *Voiny i narodonaselenie Evropy* (Moscow, 1960)

Vagts, A., *A History of Militarism* (London, 1938)

Van Creveld, M., *Supplying War: Logistics from Wallenstein to Patton* (Cambridge, 1977)

Van Deursen, A.Th., 'Holland's experience of war during the Revolt of the Netherlands', in A.C. Duke and C.A. Tanse, eds., *Britain and the Netherlands*, 6 (The Hague, 1977)

Vattel, E. de, *Le Droit des gens ou les principes de la loi naturelle*, ii (Washington, D.C., 1916)

Vignols, L., 'La Course maritime: ses conséquences économiques, sociales et internationales', *Revue d'Histoire Economique et Sociale*, xv (1927)

Western, J.R., 'Armed forces and the art of war', in *New Cambridge Modern History*, viii (Cambridge, 1965)

——, *The English Militia in the Eighteenth Century: The Story of a Political Issue, 1660–1802* (London, 1965)

Wijn, J.W., 'Military forces and warfare, 1610–48', in *New Cambridge Modern History*, ix (Cambridge, 1970)

Wilson, C., *Profit and Power: A Study of England and the Dutch Wars* (London, 1957)

Wilson, P.H., *War, State and Society in Württemberg, 1677–1793* (Cambridge, 1993)

——, 'The German 'Soldier Trade' of the seventeenth and eighteenth centuries: a reassessment', *International History Review*, 18 (1996)

Wismes, A. de, *Jean Bart et la guerre de course* (Paris, 1965)

Wright, J.W., 'Sieges and customs of war at the opening of the eighteenth century', *American Historical Review*, xxxix (1933–4)

Zeller, G., 'Le Commerce international en temps de guerre sous l'ancien régime', *Revue d'Histoire Moderne et Contemporaine*, n.s. ix (1957)

Index